KINGSHIP, POWER, AND LEGITIMACY IN ANCIENT EGYPT

In this book, Lisa K. Sabbahy presents a history of ancient Egyptian kingship in the Old Kingdom and its re-formation in the early Middle Kingdom. Beginning with an account of Egypt's history before the Old Kingdom, she examines the basis of kingship and its legitimacy. The heart of her study is an exploration of the king's constant emphasis on his relationship to his divine parents, the sun god Ra and his mother, the goddess Hathor, who were two of the most important deities backing the rule of a divine king. Sabbahy focuses on the cardinal importance of this relationship, which is reflected in the king's monuments, particularly the pyramid complexes, several of which are analyzed in detail. Sabbahy also offers new insights into the role of queens in the early history of Egypt, notably sibling royal marriages, harem conspiracies, and the possible connotations of royal female titles.

Lisa K. Sabbahy is Assistant Professor of Egyptology at the American University in Cairo.

KINGSHIP, POWER, AND LEGITIMACY IN ANCIENT EGYPT

FROM THE OLD KINGDOM TO THE MIDDLE KINGDOM

LISA K. SABBAHY

American University of Cairo

CAMBRIDGE
UNIVERSITY PRESS

University Printing House, Cambridge CB2 8BS, United Kingdom

One Liberty Plaza, 20th Floor, New York, NY 10006, USA

477 Williamstown Road, Port Melbourne, VIC 3207, Australia

314–321, 3rd Floor, Plot 3, Splendor Forum, Jasola District Centre,
New Delhi – 110025, India

79 Anson Road, #06–04/06, Singapore 079906

Cambridge University Press is part of the University of Cambridge.

It furthers the University's mission by disseminating knowledge in the pursuit of
education, learning, and research at the highest international levels of excellence.

www.cambridge.org
Information on this title: www.cambridge.org/9781108830911
DOI: 10.1017/9781108914529

© Cambridge University Press 2021

This publication is in copyright. Subject to statutory exception
and to the provisions of relevant collective licensing agreements,
no reproduction of any part may take place without the written
permission of Cambridge University Press.

First published 2021

A catalogue record for this publication is available from the British Library.

Library of Congress Cataloging-in-Publication Data
NAMES: Sabbahy, Lisa, author.
TITLE: Kingship, power, and legitimacy in ancient Egypt : from the Old Kingdom to the Middle
Kingdom / Lisa K. Sabbahy, American University of Cairo.
DESCRIPTION: Cambridge ; New York, NY : Cambridge University Press, 2021. | Includes
bibliographical references and index.
IDENTIFIERS: LCCN 2020035990 (print) | LCCN 2020035991 (ebook) | ISBN 9781108830911
(hardback) | ISBN 9781108823739 (paperback) | ISBN 9781108914529 (ebook)
SUBJECTS: LCSH: Monarchy – Egypt – Religious aspects. | Egypt – Kings and rulers. | Egypt – History –
Old Kingdom, ca. 2686–ca. 2181 B.C. | Egypt – History – Middle Kingdom, ca. 2180–ca. 1551 B.C.
CLASSIFICATION: LCC DT85 .S23 2020 (print) | LCC DT85 (ebook) | DDC 932/.012–dc23
LC record available at https://lccn.loc.gov/2020035990
LC ebook record available at https://lccn.loc.gov/2020035991

ISBN 978-1-108-83091-1 Hardback

Cambridge University Press has no responsibility for the persistence or accuracy of
URLs for external or third-party internet websites referred to in this publication
and does not guarantee that any content on such websites is, or will remain,
accurate or appropriate.

CONTENTS

List of Figures	*page* vii
Preface	ix
Acknowledgments	x
INTRODUCTION	1
1 BACKGROUND TO ANCIENT EGYPT	4
Ancient Egyptian History and Chronology	4
Early Evidence and Formation of a State	6
The Early Dynastic Period: The First Dynasty	13
The Second Dynasty	19
Basis of Egyptian Kingship	22
Beginning of Government and Administration	25
2 THE EARLY OLD KINGDOM	29
The Third Dynasty: The Reign of King Netjerikhet (2667–2648)	29
The Fourth Dynasty	40
The Reign of Sneferu (2613–2589)	41
The Reign of Khufu (2589–2566)	52
The Reign of Djedefra (2566–2558)	58
The Reign of Khafra (2558–2532)	61
The Reign of Menkaura (2532–2503) and the End of the Fourth Dynasty	68
3 THE LATER OLD KINGDOM	76
The Fifth Dynasty	76
The Reign of Userkaf (2494–2487)	77
The Reign of Sahura (2487–2475)	81
The Reign of Nyuserra (2445–2421)	83
The End of the Fifth Dynasty	92
The Reign of Unas (2375–2345) and the Pyramid Texts	93
The Sixth Dynasty	98
The Reign of King Teti (2345–2323)	98

The Reign of King Pepy I (2321–2287) 101
The Reign of King Pepy II (2278–2184) 115
The End of the Sixth Dynasty 118

4 THE EARLY MIDDLE KINGDOM REUNIFIES EGYPT 121
The Reign of Mentuhotep II (2055–2004) 122
The End of the Eleventh Dynasty 135

5 THE BEGINNING OF THE TWELFTH DYNASTY 138
The Reign of Amenemhat I (1985–1956) 138
The Reign of Senusret I (1956–1911) 146

CONCLUSION 161

Bibliography 165
Index 203

FIGURES

1	Map of Predynastic and Early Dynastic Egypt	6
2	Stela from Abydos with the name of Meretneith (JE 34450)	15
3	The wadi at Abydos	17
4	The ivory comb of King Djet from Abydos (JE 47176)	17
5	Map of the Old Kingdom and the First Intermediate Period of Egypt	30
6	Mortuary temple of the Step Pyramid at Saqqara	33
7	Four pairs of feet in the *heb sed* court of the Step Pyramid	38
8	Base of the statue of Netjerikhet with name and titles of Imhotep	40
9	Sneferu's pyramid at Meydum	43
10	Small valley temple at the Meydum pyramid	44
11	Stela at Dahshur *heb sed* temple with titulary of Sneferu (JE 89289)	49
12	Entrance into the *heb sed* temple of Sneferu	50
13	Two pottery lion goddess statues from North Saqqara	55
14	Diorite statue of Khafra from his valley temple (CG 9)	62
15	Limestone statue of Khamerernebty II from Giza (JE 48856)	67
16	Menkaura's pyramid at Giza with granite casing blocks still on the ground	69
17	Triad with Menkaura and Hathor from Giza (JE 40679)	71
18	The tomb of the queen mother, Khentkaues I, Giza	73
19	The pyramid of Userkaf, with Netjerikhet's Pyramid in the background	78
20	Summer scene from depictions of the seasons, Sun Temple of Nyuserra, Abu Ghurab (Berlin 20038)	87
21	A view across the causeway of Unas to the Step Pyramid, Saqqara	94
22	A view of the east side of the pyramid of Unas, Saqqara	95
23	Pyramid Texts on the west wall of the entrance into the antechamber, pyramid of Unas, Saqqara	96
24	The pyramid of Teti, Saqqara	99
25	The Inscription of Weni from Abydos, (CG 1435)	102
26	Decree of Pepy I from Coptos, for his mother, Queen Iput (JE 41890)	104
27	Copper statue of Pepy's son, Merenra, from Hierakonpolis (JE 23034)	108
28	Granite lintel from the mortuary temple of Queen Ankhenespepy II, South Saqqara	110
29	Granite false door reused for Queen Meritites II, South Saqqara	113
30	Map of Middle Kingdom Egypt	123
31	Seated statue of Mentuhotep II from the Bab el-Hosan Deir el-Bahari (JE36195)	128

vii

32	Damaged pillars still stand in the peristyle court, Mentuhotep II temple, Deir el-Bahari	131
33	Remains of the sanctuary at the back of the court, Mentuhotep II temple, Deir el-Bahari	132
34	Tomb of Ihy, Saqqara, across from the Teti pyramid	140
35	Colossal granite statue of Amenemhat usurped by Merenptah, found at Tanis (JE 37176)	144
36	Side of the statue with original cartouche of Amenemhat I (JE37176)	145
37	Osiride figure of Senusret I from Lisht (CG 398)	151
38	Seated statues of Senusret I found buried at Lisht (JE 31139)	152
39	Colossal standing statue of Senusret I from Memphis, usurped by Ramses II	153
40	Space in the middle of Karnak that once held the Middle Kingdom temple of Senusret I	154
41	Pillar with Osiride figure of Senusret I, Karnak (JE 48851)	155
42	Naos of Senusret I from Karnak (JE 47276)	156

PREFACE

This book presents a history of the Old Kingdom and the re-formation of a united Egypt with the beginning of the Middle Kingdom. It is not meant to be a "standard" history in the sense of events, battles, and foreign expeditions; rather, it is concerned entirely with Egypt's internal history, focusing on well-documented kings and their expression of legitimacy and power. This specific focus came about from an interest in several questions. How far back is there evidence for the king's close association with the sun god Ra? What about the queen's relationship with the goddess Hathor? Can a pattern be seen in when the king marries his sister and when he doesn't? When work on the book began, this last question was the driving force behind it. Unfortunately, at many times the evidence about the women the king marries was so scant, it was impossible to recognize much of a pattern. Not having evidence for understanding the social structure of the royal family or the harem at this time in Egypt was another problem.

The main focus then shifted to the king's monumental structures and how the layout, decoration, and statuary stated his divine position and legitimacy. Even with the damage these structures have suffered, a great deal of evidence remains. Female members of the king's family are included in the discussion whenever possible, and high officials in their role of working for and supporting the reign of the king round out the discussion.

Although this book may seem of more interest to Egyptologists and Egyptology students than other readers, the first chapter offers a complete introduction to predynastic Egypt, its formation as a state, and the Early Dynastic Period right before the beginning of the Old Kingdom, so any reader can acquire the background to understand the following discussion.

Ancient Egyptian words are written out in italicized English, followed by Unicode transliteration the first time they are used. After that, the transliterations are not added. Ancient Egyptian names, and most titles, do not have following transliteration.

There are three maps in the book showing the places mentioned in the chapters. The first map is at the beginning of the discussion of Predynastic Egypt (Figure 1), the second at the beginning of the Old Kingdom discussion (Figure 5), and the third at the beginning of the Middle Kingdom discussion (Figure 30).

ix

ACKNOWLEDGMENTS

I would like to thank the Rare Books Library staff of the American University in Cairo, especially the Egyptology librarian Amr Kamel, and Mahmoud Mostafa who endlessly scanned material for me. I also appreciated use of the Egyptian Exploration Society's library in London, which had important sources I could not find in Cairo. Thanks also to graduate student Ahmed Osman, who patiently explained and did Unicode for the transliterations. When Dr. Reinart Skumsnes was still a graduate student he worked as my research assistant, and I set him to work finding the evidence of royal sibling marriages in the Old Kingdom. Finally I have made good use of this material and must thank him.

Most importantly, I would like to thank my family and friends for being so understanding about my lack of time and attention for them. Thanks also to Beatrice Rehl of Cambridge University Press for her unfailing help and support.

INTRODUCTION

P HARAONIC EGYPT IS OFTEN VIEWED AS HAVING BEEN MONOLITHIC and unchanging. Ancient Egyptian civilization was certainly long-lasting, and throughout its 3,000 years the basic tenets of its culture endured. There was development and change, however, as kings faced evolving situations, both natural and manmade, and responded to political and economic pressures in order to keep their hold on power. From the time of the very first dynasty, however, the ideology of royal power in Egypt "contained certain key concepts that all successive pharaohs strove to maintain intact" (Valbelle 2002, 97).

Crucial to every king's reign was his legitimacy, which was founded on his relationship to the two most important deities in the ancient Egyptian pantheon for the institution of divine kingship, Osiris and the sun god Ra, as well as Ra's female companion, the goddess Hathor. From the very beginnings of ancient Egyptian kingship, the king was the falcon god Horus, son of Osiris. The king's first and oldest name was his Horus name. By the time of the Fourth Dynasty of the Old Kingdom, the king also takes a "Son of the Sun-god" name. Also beginning with the Old Kingdom, clearly by the Fifth Dynasty if not earlier, is the theme of the divinity of the king as the child of Ra and Hathor (Troy 1986, 55).

The king expressed his legitimacy and relationship to deities by building and supporting religious institutions, among which was the king's own burial complex, as the deceased king lived in his pyramid complex as a god (Stadelmann 1985, 214). All of these royal constructions were decorated with scenes of the king and the gods, depicting the king offering to the gods and the gods responding by offering him eternal life and protection, as well as handing over to him the symbols of royal rule.

The king needed a loyal and trustworthy administration to carry out his control over the country. In the beginning, all the important administrative offices were held by male relatives of the king, especially his sons, although this stops in the mid-Fifth Dynasty when high offices such as that of the vizier are filled by nonroyal men. From then on, the king's relationship to his elite officials was of prime importance, as he needed them to support his power, just as his power maintained theirs. At times, however, elite power slipped into entitlement, and this posed a problem that the king had to deal with.

Perhaps most crucial of all to the king's reign was the perpetuation of his family line with a son to follow him on the throne, and so the females and children of the king's family must have played an essential and also, at times, possibly political role. The king of ancient Egypt was not monogamous, and throughout pharaonic history kings married any number of women. Familial endogamy and exogamy are both found in ancient Egyptian royal family marriages. Keeping marriage within the royal family was a centrist approach and protected the family's hold on the throne. On the other hand, cementing alliances with powerful nonroyal families through marriage extended the reach of royal power through loyal officials. At times, evidenced clearly in the Fourth Dynasty of the Old Kingdom, and in the Twelfth Dynasty of the Middle Kingdom, the king married his own sister. This may have been to keep power concentrated in the family, as well as to display the king's divinity, for in the Heliopolitan creation myth divine brothers and sisters married. There is often not enough evidence about royal marriages, however, to be able to ascertain if the king shared a blood relationship with his wife.

Kingship based on divine backing remained a rather static institution, but kings did innovate in the way in which they stated their legitimacy and power. The mythology that backed the position of the king was unchanging, but developing political and social contexts brought about changes in how a king projected and fulfilled his divinely chosen role. Monumental building projects, depictions of the king with the gods, royal statuary, administrative positions, documents such as decrees, as well as the place of the king's family members in his reign, all fit into the larger strategy that shaped the king's individualized statement of his rule. This book hopes to add to the understanding of the manifestations of kingship, power, and legitimacy in the period that was the foundation block of pharaonic history, the Old Kingdom, and its re-formation in the beginning of the Middle Kingdom that follows. Chapter 1 presents the background material for understanding ancient Egyptian history and civilization. To properly understand kingship and its power in ancient Egypt demands an understanding of how its civilization, ruled by a divine king, came about in the first place.

CHAPTER ONE

BACKGROUND TO ANCIENT EGYPT

ANCIENT EGYPTIAN HISTORY AND CHRONOLOGY

This study covers approximately 1,000 years, centering on two broad periods of pharaonic civilization referred to by scholars as kingdoms: the Old Kingdom and the earlier part of the Middle Kingdom, when the state is reunified and reformed. Later there would be changes in the New Kingdom that follows. These, in large part, were brought about by external forces and foreign peoples, but, for the most part, New Kingdom kingship, state administration, and, in the early New Kingdom, royal marriage patterns, were based on Middle Kingdom practice developed from that of the Old Kingdom. The Old Kingdom lasted roughly from 2686 to 2181 BCE, and the Middle Kingdom from 2055 to 1650 BCE (Shaw 2004, 184).

Put simply, "kingdom" is the term applied by Egyptologists to a period of centralization and unification, when one king ruled over all of Egypt. In between these kingdoms are periods, referred to as "intermediate," when there was decentralization and different kings ruled over different parts of Egypt. The kingdoms were first named in the mid-nineteenth century, and the intermediate periods became denoted as separate spans of time somewhat later, in post–World War I Egyptological studies (Schneider 2008, 182–184).

It should be kept in mind that Egyptian history has been divided by modern scholars into periods that might not reflect divisions recognized in ancient times, and this can color our understanding of ancient Egyptian history and societal change (Malek 1989, 45–49; Redford 2008, 24). An Egyptian priest named Manetho wrote a history of Egypt, known as the *Aegyptiaca*, in the third century BCE (Waddell 1971), perhaps under the patronage of Ptolemy II, and intended for Greek consumption. It is thought that Manetho worked with temple documents to compose the King List that makes up the backbone of his work, which is preserved for us in three later copies, unfortunately all corrupted. Manetho divided the kings of Egypt into thirty dynasties or "houses"; later, the last short period of Persian rule before the victory by Alexander the Great became the Thirty-First Dynasty. Some of the divisions in the groups of kings made by Manetho match divisions in an earlier New Kingdom list known as the Turin King List, and Manetho possibly used ancient documents in parts of his work, similar to those available to the scribe of the Turin List (Malek, 1982, 104–105; Gozzoli 2006, 196–197).

The Old Kingdom, also referred to as the "Pyramid Age," comprises the Third to the Sixth Dynasties. As mentioned, the modern labeling of periods of dynastic history may, in some cases, not actually match with ancient periods and divisions. For example, some scholars see the Third Dynasty as belonging more properly in the Early Dynastic Period. "In cultural and political terms, the transition from the Third to the Fourth Dynasty certainly represents a major break, whereas there is considerable continuity between the Second and Third Dynasties" (Wilkinson 2014, 49). Others accept the Old Kingdom as lasting through the Seventh and Eighth Dynasties. The kings of those dynasties, listed after King Pepy II in the Turin King List (Baud 2006, 157), are little known but seem to have continued to rule from Memphis. Eventually a second line of kings, the Ninth Dynasty, arises at Heracleopolis and, at this point, the period known as the First Intermediate Period begins. By the time the kings of the Ninth Dynasty have become the Tenth Dynasty, another line of kings in Thebes, known as the Eleventh Dynasty, appears. Determining how long the Heracleopolitan kings ruled "is fraught with all but insurmountable difficulties" (Seidlmayer 2006, 165), but the First Intermediate Period ends when a king from Thebes unites Egypt once again, during the latter part of the Eleventh Dynasty. That part of the Eleventh Dynasty through to the Thirteenth Dynasty is the Middle Kingdom.

Ancient Egyptian cultural memory retained the idea that the king was "Ruler of the Two Lands," that is, Upper Egypt and Lower Egypt, south and north. At the time of unification, traditionally thought to be at the beginning of the First Dynasty, around 3100 BCE, the two lands were joined under the rule of one king. Now, Egyptologists accept that the formation of a single Egyptian state took place 200–300 years earlier than the First Dynasty, and this time period has been given the name "Dynasty 0," in order to clearly place it earlier. Some scholars prefer to use the term "Protodynastic Period" instead of Dynasty 0. In archaeological terms, Dynasty 0 is the same as the period of Naqada IIC–IIIB, the very end of the Predynastic Period.

EARLY EVIDENCE AND FORMATION OF A STATE

The period called Predynastic Egypt began roughly around 5000 BCE with a culture known as Fayum A, whose remains were first found on the shores of Lake Qarun in the Fayum Oasis in 1934 (Caton-Thompson and Gardner

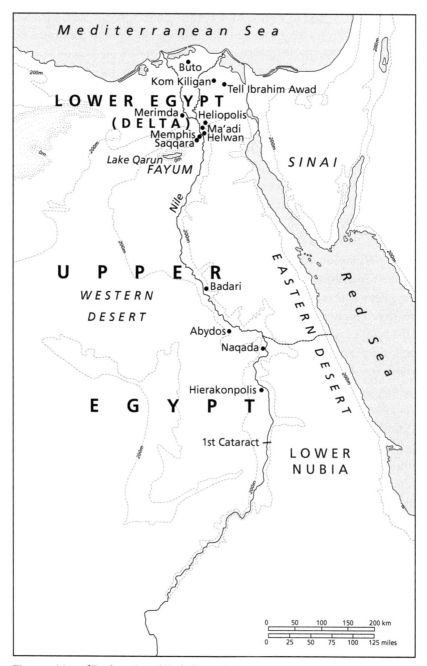

Figure 1 Map of Predynastic and Early Dynastic Egypt

1934). Fayum A is the oldest of the Neolithic cultures in ancient Egypt, Neolithic being characterized by the production of pottery and the domestication of plants and animals. Fayum A culture is represented by remains of storage pits, some still lined with matting, which were used for the storage of emmer wheat and barley (Wendrich and Cappers 2005, 12). Agricultural tools have been found, as well as baskets and rather plain, coarse pottery. Bones provide evidence of domesticated sheep and goats as well as some cattle and pigs.

A contemporary site was Merimde on the edge of the Western Delta, which produced evidence of partially subterranean, circular house remains and burials (Junker 1929–1940). The site was large, and areas of habitation were sometimes later located on top of earlier burials. The building-up of strata was possible at the site because Merimde was located on a "terrace . . . protected from the annual flood" (Tristant and Midant-Reynes 2011, 46); however, the original excavator only recognized three different strata rather late in the excavation. A newer excavation at the site, and a restudy of the material, distinguished five strata. Some of the decorated pottery in the earliest stratum, Level I, show Asiatic connections, but by Level II connections seem to be with the Sahara and Sudan (Eiwanger 1984, 61; 1992, 74). Three later levels, III–V, contain material similar to Fayum A and Omari (Midant-Reynes 1992, 109, 114).

The Omari, discovered on a plateau area by the Wadi Hof near modern-day Helwan, south of Cairo, appears to have been based around the wadi itself, and not on the flood plain of the Nile (Debono and Mortensen, 1990). Subsistence seems to have been dependent mainly on fish and domesticated animals, with a small grain component. There were pits and postholes from shelters spread over an area of about 4 kilometers; small pots made of local clay, baskets, sickle blades, other stone tools, and more than a dozen burials were found. Omari seems to have been a "local development," probably contemporary with Merimde levels II–IV and earlier than, and not related to, the Maadi culture (Debono and Mortensen 1990, 81).

There is quite a difference in the amount of evidence for Predynastic settlement in Lower Egypt, as compared with Upper Egypt. Owing to the drier environment and the nearby desert plateaus of the relatively narrow river valley, Upper Egypt offered a better chance for preservation than the much wetter Nile Delta, which also would become built up with silt during every annual inundation, burying evidence of Neolithic sites. In Lower Egypt, there are single sites known from different areas, whereas, in Upper Egypt, development in Predynastic culture can be seen over time as sites have been preserved through numerous successive strata. In terms of the material culture found in Upper and Lower Egypt, there are two main differences: the pottery from Lower Egyptian cultures is plain and undecorated, and personal items, such as jewelry, are much scarcer. Since all these items are, for the most part, found in a funerary context, the difference, however, may not reflect wealth but burial beliefs.

Slightly later than Fayum A, in about 4440 BCE, there is evidence of Predynastic settlement in Upper Egypt with the Badarian culture, found in the area of the modern-day city of Sohag. Most of the evidence for the Badarian culture comes from tombs, which were oval pits, roofed with sticks and matting. Bodies were found in a flexed position, covered by mats and hides, with some personal belongings and pottery placed around them. The Badarian culture was followed by the Naqada I culture in about 4000 BCE, although the connection between the two cultures is not entirely clear. Naqada I had similarities to the Badarian but had much more in terms of material culture, and the objects were of better quality. White-lined pottery and disk-shaped mace-heads are characteristic of Naqada I material culture.

Naqada is the material culture of Upper Egypt that evolved in stages from Naqada I through Naqada III, finally culminating in Dynasty 0. Flinders Petrie excavated sites with Naqada material culture and, based on pottery types, created his famous Sequence Dating for the Upper Egyptian Predynastic era, distinguishing three periods: Amratian, Gerzean, and Semainean, named after the most important archaeological site for each (Petrie 1901, 4–17, pl. II). Kaiser refined Petrie's system into Naqada I to III, with minor developments marked with the letters a through d (Kaiser 1957). The use of a single name for the span of this culture reflects our understanding of it as one culture that developed over time.

By the time of Naqada II, clay, not Nile mud, was being used for pottery, and pottery was decorated with boats, hints at landscape, some human figures, and animals. The same type of decoration was found in the first known decorated tomb, Tomb 100 at Hierakonpolis. The size and decoration of this tomb indicate that its owner belonged to an elite level of social stratification, and this evident stratification is another development of Naqada II. Decorated cosmetic palettes appeared, as well as large, ripple-flaked flint blades and the pear-shaped mace, known as the "white" mace, which continued to be wielded by the king of Egypt throughout pharaonic history.

Material remains of other cultures have been uncovered in Lower Egypt contemporary with Naqada II. The Maadi culture, named after the modern suburb south of Cairo, has been found in Maadi, Heliopolis, and Wadi Digla. In Maadi, subterranean houses have been found, as well as a structure that may have had a religious purpose, as there was no evidence of domestic use. The Maadi cultural material reveals connections in tool types (Rizkana and Seeher 1988, 29–31, pl. 50ff.), pottery (Rizkana and Seeher 1987, 73–77), and house structure (Rizkana and Seeher 1989, 53) with southern Palestine Early Bronze I culture, and there was possibly a "foreign Levantine" community at the site (Guyot 2008, 709). Maadi had trade connections with the copper mines in the

Sinai, and may have been a site of copper production, as numerous copper objects, as well as three ingots, were found (Rizkana and Seeher 1989, 13–18). By the time of Naqada II in Upper Egypt, Maadi pottery is found in other Delta sites, such as Buto (Tell el-Fara'in). Buto also had a foreign community, evidenced by types of foreign pottery made with Nile mud (Faltings 2002, 166–168), as well as trade connections to the Levant and Mesopotamia by land and via access to the Mediterranean (von der Way 1992, 3; Guyot 2008, 709–710).

By the time of the later Naqada II, at the Lower Egyptian sites of Buto, Tell Ibrahim Awad, and Kom Kiligan, material objects of the Maadi-Buto culture begin to disappear from burials (von der Way 1992, 3) and Naqada material culture is found instead. By Naqada III, Maadi-Buto culture is gone, and Naqada III material culture is found throughout Egypt. The actual taking over of the Delta by Naqada III material culture is not fully understood. Did the material culture of the south simply become the standard in funerary contexts, or was there an actual invasion of the north by the south? Did the adoption of a new material culture lead to political unity? One important point is that trade to the Sinai and the Near East was concentrated in Lower Egypt (Chlodnicki 2008). Was it therefore economically expedient for the newly based rulers in Abydos to take over Lower Egypt and become a single, unified state? Egypt's unification, and how it was brought about, is a topic that has still not been settled (Köhler 2008b).

One site in Upper Egypt, Hierakonpolis, stands out in importance in the later Predynastic Period as having had a local line of rulers, as well as a ceremonial center in which their power and control were celebrated in ways and with symbols that were retained once there were kings ruling over a united Egypt. Site HK6 has uncovered large tombs with high-quality objects as well as surrounding subsidiary tombs with both humans and animals. Tomb 16 dates to Naqada IIA. It had been both plundered and reused but still contained more than a hundred pottery vessels; two ceramic masks; beads, including two of gold; ivory fragments; and arrowheads (Friedman, Van Neer, and Linseel 2011, 159–160). Immediately next to Tomb 16 were thirteen other burials, with a total of thirty-six men, women, and children (Friedman, Van Neer, and Linseele 2011, 172–174), and located beyond these, the burials of twenty-eight different animals. The animals were both wild – elephant, auroch, hartebeest, and baboon – and domestic – bull, dog, and cat (Friedman, Van Neer, and Linseele 2011, 175–185). As of 2015, thirty-eight wild animals, from twelve different species, have been found at HK6 in the area around Tomb 16 and a nearby area called the East Complex (Van Neer et al. 2017, 1–3). It has been suggested that not only is the capture and killing of these animals a show of power but, for the chieftain in Tomb 16 to bury them nearby, means he "takes their powerful natural attributes" for himself, reflecting "the physical reality behind the animal-based royal iconography of the Early Dynasty Period" (Friedman, Van Neer, and Linseele 2011, 186). Kemp has termed the capture and killing of wild animals the "containment of unrule" (Kemp 2006, 92–94), and this symbolic expression of power in the late Predynastic era became a political statement that continued to be made throughout the whole of Pharaonic history.

The slightly later Naqada IIB Tomb 23 at site HK6 is perhaps "the largest tomb of its time" (Friedman 2008, 1188), a time when Hierakonpolis functioned as a major center in the southern part of Upper Egypt. Although badly plundered, the tomb still contained fragments of ceramic masks, ivory objects, and a stone vessel, all indicative of an elite burial (Friedman 2005, 4). This tomb and another small structure, possibly an offering chapel on its northeast side, were enclosed by a rectangular wooden wall. More than 500 fragments from a smashed, near life-size, limestone statue, were found in the area of the chapel, including fragments that could be identified as ears and a nose (Jaeschke 2004, Harrington, 2004). Northeast of the chapel, still within the wooden enclosure, were ritual deposits of vessels, such as those found at the ceremonial center HK29A, and flint animal figurines like those found in other elite tomb and temple contexts at Hierakonpolis and Abydos (Friedman 2005, 5; 2008, 1167–1169).

The ceremonial center HK29A underwent three phases of construction from Naqada IIB to the time of the First Dynasty, when it ceased to be used – a period of about 500 years (Friedman 2009, 91–99, fig. 9). It had an oval courtyard about 135 feet long and around 40 feet wide, marked off with a gated wall and, based on the potholes, some type of pillared structure, perhaps a "viewing pavilion," on both the north and south sides (Friedman 2009, 92, figs. 8–9). In a second phase of construction, a 14-foot-wide platform was added on the north side of the courtyard; it has been pointed out that this platform may have been like the one King Narmer sits on in the scene on his ceremonial mace-head, found at the Horus Temple at Hierakonpolis (Friedman 1996, 33, fig. 12).

Both the pottery and the faunal remains from HK29A have been studied in detail and would seem to indicate that this location was used for rituals and ceremonies. The bone remains show that the different wild and domestic species brought to the complex differed from those found in the rest of the settlement site. Some of the species seem to have been brought into the complex to be slain for ritual purposes and others brought to be butchered and eaten. The large number of flint debris recovered at HK29A suggests the sharpening of knife blades. There was plentiful evidence of the bones of very large Nile perch as well as young cattle, which were not found at domestic sites at Hierakonpolis and probably considered "high-status" food. There were also species of wild animals such as "fennec, hyena, hartebeest" and "remains from crocodile and softshell turtle" not found anywhere else at Hierakonpolis (Linseele, Van Neer, and Friedman 2009, 132). These creatures may represent elite hunting trophies or, in the case of hippopotamuses, were animals killed in a ritual ceremony intended to control and overcome chaos. King Narmer's ceremonial mace-head also depicts an oval enclosure with wild animals running in it. There are clear similarities between the activities that seem to have taken place in the ceremonial center HK29A and those portrayed in images on late Predynastic and Protodynastic objects, such as the capturing, subjugation, and sacrificing of wild and powerful animals (Perry 2011, 1282). Morenz proposes that the scenes on the ceremonial palettes of the Protodynastic Period "are used to convey a sacro-political message" and they correspond to "central festivals celebrating the ruler – enthronement, victory, agricultural rituals" (Morenz 2013, 138). The decoration on the mace-heads must have served the same purpose.

Numerous pottery sherds from two types of vessels also indicate ritual use. Tall, red-washed jars and polished, small egg-shaped black vessels, discarded after minimal use, were found in refuse pits at the ceremonial center. Possibly these two vessels, whose shapes represent "over 45% of the rim, base and body sherd collection" (Friedman 1996, 29), represent the Red Land and the Black Land, the desert and the Nile Valley. The remains of fauna in the refuse pits suggest that the rituals in the ceremonial center were tied "with the coming of the Nile flood, an especially chaotic moment in the cosmic cycle of renewal" (Friedman 2011, 36; Perry 2011, 1280).

It has been suggested that the site of Hierakonpolis was the source of ancient Egyptian kingship and that this can be seen in the rituals of a ceremonial center, such as HK29A, that " 'materialized' the role of the elite as intermediaries in an emerging ideological system" (Perry 2011, 1278). Moreno García has suggested early "royal" authority developed and existed in the area of Hierakonpolis, and later these kings moved to Abydos, an area with a larger agricultural potential and better situated for control over Egypt and also over foreign trade (Moreno García 2013, 188–190), although Hierakonpolis may have continued to have status as Egypt's old and "glorious past" (Friedman 2008b, 26). Other scholars think this is going too far and that this may be more of a case of the fact that "kings legitimize themselves by reference to antiquity" (Baines 1995, 98).

Quite a number of elements seen later in the symbolism backing pharaonic kingship and in the architectural details of royal burials, can be found at late Predynastic Hierakonpolis, however. It is possible that sacrificial burials were associated with elite burials such as Tomb 16 (Friedman 2011, 39), and these kinds of burials are found in association with the later royal burials in Abydos. Tomb 16 and other elite burials at Hierakonpolis also offer evidence of separate superstructures tied to funerary ritual. These superstructures are clearly seen on a massive scale at Abydos. Rulers associated with powerful animals, and the importance of control over them as a symbolic controlling of chaos is clearly seen in the artistic representations of pharaonic kingship.

The period at the end of Naqada III has been named Dynasty 0 (also referred to as the Protodynastic Period), and Egypt appears united, ruled by a line of kings. The names of possible Dynasty 0 kings are known, although not all scholars agree on the reading of the hieroglyphs that make up their names. There appear to have been at least four to five kings, the last of whom is Narmer. His rule has been suggested as possibly spanning the change of Dynasty 0 to the First Dynasty; alternatively, Narmer may be synonymous with Menes, the traditional first king of Egypt (Hassan, Jimenez-Serrano, and Tassie 2006, 689–697). The tombs of these early kings have been found at Abydos. Cemetery U is the oldest and dates from Naqada I down to Naqada III, or Dynasty 0. The largest tomb is Uj, which has been attributed to King Scorpion I, based on the large amount of pottery in the tomb from the "estate of Scorpion" (Dreyer 1992, 297). Just to the south is Cemetery B with the tombs of Iry-Hor, Ka, and Narmer, the last king of Dynasty 0, as well as Aha, the first king of the First Dynasty. Slightly farther to the southwest is the Umm el-Qa'ab with tombs of the kings of the First and Second Dynasties.

Tomb Uj, the largest tomb in Cemetery U, was excavated in 1988. It had been robbed in ancient times and parts of it were carelessly dug up in the 1890s by Émile Amélineau; Petrie apparently called Amélineau's work at Abydos "scandalous" (Spencer 2011, 19–20). This tomb is particularly important not only for containing the earliest evidence of hieroglyphic writing but for its architecture and contents, providing the equivalent of a palace for the deceased (Wilkinson 2004, 1132). The tomb has twelve chambers that seem to "correspond to rooms of a house or palace" (Dreyer 2011, 130). Although plundered, it still retained a number of objects, some in obsidian, gold, and ivory. Three chambers had been filled with wine jars of Palestinian style; 700 were still in situ. The burial chamber contained a wooden shrine, possibly a forerunner to later royal burial shrines. An ivory *heka* (*ḥkȝ*) scepter was also found in this chamber (Dreyer 2011, 131–133); the *heka* scepter, or "crook," is an important part of later pharaonic regalia. The reliability of using these objects and symbols to establish that there was an early king, or early ideas of kingship, however, has been questioned by some (Bestock 2009, 5–7; Papazian, 2012, 43–45).

The oldest hieroglyphs known are those found on the small bone labels in tomb Uj. There are about 150 of them, many from a large chamber in the southwest of the tomb that seemed to have held the more valuable objects. The labels are "incised with numbers or 1–4 hieroglyphic signs," giving amounts or sizes along with the origin of the particular object (Dreyer 1992, 297, pl. 6). The creation of writing is to be seen as part of the "court culture" that formed in the area of Abydos in the very late Predynastic Period and then expanded north, bringing about the "establishment of a highly-centralized state" (Regulski 2008, 1002) with its capital at Memphis, which had already "become a major administrative centre" by the time of Narmer (Regulski 2010, 697).

THE EARLY DYNASTIC PERIOD: THE FIRST DYNASTY

The most important archaeological evidence for the First Dynasty are the tombs of seven kings and one king's mother at Abydos, tombs of royal family members and high officials at North Saqqara, and tombs of some royal offspring and lesser officials at Helwan. The royal tombs of the early Second Dynasty are at Saqqara, although only the substructures remain, and the last kings of the Second Dynasty returned to Abydos to be buried. The Abydos tombs of both these dynasties consist of mud-brick–built chambers in large pits cut down into the sand and rock below at the Umm el-Qa'ab. Some of these early chambers had wood in the interior, such as a wooden floor, and, in the later First Dynasty, the tomb of King Den had the main chamber partly done in red granite (Petrie 1900, 11). Den's tomb also had the addition of a staircase leading down into the tomb; staircases appear in tombs after his, as they must have afforded an efficient means not only for work on the tomb but for carrying out the actual burial. A stairway entrance also allowed the tomb to be constructed in full before the death of the king, as the roofing and covering of the tomb chamber did not have to wait until after the burial (Ormeling 2017).

Den's tomb had one other architectural difference from the other Umm el-Qa'ab tombs. In the southwest corner was a small chamber (S4b) that has been explained as a statue chamber, or serdab, that must have held a statue of the king (Dreyer 1990, 78, figs. 7–8). A small staircase led up from this chamber to the outside, perhaps as a means for the king's spirit to travel to the west (Bárta 2019, 63).

The tomb chambers were roofed in wood, and, above the roof, but still below the surface, a mound was constructed, supported by brick walls and plastered over. These mounds were not visible once the tomb was covered over, and they must have provided "some kind of service to the deceased" (O'Connor 2009, 152). Finally, a similar but much larger mound was constructed over the entire tomb. There would have been two large stone stelae bearing the king's Horus name on the east side of this mound; two stelae were found for kings Peribsen and Khasekhemwy, although not in situ. None of the tombs have any evidence left of a chapel on the surface, but there must have been one where the stelae were placed (O'Connor 2009, 155).

All of the First Dynasty tombs, beginning with that of King Aha, have subsidiary tombs with burials that seem to have taken place at the same time as that of the king. Three hundred and seventeen subsidiary tombs, the highest number known, surrounded the tomb of King Djer, Aha's successor. Although both males and females were found in these subsidiary graves, the majority were male and young, none being older than twenty-five (van Dijk 2007, 138–139; Morris 2008, 17–20). However, these burials stop at the end of the First Dynasty.

In the case of King Aha, the burials, a total of thirty-six in three rows, are placed around the burial chamber of the king, and seem to have been roofed over at the same time as the king's burial. The skeletal remains are all of young adult men aged twenty to thirty, and presumably they would have been royal guards (Bestock 2009, 28). It would appear that they must have been put to death at the time of the king's burial, but there is no actual evidence to show how they died. Such sacrifices demonstrated the king's ultimate control over the victims' lives and deaths (Wengrow 2006, 224, 252). At least seven lions were also buried with King Aha, and graves of hunting dogs and donkeys are also known (O'Connor 2009, 173).

It is possible that there is also evidence for the woman who was either the mother or wife of King Aha. In 1897, Jacques de Morgan discovered a very large First Dynasty mastaba at Naqada, decorated with a serekh-façade, a stylized drawing of the royal palace. In some of the interior chambers, he found small ivory labels with the name Neithhotep, as well as two with the name of King Aha (de Morgan 1897, figs. 521, 550, 556–557). It has been suggested that, since her name contains the name of Neith, a Delta goddess, this woman is the "daughter of Delta royalty" and was married to Aha for "strategic" reasons (Wenke 2009, 242). In addition, it has been suggested that Neithhotep was from a prominent Naqada family and became the wife of Narmer to join together the two powers of Naqada and Abydos (Wilkinson 1999, 70). A 2001 study of all the objects from this tomb concludes that they were richer than those found in contemporary large tombs at Saqqara, and that the tomb must have belonged to the highest ranked person whose name was found in the tomb, that person being Queen Neithhotep (Kahl et al. 2001, 184–185), although her family and origins are still unknown.

In conjunction with each of the tombs in the Umm el-Qa'ab, so-called funerary forts were constructed close to the edge of cultivation near the temple of the god Osiris. There are now eight known funerary forts from the First Dynasty, including three dating to the reign of King Aha (O'Connor 2009, 166) and two from the Second Dynasty. These "forts" were large, mud-brick rectangular structures meant as spaces for royal rituals, probably connected to the presentation of offerings (Bestock 2009, 60). In 2004–2005, two additional small enclosures were found that date to the reign of Aha. This king, then, had three enclosures, although probably the largest was his and the two smaller enclosures possibly belonged to members of his family (Bestock 2008a, 51; 2009, 88–89). Like Aha's tomb, and the other First Dynasty tombs at the Umm el-Qa'ab, the funerary enclosures also have subsidiary tombs. The enclosure known as the "Western Mastaba" has fourteen boat burials associated with it (O'Connor 2009, 166).

These enclosures provided a large interior space, and the ones better preserved have a structure, perhaps a chapel for a statue, or possibly a stela, of the king, in the southeast corner. In the chapel of Khasekhemwy's enclosure, evidence was found of "incense burning and libations" (O'Connor 2009, 172). There are two gateways into the enclosure, the main one in the east and a secondary one in the north. There is evidence of "intentional destruction" of all of these structures (Bestock 2009, 55), probably in conjunction with the burial of the king; only Khasekhemwy's enclosure, the last one built, was left intact (Adams and O'Connor 2003, 84).

One of the First Dynasty tombs at Abydos belonged to Meretneith, accepted as the mother of King Den, who held the reins of power when her husband, Den's father, King Djet, died and Den was still a young boy. The name Meretneith was found on two limestone stelae from the tomb, one complete and one broken, as well as on fragments of stone vessels (Petrie 1900, 10–11, pls. V, LXIV; Kaplony 1963, 494) (Figure 2). The evidence for this family

Figure 2 Stela from Abydos with the name of Meretneith (JE 34450). Photo: Sally el-Sabbahy. Courtesy of the Egyptian Museum, Cairo.

relationship is based on the fact that Meretneith is named as the mother of Den in the Palermo Stone, as her name follows his (Schäfer 1902, 42, pl. 1; Helck 1987, 124–125; Roth 2001, 520, fig. 2). Her position as king's mother and regent seems to be clear by including her, with her title of "King's Mother," in a list of kings' names on a clay sealing found at Abydos (Dreyer 1987, 36–37, fig. 3), her secondary importance shown by her name following her son's (Kahl 2006, 97). Manetho's *Aegyptiaca* states that, in the Second Dynasty, women were allowed to rule, perhaps a reflection of the case of Meretneith, the king's mother, serving as regent (Waddell 1971, 37). Meretneith only holds the title "King's Mother," and the large stelae from her tomb do not show her name in a serekh-façade. She is not king but rules in the name of her son. This evidence for Meretneith and her position, however, is particularly important because it is the first time we get any kind of glimpse into the members of an ancient Egyptian royal family and, especially, the importance of a female member of the royal family.

Meretneith's tomb was constructed next to that of her husband, Djet, and just northwest of that of her son, Den, and clay sealings with his Horus name were found in her tomb (Petrie 1900, pl. XXI). Her burial chamber is about 9 by 7 meters, and eight small, rectangular rooms, probably storage magazines, were built on all sides. This structure is then surrounded by a rectangle of forty-one subsidiary burials except for a gap in the south corner. In fact, all the First Dynasty tombs beginning with that of King Djer have a gap in the line of subsidiary tombs in the southwest corner, which would have allowed their souls to travel unimpeded into their afterlife in the west (Bárta 2019, 63). The wadi southwest of these royal tombs was thought to lead into the afterlife (Figure 3).

The number of subsidiary tombs is fewer than those around the earlier royal tombs built, but perhaps because Meretneith was not actually a king she had fewer (Bestock 2009, 39–40). Like all the other royal tombs at Abydos, Meretneith also has a separate funerary enclosure to the north. The enclosure accepted as hers only has slight remains of two of the walls and some of the subsidiary burials.

An ivory comb belonging to King Djet may be the "oldest evidence for a link between the sun god and the king" (Cervello-Autuori 2011, 1133) and provides evidence for the "prominence of the solar cult" (Lieven 2010, 29–30) (Figure 4). The comb is decorated with the Horus name of the king, and then above that is "an outstretched pair of wings upon which another falcon sails in an archaic boat" (Quirke 1992 21). Thus, the falcon Horus, who is the king, is "assimilated to the Sun" (Cervello-Autuori 2003, 53). Berlev expresses this as there being "two suns," one terrestrial and one celestial (Berlev 2003, 30). The iconography on the comb has been compared to that on a column in Sahura's Fifth Dynasty funerary temple, as well as the upper part of an obelisk of King Teti of the Sixth Dynasty from Heliopolis (Cervello- Autuori 2011, 1134–1135).

THE EARLY DYNASTIC PERIOD: THE FIRST DYNASTY 17

Figure 3 The wadi at Abydos. Photo: Lisa Sabbahy

Figure 4 The ivory comb of King Djet from Abydos (JE 47176). Photo: Sally el-Sabbahy. Courtesy of the Egyptian Museum, Cairo.

A king named Adjb (or Anedjib) ruled after King Den and may have been his son, although no evidence has been found to prove a family relationship. His tomb, next to those of Meretneith and Den, seems to have been hurriedly completed. *Hwt-ka* (*ḥwt-k 3*), or "soul house," on two stone vessels with his Horus name appear to be the earliest evidence for a cult of the king's *ka*, or soul (Kaplony 1968, 16, fig. 31). King Adjib is discussed further in Chapter 2, as the stepping of a tomb at Saqqara dated to his reign may have been an early development that helped lead to the later Step Pyramid of King Netjerikhet of the Third Dynasty.

Contemporary with the First Dynasty royal tombs at the Umm el-Qa'ab are fifteen large mastaba tombs on the edge of the plateau at North Saqqara. Walter Emery excavated them, beginning in the 1930s and, based on their large size and clear evidence of burials, decided he had found the royal tombs of the First Dynasty (Emery 1949, 1954, 1958). These tombs were well provisioned with high-quality objects, and Emery found clay sealings with royal names and the names of officials. The tombs at Saqqara, not as elaborate and without clear traces of burials, were interpreted as cenotaphs. It was suggested that, since these kings originated from the Abydos area but ruled in the Memphite area, they chose to build a tomb in both places, although they were buried in the tombs at Saqqara. The Saqqara tombs do share elements with the royal tombs and enclosures in Abydos, such as serekh-façades, subsidiary burials at some of the tombs, although not in great numbers, as well as a sand tumulus covering the burial chamber, and boat burials.

Kemp has pointed out, however, that the tombs at Abydos were all tied to a matching funerary enclosure and that this two-part complex was certainly much larger than the Saqqara tombs, concluding that the Saqqara tombs belonged to high officials and the royal tombs were indeed those at Abydos (Kemp 1967). His interpretation has generally been widely accepted (Hendrickx 2008), but recently the question of whether or not the Saqqara tombs belonged to high officials has been brought up again. In particular, questions remain about whether Tomb S3505 belongs to the high official Merka or whether his was a subsidiary tomb within the main tomb. In his discussion, O'Connor draws no firm conclusion but suggests "the ascription of ownership to the elite First Dynasty tombs at Saqqara be treated as a more open issue than is presently the case" (O'Connor 2005, 230). Morris suggests that the Saqqara tombs may have been for members of the royal family, such as queens and even sons who were not in line for the throne (Morris 2007, 187–188). Stadelmann agrees that these tombs were for "the highest members of the royal family" (Stadelmann 2011b, 375).

THE SECOND DYNASTY

In the Second Dynasty, there were seven kings, and there is evidence for five of their tombs. The first three kings of the dynasty built their tombs at Saqqara, south of the area where Djoser later built his Step Pyramid. Only the substructures, underground complexes of rooms, remain. One substructure belongs to Hetepsekhemwy and possibly also a second king, Raneb, because seals with both their names have been found (Lacher 2008, 427–428) as well as inscriptions for both giving their Horus names and, for Raneb, mention of his *hwt-ka* (Kaplony, 1968, 34–36). Another substructure belonged to King Ninetjer. There are enclosures, such as the Gisr el-Mudir (Regulski 2009, 226–228; Mathieson 2000, 37), in the desert west of the Step Pyramid of King Djoser, and these must be related to the tombs, in the way that the funerary forts at Abydos related to the tombs there.

Peribsen and Khasekhemwy, the last two kings of the dynasty, built their tombs at the Umm el-Qa'ab at Abydos, just west of the tombs of the First Dynasty. The tomb of Peribsen was very much in the style of the earlier First Dynasty tombs, while Khasekhemwy's, when completed after four different phases of construction, was much larger and longer and had a great number of storage magazines. In the center of his tomb was a stone-lined burial chamber, surrounded by fifty-eight storage rooms in which the funerary provisions had been clearly organized by type. The final plan of the tomb had two entrances, one from the north and one from the south (Dreyer et al. 2003, 108–114; Angevin 2015, 822, 829). Wilkinson suggests that the corridor into the tomb from the north foreshadows the later Old Kingdom pyramids' corridors, facing north to direct the king's spirit up to the circumpolar stars to become one of the "Indestructibles" (Wilkinson 2004, 1139).

One noticeable difference between the First and Second Dynasty royal tombs and funerary enclosures is that those of the Second Dynasty have no sacrificial burials. The last subsidiary burials were the twenty-one found around the tomb of Qa'a, the last king of the First Dynasty (Engel 2008, 39). Having sacrificial burials around the royal tomb has been called an "exercise in absolute power" (Wilkinson 1999, 266). The disappearance of the practice in the Second Dynasty has been described as a "renunciation" of this kind of power and a subordination of the king "under divine forces" (Kahl 2007, 61), particularly that of the sun god.

It has been pointed out that "Early Dynastic society at Memphis was highly structured" (Regulski 2010, 697) and that this can be seen by the placement of tombs either on the west of the Nile at North Saqqara, the most elite place, or in the east at Helwan, where tombs are still those of the elite or even belong to members of the royal family but they were figures who were not as important. There seem to be clear spatial divisions in these cemeteries between ranks of officials as well as between royal and nonroyal persons (Van Wetering 2004, 1062). This reflects the social complexity brought about by "integrating the north and south of Egypt into one polity" and would have been reflected most at Memphis (Köhler 2008, 383). If the location of one's tomb was of significance, Helwan seems to have been an inferior site, while "individuals buried at Saqqara were members of the 'inner circle' at the court" (Köhler 2008, 389). There were, however, at least one royal son and two royal daughters who had their tombs at Helwan, although their tomb stelae appear to be of lesser quality than those found at Saqqara (Köhler and Jones 2009; Solá-Sagalés 2015, 1558). It has also been pointed out that most of the tombs at Helwan were "built more economically, resulting in fewer materials and labor resources being required in their construction" than the tombs at North Saqqara (La Loggia 2009, 178).

There are two further points that must be brought up in a discussion of the Second Dynasty that may well shed more light on both the political power and the religious role of the king. The first is that the stela of King Raneb, second king of the dynasty, supposedly found at Mit Rahina but probably originally from Saqqara, incorporates Ra, the name of the sun god into the king's name (Roehrig and Serotta 2011, 210). This name can be translated as "Lord of the Sun," "The Sun is the Lord," or "My Lord is the Sun God" (Leprohon 2013, 28; Kahl 2007, 7). It is often stated that the first evidence for the actual cult of the sun god seems to be from the Third Dynasty, evidenced by the names of high officials compounded with Ra, such as Hesira (Kahl 2007, 34ff.) and the fact that the title "The One who Sees the Great One," said to be that of the High Priest of Ra, appears among the titles of Imhotep, although the earliest evidence for this title may go back to the time of King Den in the First Dynasty (Moursi 1972, 12), and, as seen in the previous section, the solar iconography on the ivory comb of King Djet seems to be further evidence of a First Dynasty solar cult.

Most scholars accept that the importance of the relationship of the sun god with the king can first be seen in the Fourth Dynasty when King Radjedef "was the first to use the designation *s3-rʿ*, 'the son of Re' to introduce his Throne name" (Leprohon 2013, 36n35). There were, and are now again being put forth, theories that the cult of Ra can be seen much earlier than the Old Kingdom. In *Archaic Egypt*, published in 1961, Emery stated that the Abydos kings must have been influenced by the worship of the sun god at Heliopolis, and by the Second Dynasty there "appears to have been a fusion of the sky-god Horus with the sun-god Rê, as a composite deity Rê-Harakhte and the king identified with Horus became the son of Rê" (Emery 1961, 121). Perhaps the title "Son of Ra" used by Radjedef, whose name can also be read Djedefra, is not the beginning of the importance of the relationship of the king and Ra but should "be regarded as the end of an evolutionary phase" (Reader 2014, 428) that ushers in the so-called Sun Kings of the Fifth Dynasty.

In the chapters that follow, there will be an emphasis on the relationship between the king and Ra, particularly in the reigns of kings who clearly deify themselves as the sun god. The importance of this relationship also affects the position of royal women because "the women around the king relate to him as Hathor relates to Re" (Quirke 2001, 31). In mythology, when Ra needs a female counterpart, mother, daughter, or wife, the goddess Hathor fills that role, so when "the king plays the part of god, above all Ra . . . a woman styled 'king's wife' becomes his Hathor" (Quirke 2001, 7). The ramifications of this divine role for royal women have never been considered from the point of view of how the king's divinity might affect his choice of spouse, as well as affect her position and status. Whenever there is evidence for the queen's possible family relationship to the king, or her status, these details will be brought into the discussion.

The second point to be brought up is that, in the later part of the Second Dynasty, King Peribsen had a Seth name, not a Horus name. There seems to be little evidence for this king outside of Upper Egypt, and his tomb was in Abydos, not Saqqara. It is possible that there was some type of political break with Memphis at this time, but there is no hard evidence on which to base such a conclusion. One interesting point is that there appears to be a sun disk over the Seth figure above his name, in at least one instance (Kaplony 1963, pl. 80, 302), leading some scholars to accept a Seth-Ra title for this king, although its meaning can only be speculated about (Saied 2005, 290; Kahl 2007, 42–44).

King Khasekhemwy, who followed Peribsen, also seems to have had a power base in the south, with all early evidence of him coming from Hierakonpolis. He may have first constructed a funerary enclosure there, planning for a burial at Hierakonpolis, but more recent work at the site concludes that this enclosure had a "special function that served a living king and not his spirit or memory" (Friedman 2007, 326–328). Directly in the center of the square enclosure was a structure with evidence still remaining of a granite column base, probably one of two, and smashed pieces of an inscribed granite block that might have been a lintel. Matching pieces had been found earlier by Ambrose Lansing, and one piece preserves a serekh-façade with the name of Khasekhemwy (Lansing 1935, 43, fig. 11), the later form of the name Khasekhem. Khasekhem, whose name meant "The Power Has Appeared," changed his name to the dual form, Khasekhemwy, "The Two Powers Have Appeared," and both Horus and Seth appear above his name in the serekh-façade. There is also an epithet following this name, which adds "the Two Lords are at peace in him," which seems to be based on the name of the first king of the Second Dynasty, Hetepsekhemwy (Wilkinson 1999, 91), perhaps purposefully to suggest a new beginning (Kaiser 1992, 184n44).

Four other fragments depict the king in "scenes of ritual character" and one has a figure that can only be that of the king's ka, or soul (Alexanian 1997, pls. 2–3; Alexanian 1999, 14–15). The pottery found at the Hierakonpolis enclosure all dates from the middle of his reign and, although only a small sample, "points to domestic or secular context" and does not match the pottery types found with Khasekhemwy's funeral objects in Abydos (Raue 1999, 13). Khasekhemwy's enclosure, or "fort," must have been connected to kingly celebrations (Alexanian 1997, 21), such as his reunification of Egypt and his change of name, or his *heb sed* (*ḥb-sd*). There are also similar granite fragments from El Kab on the east side of the river from Hierakonpolis. One of the fragments has Khasekhemwy's name (Smith 1946, 131n1). Two block fragments from Gebelein (Morenz 1994, figs. 1, 2), dated stylistically to the late Second Dynasty (Smith 1946, 138) and depicting what seems to be a temple foundation ceremony, possibly of the early Hathor temple there (Wilkinson 1999, 312), are probably also to be attributed to Khasekhemwy. Seidlmayer makes the point that the early temple building of Khasekhemwy at Gebelein, the temple of Hathor, and then the blocks from a chapel of King Djoser at Heliopolis, the temple of Ra, or at that early time, Atum, show that these early rulers were "focusing very much on the ideological foundations of divine kingship" (Seidlmayer 1996, 116). Hathor, in particular, is important in her relationship to kingship, and her temples are a focus of royal activity in the early Old Kingdom (Warden 2015, 474), as will be discussed in Chapter 2.

Two statues of Khasekhemwy, found at Hierakonpolis, have defeated and dead enemies depicted on the front and sides of their bases (Quibell 1900, pls. 39–40; Smith 1998, 23), and there is also evidence for warfare from fragmentary stelae found in the temple area at Hierakonpolis (Hamilton 2016, 110; Wilkinson 1999, 92), as well as stone vessels mentioning "the year of Fighting the Northern Enemy" (Quibell 1900, pl. 38). It would appear that, toward the end of the Second Dynasty, under Peribsen, there was some sort of split between Upper and Lower Egypt and that this was settled in the reign of Khasekhem, who then changed his name to reflect the union of these two forces.

BASIS OF EGYPTIAN KINGSHIP

Mythology defined and supported the position and power of the ancient Egyptian king. He was Horus, the falcon god, "on the throne of the living," son of the god Osiris. The myth of Osiris, the core of which is contained in the Pyramid Texts of the Old Kingdom, (Griffiths 1980, 7–17) explains how this god was once king of Egypt but was killed by his jealous brother, the god Seth, who wished to rule as king. Osiris's sister-wife, Isis, lovingly cared for his body, and Osiris lived again in the afterworld, ruling as its king. Horus fought Seth to avenge his father and dragged him before the tribunal of gods in Heliopolis, who proclaimed that the throne of Egypt belonged to Horus, and thus kinship in Egypt was to be passed down from father to son.

A second myth backing the rule of the king was that of the creator god, the sun god, Ra. Ra created all the other gods, as laid out in the Heliopolitan Creation Myth also contained in the Pyramid Texts. He created a series of brother–sister, male–female pairs, the last of which was Osiris and Isis, the parents of Horus. Horus was Ra's descendant, and so the king as Horus was the descendant or "Son of Ra" and functioned as agent of the sun god on earth (Quirke 2001, 31, 38). The king's relationship with the god Ra is dominant throughout ancient Egyptian history and may have been since the Early Dynastic Period (Kahl 2007).

The kings of ancient Egypt each had a fivefold titulary that was announced at the time of their coronation. The names proclaimed divine associations, hinted at policy, and sometimes announced accomplishments. Some kings patterned their names on earlier kings, in order to emulate them. These five names could also be changed during a king's reign because of an event, like a *heb sed*, or the building of an important monument, such as a new temple (Leprohon 2013, 12, 109).

This set of five names was completely developed by the time of the Fifth Dynasty (Lloyd 2014, 65). The Horus name, the first and oldest known royal name of the ancient Egyptian king, appeared in Dynasty 0. The name of the king is written within a serekh-façade, topped by the Horus falcon. This name literally states that so-and-so is Horus, the falcon, in the midst of the palace. The Horus name expressed that the god Horus was "the link between the heavenly royalty of the gods and the terrestrial royalty of men" (Valbelle 2002, 97) and always remained the first of the five names held by every king when his full titulary was written out.

The second name written in the full titulary is called the "Two Ladies" name, referring to the two protective goddesses, Wadjit, the cobra of Lower Egypt, and Nekhbet, the vulture of Upper Egypt, and this name places the king under the protection of these two goddesses. The earliest known example of this name is of King Aha in the First Dynasty (Leprohon 2013, 15). The Two Ladies name is followed by the "Horus of Gold" name, which is first found written in the Old Kingdom but does not become standardized until the Middle Kingdom (Leprohon 2013, 16). The meaning of the name is not entirely clear. Gold is a substance connected to the gods, particularly the sun god, Ra, and was thought to be the "flesh" of the gods. It has also been suggested – since this title is written with the Horus falcon standing on the sign for gold and because the name for gold is "Nubt," the name of the ancient town of Naqada, the cult center of the god Seth – that this name represents the "king as champion of Maat and defender of the cosmic order against the forces of chaos" (Wilkinson 1999, 177); in other words, Horus as triumphant over Seth.

The throne name of the Egyptian king, another of his five names, was preceded by the phrase *nesu-bit* (*nsw bit*), "the one who belongs to the sedge and the bee"(Leprohon 2013, 17); the sedge plant represents Upper Egypt and the bee Lower Egypt. The king has this name by the time of the Fourth Dynasty, and it is one of two names surrounded by a cartouche, or the sign known as *shen* (*šn*), a protective rope encircling and protecting the king's name.

Symbols of the two lands combined into one are ubiquitous in royal iconography. The motif of the *sema-tawy* (*smȝ tȝwy*), the tying together of the lotus flower of Upper Egypt with the papyrus of Lower Egypt, decorates the side of the king's throne. The king's headgear included two crowns – the White Crown of Upper Egypt and the Red Crown of Lower Egypt – which could be combined into one crown, called the Double Crown. All these royal symbols proclaim that it is the king who binds these dualities together and holds together the land of Egypt.

The king occupied a central position between the gods and humankind. He was a human being while at the same time divine. The king has been described as a god "confined to earth as Horus in human form" (Morales 2014, 48). This situation of the king being human and divine at the same time, or having two bodies, was perhaps most clear in the Fifth Dynasty, when, as a mortal, the king was "connected to the funerary aspects of the royal afterlife and ideology," while at the same time, as the son of the sun, he was "eternally perpetuated and celebrated in a specific and new temple," his sun temple (Nuzzolo 2017, 192).

The king's most important responsibility was to uphold *Maat* (*mȝ‘t*). *Maat* existed at the time of creation and was sometimes referred to by the ancient Egyptians as the "daughter of Ra." *Maat* symbolized cosmic order, as well as truth and justice at the everyday human level. To carry out this responsibility, the king had to serve the gods and keep them content, which was accomplished in a number of ways. One was the construction of temples, which were the gods' houses for their manifestations on earth. Another was the care and feeding of the gods in their temples, which needed to be done on a daily basis, as the ancient Egyptians believed that deities had the same physical needs as both the living and the dead. To carry out the daily ritual of care and feeding for the gods and goddesses, the king was High Priest of all the temple cults in Egypt, although, in reality, priests carried out these duties in the king's name.

Another way the king fulfilled his responsibility to uphold *Maat* was by undertaking military campaigns to defeat Egypt's enemies, those outside of the created world directed by the concept of *Maat* and antithetical to Egyptian world order. The smiting scenes, which show the king striding and striking enemies on the head with his stone mace, placed prominently on temple pylons, proclaimed the king's defeat of *isfet* (*isft*) or chaos. In the New

Kingdom, it was common for the king to lead a military expedition to a foreign country in the first year of his reign. Many scholars think this was a public statement of the king's upholding of *Maat*, while others suggest that the beginning of a new king's reign was a time of weakness and enemies might have taken the chance to rebel or attack. Also, beginning later in the New Kingdom, the king offers *Maat* to the gods in temple scenes by offering a figure of the goddess to them, expressing his upholding of the world order and therefore his legitimacy as a ruler.

BEGINNING OF GOVERNMENT AND ADMINISTRATION

Not only did the king head the government but he and the royal household comprised the core of Egypt's government and administration until into the Fifth Dynasty of the Old Kingdom. At that time, during the reign of King Nyuserra, even the highest office of the land, that of the vizier, was filled by a nonroyal man. Theoretically, the king "owned the entirety of the country," and the bureaucracy that developed was the means by which to collect and redistribute "the produce of Egypt on behalf of the ruler" (Bryan 2006, 69). The collecting, storing, and redistributing of the produce collected as taxes were carried out by the department known as the "Treasury," which was first named in seal impressions belonging to King Den of the First Dynasty (Wilkinson 1999, 125). Attested from the reign of King Aha in the First Dynasty is the biannual "Following of Horus," the king's journey across the country to collect taxes and settle disputes (Engel 2013, 27). This inspection tour maintained control over the country's resources, as well as reinforcing the people's "ties of loyalty" to the king (Wilkinson 1999, 221). The use of this royal inspection of the land to collect taxes has been questioned more recently by Warden, who sees no evidence that the Following of Horus was tied to taxation and suggests that the mention of the Following of Horus on the Palermo Stone indicates that it "has a very important role vis-à-vis the king and his divine role as mediator to the gods" (Warden 2015, 474). Bussmann also has suggested that the state may well have had little to do with provincial Egypt or "institutions off the radar of central administration" at this early time (Bussmann 2014, 88).

Scholars assume that with the beginning of a single state the important officials surrounding the king were all related to him, and, in particular, princes would have held the highest offices. These members of the royal family, along with high officials, formed the elite ruling group called the *pa'at* ($p^{c}t$) (Malek 1986, 34–35). Officials with the title *pa'at* could be part of the royal family and perhaps even sons of the king (Emery 1958, 60; Wilkinson 1999, 148), but in the First Dynasty there was no clear title showing a familial relationship with the king. The titles of both "King's Son" and "King's Daughter" first appear in the Second Dynasty. This is also the time when the royal female title of "King's Wife" is first known, while the title "King's Mother" can be traced to the First Dynasty. Both of these titles are held by Nymaathap (Ny-ma'at-hap), who was probably the wife of King Khasekhemwy and mother of King Netjerikhet (later known as Djoser) of the Third Dynasty.

The vizier, *tjaty* (t͜ʒty), was the most important official under the king, and he remained a constant feature of ancient Egyptian government throughout the periods of the Old and Middle Kingdoms covered in this book. Possibly, the first vizier known by name is Menka, who is mentioned in ink inscriptions on stone vessels dating to the mid-Second Dynasty from the Step Pyramid at Saqqara (Strudwick 1985, 300; Wilkinson 1999, 137). The next attested use of the title is in the early Fourth Dynasty, when it is held by Nefermaat, the eldest son of King Sneferu (Studwick 1985, 301). The actual duties of the vizier are not evident this early on, but a much later text makes clear that the vizier oversaw all government departments, including the royal household and royal activities, and was also the highest judicial official. The New Kingdom text called *The Duties of the Vizier*, known from the tomb of the vizier Rekmire (TT 100) on the West Bank of Thebes, spells out the vizier's duties, the three main aspects of which are managing the royal palace, being the head of the civil administration, and serving as the king's deputy (van der Boorn 1988, 310–331; Bryan 2006, 70–77). At times in the later Old Kingdom, and in the New Kingdom, there could also be two viziers, one for Upper Egypt and one at the royal court at Memphis or, in the later New Kingdom, at Per-Ramses (Haring 2014, 221).

Our understanding of administrative departments and their officials is based in the Old and Middle Kingdoms on the evidence from titles, since before the New Kingdom few administrative documents are known. The problem with relying on titles is that they do not necessarily describe the official's function, as many of the titles reflect status, or position, and not duties (Moreno García 2013, 6). Many official titles simply placed a man in a position of authority and he could then be expected to carry out whatever task the king wanted to be done.

Mastaba S3505 at North Saqqara was the burial site of an official named Merka dating to the late First Dynasty reign of King Qa'a. A roughly shaped, rectangular limestone stela from the tomb gives a rather disordered list of Merka's titles above his seated figure (Emery 1958, 30–31, pl. 39). He had the title *pa'at* that signified he was "a member of the group of royal kinsmen that constituted the ruling elite in the First Dynasty" (Wilkinson 1999, 148). He had religious titles, such as "priest of the goddess Neith," although this title may have been important in reflecting his possible ties to royal women and the court, since the goddess Neith was associated with two royal mothers, as discussed in the section "The Early Dynastic Period: The First Dynasty." Merka also had the title *s(t)m-* priest (*sm* or *stm*), although it is suggested that at this early time the title might have been connected to the king's wardrobe (Wilkinson 2016, 553) rather than to a priestly position. As well, Merka held administrative titles such as "District Administrator of the Desert," a title "that probably involved the organizations of quarrying and mining" (Köhler 2008a, 387), and he was also a "Follower of the King," meaning that he took part in the biannual taxation tour through the country. Still other titles indicate that Merka was tied to the functioning of the palace, such as "Controller of the Palace" and "Controller of the Audience Hall." The majority of his titles could be interpreted as centering on the king and royal court, and Wilkinson suggests that, in the Early Dynastic Period, monarchy was absolute and "all actions, administrative and religious, centered on the person of the king" (Wilkinson 2016, 557).

There is not a great deal of evidence, other than seal impressions, upon which to construct the early administration of the Egyptian state. Based on seal impressions, Müller has been able to point out structure and change in the administration of royal domains, particularly in the First Dynasty reign of King Den as well as immediately after, although it is not clear how much this can help with understanding the administration of the country at large (Müller 2012, 17). Domains were the land that produced the commodities used for the royal mortuary cults. They were of two types, the *hwt* (*hwt*), which might have been some type of administrative collection center, and the *niwt* (*niwt*), probably a village with agricultural land (Khaled 2008a, 28–35). Domains seem to have been based primarily in the Delta, undoubtedly because the most extensive agricultural land is in that area.

Wilkinson has suggested that such control of natural resources and agricultural produce led to a central administration and the division of the country into *sepat* (*sp3t*), or nomes, for tax collection and that the royal domains were the earliest form of a mechanism for "imposing effective economic management"; he sees the "beginning of a nome-based economic system" in the late Third to early Fourth Dynasties (Wilkinson 1999, 117–118). Engel suggests that the division into nomes might have originated as early as the reign of King Den in the First Dynasty (Engel 2006, 2013, 31). Engel also points out seal impression evidence for the department of the Treasury, the *per-hjed* (*pr-ḥḏ*), in the reign of King Den, indicating again that this part of the late First Dynasty was a formulative period of growth and organization in state administration (Engel 2013, 21; Kaplony 1963, pl. 37, fig. 121). State administration and officials will be an important part of the discussion to come, beginning in Chapter 2 on the Old Kingdom.

The study pursued in the chapters that follow will discuss the Old Kingdom, the First Intermediate Period that follows, and then the early part of the Middle Kingdom, in terms of particular kings' reigns and how their rule is reflected in evidence such as (1) monuments and inscriptions expressing power and religious ideology and the king's place within it – this mainly focuses on the king's building of religious structures including his burial complex, which was perhaps always his most important architectural statement; (2) the royal family and what evidence there is that can shed light on their role in the king's position and status – the focus here is on the female members of the family, particularly the royal wives, although this evidence is often scanty at best; (3) key governmental departments and officials and their status under each of these kings, as well as changes in offices and the creation of new positions.

Not every king will be discussed or discussed in detail or with the same level of detail as for another king. This work is not intended to be a comprehensive history of ancient Egypt in the span of the Old Kingdom to early Middle Kingdom but rather an exploration of the evolving politico-religious position of ancient Egyptian kingship and its power, throughout that time. Where possible, this study includes a focus on the role of the royal family. The evidence for each king's reign and each dynasty varies greatly; for example, in the late Fifth Dynasty there were large numbers of administrative titles providing evidence for government structure. Yet, for certain kings, very little evidence exists that refers to members of the royal family. Therefore, the discussion will be uneven at times, but it is dependent on the vagaries of archaeological preservation. (The dates of the king's reign following his name in the chapter headings are those found in Shaw 2000.)

CHAPTER TWO

THE EARLY OLD KINGDOM

T HE OLD KINGDOM COVERS ROUGHLY THE PERIOD 2682–2060 BCE and comprises primarily the Third to Sixth Dynasties. Technically, the rule of a single king at Memphis continued into the Eighth Dynasty (Papazian 2015), but because little evidence outside of the names of kings, particularly in the Abydos King List, is preserved, the Old Kingdom after the Sixth Dynasty is not included in this study. The Old Kingdom begins with the Third Dynasty, for which the Turin King List gives the names of five kings and a total number of seventy-four years for their reigns. Five Horus names of kings are known from inscriptional evidence dating to this dynasty, but there are difficulties matching these Horus names with the *nsw-bit* (*nsw bit*), or "King of Upper and Lower Egypt," crown names used in the Turin List. Furthermore, there are scholarly disputes over the order in which these kings are listed (Wilkinson 1999, 94). It is now accepted by almost all scholars that Djoser, Horus name Netjerikhet, was the first king of the Third Dynasty and Huni was the last.

THE THIRD DYNASTY: THE REIGN OF KING NETJERIKHET (2667–2648)

Netjerikhet is by far the most important king of this dynasty, particularly in terms of the monuments dating to his reign; even in ancient times, tourists visited his Step Pyramid complex at Saqqara. The graffito by an Eighteenth Dynasty scribe named Ahmose, written on the wall in the "Northern Palace,"

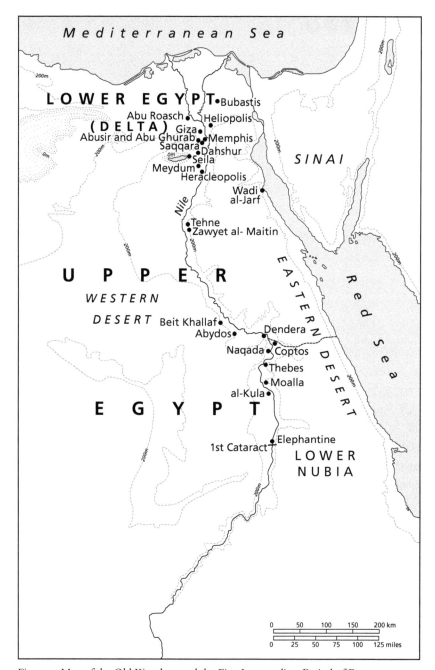

Figure 5 Map of the Old Kingdom and the First Intermediate Period of Egypt

describes his awe of the pyramid, "as if there were heaven in it, Ra rising in it." Ahmose requests all good things for the soul of Djoser, including "may heaven send down myrrh and provide incense" (Navrátilová 2007, 75–76). In the Turin King List, the New Kingdom scribe who wrote it switched from black ink to red when he wrote the title "King of Upper and Lower Egypt" for Djoser (Gardiner 1959, pl. II; Wildung 1969b, 65), "thus acknowledging the reputation Djoser (Netjerikhet) enjoyed at that time" (Malek 1986, 37). There is no evidence for the name Djoser in the Third Dynasty; it appears in later texts, beginning in the Middle Kingdom (Leprohon 2013, 32n4). Based on clay sealings with the name of Netjerikhet found in the tomb of Khasekhemwy at Abydos, Netjerikhet is accepted as the son and successor of Khasekhemwy, the last ruler of the Second Dynasty (Dreyer 1998, 32–33). Netjerikhet's name "may state that he is 'the Divine One of the Corporation (of gods),'" and in the same way his funerary complex "expresses his overweening aspirations" (Baines 1995, 143).

Accidents of preservation play a large role in determining what the modern world understands about any period of ancient history, but even with the loss of archaeological evidence, it is clear that great changes took place in the reign of Netjerikhet, which according to the Turin King List lasted nineteen years. His mortuary complex presents a remarkable leap forward in the quarrying and handling of stone, as well as new visions of size and form. The building of his complex demanded skilled professionals, as well as an efficient system for procuring the materials, such as the Turah limestone and Aswan granite, needed to construct it.

With Netjerikhet's reign there is solid written evidence for officials and their titles and offices. For the first time, there is also clear evidence for the king's female relatives, and their titles and depictions suggest they served an important role in the king's divinity. The theology backing his rule is stated not only by the relief decoration found in his pyramid complex but also by the very words of the gods on the fragments of a shrine discovered at Heliopolis, on which gods such as Geb and Seth request *heb seds* for the king. These points will be addressed, but because Netjerikhet's Step Pyramid complex at Saqqara contains the most evidence we have for this king and his family, the discussion of Netjerikhet begins with this monument. With later kings, there will be much more diverse and written evidence for their reigns, and the discussion will not necessarily be so heavily based on monuments.

Many of the separate architectural elements of Netjerikhet's Step Pyramid complex can be traced directly to the architecture of the First and Second Dynasties at Abydos and North Saqqara. Rather than having a mastaba tomb for the burial and a funerary "fort" for rituals, such as is found at Abydos, the Step Pyramid complex merges these two disparate structures together, setting the burial within the funerary fort. The complex is oriented north–south, the north aligns to the so-called imperishable stars that the king joins in his afterlife and the south aligns to the stars in Orion's Belt (Faulkner 1966).

The stepped pyramid started out as a square mastaba with finished "external faces" that show it was "a finished monument" (O'Connor 2009, 195). Some time later, the square mastaba was enlarged in at least five different additional construction phases, resulting in a six-step pyramid (Lehner 1997, 84). The mastaba was first extended by adding to the sides, which, on the east side with the extension labeled "M3," covered the openings of eleven shafts dug down to burial chambers. The five most northern of these shaft tombs seemed to have been used for members of the king's family, based on fragments of wooden coffins and in Shaft 5 fragments of two alabaster sarcophagi or possibly canopic boxes (Stadelmann 1987b, 252–253). The rest of the shafts were filled with Early Dynastic stone vessels that may well have come from earlier tombs intruded upon by Netjerikhet's workmen. When covered, these shafts were reached by another shaft purposefully cut down to the first shaft, which then led to a corridor that cut through all of the shafts, making them reachable.

After these extensions to the sides, at least two larger extensions added steps as well as greatly enlarging the area covered by the pyramid (Lauer 1948, fig. 6; Lehner 1997, 87). It should be pointed out that some sources suggest the antecedent of the original mastaba of the Step Pyramid was based on a mound found in the funerary fort of Khasekhemwy at Abydos (O'Connor 1989, 82; Friedman 1996, 338; Cervelló-Autuori 2002, 31;), but further excavation at Abydos has shown that there was no such mound in Khasekhemwy's funerary fort (Bestock 2009, 52).

A structure on the north side of the pyramid probably served as the mortuary temple, although some scholars accept Ricke's opinion that Netjerikhet's structure was intended to be a "royal cult palace" (Arnold 1997, 42) (Figure 6). The layout of the building, with two main parallel courts surrounded by numerous corridors and small spaces (Firth and Quibell 1935, 2:pl. 27; Stadelmann 1985, 64, fig. 17), does not seem to match the plan of a temple, although a possible parallel for this structure can be found in a funerary temple attached to Tomb 3505 at North Saqqara and is therefore possible evidence of a "Memphite influence" in the Step Pyramid complex (Emery 1958, 10, pl. 2; Lauer 1979, 359; Cervelló-Autuori 2002, 44–45). Descending from the outside north wall of this building is the main access corridor into Netjerikhet's burial chamber in the substructure of the Step Pyramid. On the east side of the mortuary temple is a serdab for the king's *ka* statue. At the far south of the complex, right at the southern wall, is a very similar but much smaller version of the king's burial chamber, the so-called South Tomb. This appears to have functioned as the burial place for the king's *ka* (*k3*) and also may have been symbolic of a royal burial in the south at Abydos.

In both of these underground spaces, the king's tomb and the South Tomb, are three panels, arranged from north to south, depicting the king either running or standing. Under the pyramid, in a gallery east of the burial shaft,

Figure 6 Mortuary temple of the Step Pyramid at Saqqara. Photo: Lisa Sabbahy

the king is shown standing in the first panel and running in the next two; the panels in the South Tomb show the king running in the first panel and standing in the last two (Friedman 1995, 12, fig. 7a). Friedman's study of the panels suggests that the scenes are tied to *heb sed* rituals. The standing king in the panels is like the statue of the king set in the doorways of the southern-facing chapels of the *heb sed* court (Friedman 1995, 34, fig. 20) "recrowned as eternal monarch of Egypt" and the running king in the panels carries out two rituals symbolizing control over Egypt (Friedman 1995, 42; Friedman 1996, 339–340). The king running around the boundary markers in the Great Court reclaims his rule over Egypt, and when the king runs south and out of the gate of the complex he enacts the ritual of "circuiting the capital walls," which happened at the king's coronation and his *heb sed*, each of which asserted his authority over the land (Friedman 1996, 341). Although its purpose is not completely understood, it has been suggested that the Dry Moat, possibly created by quarrying material for the building of the complex, also served a religious function, creating a parallel underground space along with the king's tomb and South Tomb for the king's afterlife (Myśliwiec 2006, 233; Kuraszkiewicz 2011).

The funeral temple was constructed after the last expansion of the stepped pyramid was carried out. Altenmüller has suggested that the court at the far northern end of the enclosure, just beyond this temple, was also part of this construction phase (Altenmüller 1972, 7–8). The court has a square, rock-cut platform against the middle of the north wall, approached by stairs. In the middle of the platform are remains of what may have been an obelisk (Firth and Quibell 1935, 77, pl. 84) or possibly an altar, and Altenmüller suggests that there was a sun cult here (Altenmüller 1972, 11), although others suggest it was simply a place for offerings (Stadelmann, 1969, 373–378) or was used during the *heb sed* (Kahl 1994, 82).

There are other reasons for considering that a sun cult existed at Netjerikhet's pyramid complex. The "step pyramid itself is a clear ascensional monument" and states the relationship of the king with the sun god (Cervelló-Autuori 2011, 1128). The stepping of the pyramid may have been influenced by an earlier stepped mastaba of the First Dynasty, Mastaba 3038 at North Saqqara, which belonged to an official named Nebitka from the time of King Adjib (variation: Anedjib), based on sealings found in the mastaba (Emery 1961, 82). This mastaba went through three successive building changes. In the first one, it was constructed with eight steps, built with bricks on three sides, north, south, and west, and the entrance down into the tomb chamber was on the east. In a second phase, brick terraces were built up to the fourth step, but for a period of time the mastaba was a visible, 5-meter-high, truncated step pyramid (Cervelló-Autuori 2002, 47). Then, the mastaba was walled in by a niched enclosure and the steps covered by sand (Emery 1949, 82–88; Lehner 1997, 80). Emery, the excavator of Mastaba 3038, viewed it as directly ancestral to the Step Pyramid (Emery 1961, fig. 85).

This same type of stepped truncated form is shown in inscriptions on stone vessels discovered in the galleries of the Step Pyramid (Lacau and Lauer 1959, pl. 6) as well as pot marks from Abydos (Emery 1949, 82, fig. 47). All these show a serekh with the Horus name of King Adjib and then, behind it, a three-stepped platform with a square above it which contains hieroglyphs for "Protection is behind Horus." Further evidence for stepped tombs, which might be a "Memphite influence," comes from Abusir; small mastabas of the later First Dynasty have been found having three steps (Radwan 2003, 95). Stepping as a way for the deceased king to reach the sky is stated in Pyramid Texts, such as PT 267: "A stairway to the sky is set up for me that I may ascend on it to the sky"; and PT 619: "a stairway has been set up to the sky that you may ascend" (Faulkner 1969).

Netjerikhet is the only Third Dynasty king for whom female family members are known. The name of Nymaathap, given the title "Mother of the King's Children," was found on a sealing in Khasekhemwy's tomb (Petrie 1901, 12) and she is assumed to be Khasekhemwy's wife and the mother of Netjerikhet (Dreyer 1998, 33). A second title on this seal, "Who Says Anything and It Is Done for Her," is found later in the Fourth Dynasty and always refers to a king's mother (Sabbahy 1982, 30), so it is probable that Nymaathap was

Netjerikhet's mother. Nymaathap has these same two titles on clay sealings from Tomb K1 at Beit Khallaf, north of Abydos, along with a third title, "Follower of Horus," which is also a well-known queen's title in the Fourth Dynasty (Garstang 1901, pl. X; Kaplony 1963, fig. 326; Kahl, Kloth, and Zimmermann 1995, 22).

The Beit Khallaf tomb is dated to the reign of Netjerikhet, based on the large number of clay sealings with his name found throughout the tomb. More than a hundred sealings had his Horus name and more than twenty had his *nsw-bit*, or crown name (Garstang 1901, 11). So it is possible that this is the mastaba tomb of his mother, as it is the largest, at 85 meters long and 45 meters wide (Garstang 1901, 8), of several mastabas at the site that date to the reign of Netjerikhet (Wilkinson 1999, 97). Evidence that might suggest the king's mother was buried at Saqqara instead of Beit Khallaf was found in the Saqqara tomb inscription of the early Fourth Dynasty official Metjen, stating that he was granted "one hundred loaves of bread every day from the funerary temple of the mother of the king's children, Nymaathap" (Sethe 1903, 4, 9), although a chapel for her could also have been erected at Saqqara.

There is a fragment of a stone vessel, in a private collection, that gives Nymaathap the titles "King's Mother, (king's) Wife," the word "King" written only once in honorific transposition at the top of the vertical line of the inscription with the titles (Kaplony 1963, 3:pl. 150, fig. 866). This is the first known instance of the queen's title, *hemet-nsw* (*ḥmt-nsw*), "King's Wife," although here it is not fully written out. The next evidence we have for this title is at the beginning of the Fourth Dynasty, when it is held by Hetepheres I, the queen of Sneferu, and from then on it is the most commonly held queen's title.

There are two other royal women known from the reign of King Netjerikhet besides the king's mother, his wife, Hetephernebty, and his daughter, Intkaues. The names of these two women appear on stelae from the Step Pyramid complex, as well as from blocks of what were once tall incense burners or offering stands, along with the name of Netjerikhet. There are roughly fifty of the stelae (Firth and Quibell 1935, pl. 86) and thirty to forty stands (Firth and Quibell 1935, pl. 87; Arnold 2007, 157). Both the stelae and the stands were rather crudely made and then reused as building blocks in parts of the complex, particularly in the walls of the south court and the walls of the serdab court (Espinel 2003, 215). The blocks were placed such that the inscriptions were not visible (Firth and Quibell 1935, 119), so, clearly, they were made in order "to be discarded after serving a limited ritual function" (Arnold 2007, 161).

All the stelae and stands have the same inscription. On the right side is the *imiut*-fetish (*imywt*), a symbol of the jackal god Anubis, which can also be a symbol of a cemetery, and just to its left and facing it, the Horus name of

Netjerikhet. Then, behind the Horus name, are two vertical rows, the first with the titles and name of Hetephernebty and the second with the title and name of Intkaues. The two titles of Hetephernebty are "The One Who Sees Horus" and "King's Daughter." If Hetephernebty is a king's daughter, one could assume that her father was Khasekhemwy, and so Netjerikhet married his sister or half-sister. This could possibly point to a sibling royal marriage.

The title "The One Who Sees Horus" is found beginning in the First Dynasty, but the complete form of the title, "The One Who Sees Horus and Seth," does not appear until the early Fourth Dynasty in the titles of Henutsen, one of the wives of King Khufu, and then is used throughout the rest of the Old Kingdom (Sabbahy 1982, 53). The title is an expression of the woman's relationship and closeness to the king as a god. Intkaues has only the title "King's Daughter." On all the stelae and stands, above their names and titles, is a short horizontal line that reads "foremost of the sacred land" followed by the figure of a recumbent Anubis.

It is not clear why these stelae and stands were made. Considering their number, they probably lined something, perhaps in connection with the finishing of a stage or part of the Step Pyramid complex. Logan has pointed out that, on slightly earlier objects, the *imiut*-fetish is tied to the king's opening of an important building (Logan 1990, 69). Another suggestion is that the stelae could have been used as markers lining a route, while the stands could have been used to hold oil lamps, such as those used in the ceremony of "illuminating the thrones," which came before the *heb sed*. When this ceremony was completed the stelae had no further purpose and were reused (Kuraszkiewicz 2006, 280–281; Wilson 1936).

As to why it was necessary to have names and titles of the royal women on these objects is another question, and this must be tied to their importance in the regeneration and renewal of kingship. Troy has pointed out that "kingship is a manifestation of the power of the creator, placed in the context of the role of mortal sovereign" (Troy 1986, 2). The creator god, Ra, created everything else by himself and therefore must be androgynous. As such, kingship, the power of the creator on earth, must also be both male and female, and so the king's female relatives represent the female half of kingship. In other words, kingship and queenship are the two halves of monarchical rule in ancient Egypt.

The role of royal women is based on that of Hathor, who "as uterine disc is mother to the solar child" and, as the eye of the sun, is "daughter to the heavenly father" (Troy 1986, 23). The generational mother–daughter continuum "functions as the mediator for the transition of the male element from father to son" (Troy 1986, 23). The representations of Hetephernebty and Intkaues, mother and daughter, on these stelae and stands are the earliest examples "of the presentation of queenship as a duality" (Troy 1986, 110).

This author suggests that this interpretation of kingship and regeneration also backs sibling marriages, because the king would not be marrying his sister so much as he is marrying the female half of his father's renewal and regeneration. Troy goes on to state: "The duality of two successive female generations is used as a motif to relate the royal family to the pattern of cosmic renewal" (Troy 1986, 3). Sibling marriage has to be seen as a similar motif.

These two women, wife and daughter, are depicted on a fragment of relief from a small shrine, which Ernesto Schiaparelli found at Heliopolis in 1903 (Smith 1946, 133; Kahl, Kloth, and Zimmermann 1995, 114; Morenz 2002, 158). The fragment shows the lower part of a seated king with three small figures at his feet. One woman kneels behind his leg, with her left arm embracing his ankle. Hetephernebty and Intkaues stand in front of his feet, facing in the same direction as the king, with their title and name inscribed vertically above them. Hetephernebty has both of her arms bent at the elbow and crossed over her chest. She is wearing a long garment that comes up over her shoulders and comes together at her crossed hands and a short wig that sits oddly back off her forehead. There are two instances known from the Fourth Dynasty when queens wear this exact same cloak and wig, and it is when they appear with one of their children (Sabbahy 1982, 310–312).

It has been suggested that the third woman behind the king's foot is his mother, Nymaathap, as suggested by Troy (1986, 152), although it is difficult to read the damaged hieroglyphs above her. The top hieroglyphic bird sign can be read *wrt* (*wrt*), "great," and this could be the title "Great of Affection (?)," possibly used earlier in the First Dynasty and which was occasionally used later in the Old Kingdom (Sabbahy 1982, 22). This scene represents a family of four, the king and three female relatives. Roth points out that this is the first time a king's family has been depicted together, and perhaps this is a reflection of the growing importance of the cult of Ra, with its "stress on family, children, and posterity" (Roth 1993, 54). If these women were the king's mother, wife, and daughter, they would represent the complete female multigenerational continuance of Netjerikhet's kingship.

This type of family grouping might also have been portrayed in statuary at least once in the Step Pyramid complex. At the north end of the *heb sed* court are the remains of four sets of feet (Firth and Quibell 1935, 114, pl. 63; Stadelmann 1999, 174), two larger and two smaller, although there is no evidence as to whom the feet belong, other than assuming that at least one pair of the larger feet must be the king's and perhaps the two smaller pairs belong to his wife and daughter (Figure 7). Since these figures are in the *heb sed* court, Seidel suggests that both pairs of larger feet were the king's, one pair representing the White Crown and one pair the Red, and the smaller feet were the goddesses Nekhbet, the vulture goddess of upper Egypt, and Wadjit, the cobra goddess of Lower Egypt (Seidel 1996, 9).

Figure 7 Four pairs of feet in the *heb sed* court of the Step Pyramid. Photo: Lisa Sabbahy

The abovementioned fragment of relief found at Heliopolis by Schiaparelli with King Netjerikhet and his female family was just one of thirty-nine fragments, all of which are now in the Turin Museum in Italy (Weill 1911, 9–16; Smith 1946, figs. 48–53). As pointed out in a 2017 study, these block fragments are the main evidence used to substantiate the claim that Heliopolis was the center of the cult of Ra at this early time (Nuzzolo and Krejčí 2017, 361). However, some scholars have questioned whether or not these fragments were originally part of a shrine or chapel, perhaps at the Step Pyramid complex, and were only later moved to Heliopolis (Quirke 2001, 84). There may not be any evidence for a cult temple of Ra at Heliopolis before the Sixth Dynasty with the obelisk of King Teti. This would not mean there was not yet a sun cult or solar influence, but perhaps the cult was not yet located at Heliopolis.

A number of the Heliopolis block fragments of Netjerikhet fit together into a relief scene with seated figures of gods, one certainly Seth and another possibly Geb, separated by bands of vertical inscription (Smith 1946, fig. 50). The inscriptions are connected to the celebration of the *heb sed*: "Words spoken: I have caused that he celebrate heb-seds" (Kahl, Kloth, and Zimmermann 1995, 116–117). This might also seem to indicate that this monument was originally located at the Step Pyramid since *heb sed* buildings and courts are a large part of the Step Pyramid complex, although had the king celebrated an actual *heb sed*, it undoubtedly would have been at Memphis.

There are a few salient points to bring in about officials and their titles in the reign of Netjerikhet. One is that personal names began to use the name Ra, as an element, indicating the "veneration" of Ra at this time, such as Hesy-ra, "The Praised One of Ra" (Kahl 2007, 29–30). There are thirteen men with scribal titles known in the Third Dynasty, and five of them have the element "Ra" in their name. Kahl makes the observation that these men are "of highest rank in the scribal administration," suggesting that perhaps they took these as "professional names"; this might point to the importance of scribes in the dissemination of the worship of the god Ra (Kahl 2007, 38–39). Hesy-Ra was "Overseer of the Royal Scribes" as well as being attached to the royal treasury, and, having an administration position, "Greatest of the Tens of Upper Egypt," which involved recruiting labor for royal building projects (Wilkinson 2007, 30–32).

Hesy-Ra's tomb (S2405) at Saqqara had a series of wooden panels in it, six of which were removed in 1876 and are in the collection of the Cairo Museum. On five of them, Hesy-Ra is shown standing, with his titles above him, and on the sixth he is seated at an offering table. In all of them he either holds or has over his shoulder his scribal equipment. One of the panels is badly damaged in the middle, but Hesy-Ra's legs can be seen at the bottom. His left hand extends in front, holding a *hes*-vessel (*ḥs*), and his right hand is down at his side behind him, holding a round disk (Wood 1978, pl. 2c; Kahl 2007, 31; Fischer 1972, figs. 11, 25). Fischer suggests that the two objects held are an emblematic writing of Hesy-Ra's name (Fischer 1972: 19).

Another, much more important official of Netjerikhet's, was Imhotep, who is considered to have been the architect of the Step Pyramid complex. His importance is reflected in the fact that his name and titles are inscribed on the base of a limestone statue of the king (JE 49889) found at Saqqara inside the entrance to the complex on the south side, at the beginning of the colonnade. Imhotep's titles are "Seal Bearer of Lower Egypt, Foremost under the King, Administrator of the Estate, *iry-pat* (*iry- pꜥt*)," "One of the Elite," "Greatest of Seers, Overseer of Sculptors" (Kahl, Kloth, and Zimmermann 1995, 70; Strudwick 2005, 129); the very last part of the inscription is broken away (Figure 8). "Greatest of Seers," *wr mꜣw*, can also be read as "Seer of the Great One," *mꜣ wr* (*mꜣ-wr*). By the time of the Middle Kingdom, the title is clearly written "Greatest of Seers," and the official with this title is the High Priest of Ra (Moursi 1972, 154). Quirke has pointed out that before the Middle Kingdom there were not actually high priests tied to cult centers, but such titles belonged to officials of the king's court who had particular religious responsibilities (Quirke 2001, 106); this was true of the title "Greatest of Seers" or "Seer of the Great One" until the Middle Kingdom.

Figure 8 Base of the statue of Netjerikhet with name and titles of Imhotep (JE 49889). Photo: Lisa Sabbahy, Courtesy of the Imhotep Museum, Saqqara

THE FOURTH DYNASTY

The Fourth Dynasty had six kings and lasted from 2613 to 2494 BCE. Several changes take place, perhaps the most dramatic being that the king now builds a true pyramid complex in which to be buried, which has a completely different architectural layout than that of a step pyramid complex. There are more inscriptions from the Fourth Dynasty than earlier dynasties, including what is called the first autobiography, and therefore more evidence about government structure, officials, and members of the royal family. The king's titulary fully develops into five titles with the addition of the king's birth name as his son of the Sun god name. The most important royal sites of the Fourth Dynasty are Dahshur and Giza.

With the Fourth Dynasty, ancient Egypt is often referred to as a centrist state. For the most part, royalty and the elite are based at Memphis, and their burials are at the nearby Memphite cemeteries. The king was considered a god, and his power was unquestioned. Enormous pyramids stated the king's position and control. "There is some evidence that the need to express power through the medium of monumental architecture may be greater … when the degree of central power is increasing" (Trigger 1990, 127). The labor that goes into the building of monumental structures uses massive amounts of energy, and "the control of energy constitutes the most fundamental and universally recognized measure of political power" (Trigger 1990, 128).

During the Fourth Dynasty, royal relatives held the most important positions under the king, with the rest of the bureaucracy below them. Royal estates were located throughout Egypt and supplied the royal house and royal funerary cults with necessary goods. The majority peasant population was called up when necessary to procure building materials and to labor in the construction of royal projects, for the most part the construction of the royal funerary complexes with their pyramids.

THE REIGN OF SNEFERU (2613–2589)

King Sneferu's throne name means "God has made me perfect." Both his Horus and his Two Ladies names were the same, "Possessor of *Maat*" (Leprohon 2013, 35), which perhaps can be seen as a bold statement of his legitimacy since *Maat* represented cosmic order and justice and was tied closely to the sun god Ra (Bárta and Dulikova 2017, 27–28). Like Netjerikhet, Sneferu was a king who was venerated in later times. His cult at Dahshur was restored in the Middle Kingdom (Fakhry, 1961b), and his reign was used as the setting for Middle Kingdom stories and tales (Graefe 1990; Parkinson 2002, 182–187).

Sneferu is accepted as the son of King Huni, the last king of the Third Dynasty, although there is no clear proof of this relationship (Dodson and Hilton 2004, 51). The name of his mother was Meresankh, which is known from the Palermo Stone (Sabbahy 1982, 32). His queen is accepted to be Hetepheres I, based on the fact that Sneferu's name is on the gold-covered bed canopy box found in her tomb at Giza (Reisner 1955, figs. 28–29), although this is not absolute proof of their relationship (Der Manuelian 2017, 18). Hetepheres holds the title of "King's Mother," referring to King Khufu, her son, whose name is on the sealings that closed the boxes in her tomb. She must have either died or, as is also suggested, was reburied during his reign after her original burial was disturbed (Reisner 1955, 48, 59). This second suggestion is based on the fact that the tomb of Hetepheres is near Khufu's pyramid at Giza, whereas a queen was normally buried near the pyramid of her husband, along with the fact that her body is not included in the burial and therefore may have been destroyed when her original tomb was looted. There is no known evidence of an original tomb for Hetepheres I, however (Jánosi 1996, 8).

Hetepheres I also had the title "God's Daughter," which indicates that her father was the deceased king and therefore King Huni. If Sneferu was also Huni's son and married Hetepheres, they would have had a brother–sister marriage. No other queen's name is known from his reign, but certainly Sneferu could have had other wives. Along with her two titles "King's Mother" and "God's Daughter," Hetepheres I also had the additional title

"Anything She Says Is Done for Her," and these three titles are the ones that distinguish a king's mother (Sabbahy 1982, 45).

The titulary of King Sneferu is carved vertically down the wooden jambs of the bed canopy of Hetepheres I (Reisner 1932, 58). On each jamb, after his name Sneferu in a cartouche, is the epithet *neb hepet* (*nb ḥpt*), which Reisner translates as "lord of the *hpt* (ceremony?)" (Reisner 1955, 25). However, this word has to do with boat travel and, later in the reign of Mentuhotep II, has a solar context and refers to Ra's crossing of the sky. As pointed out by Postel, a solar context is not exactly missing with Sneferu, as he is the first king to set his burial complex on the east–west axis of the sun and his name is in a cartouche, which has solar connotations (Postel 2004, 210). The use of the cartouche starts in the Third Dynasty and "it confirms the solarization of kingship," since the encircling ring of the cartouche stands for "all that the sun disk circles" (Quirke 2001, 123). Sneferu is the only Fourth Dynasty king for whom the epithet *neb hepet* is known, however (Dobrev 1993, 199).

Sneferu's reign was fairly lengthy; it lasted at least forty-six years and perhaps up to forty-eight. This is based on the fact that the Turin King List gives Sneferu's reign as twenty-four years, although Old Kingdom regnal years were based on the "cattle count" every two years and so that total needs to be doubled (Stadelmann 2008, 110). The most important development brought about during Sneferu's reign was the building of the first true, smooth-sided pyramids and the creation of a pyramid complex that was not within an enclosure but set out on an east–west axis following the path of the sun (Stadelmann 1997, 2). Although some of the details from step pyramid complexes, such as the entrance into the pyramid from the north side and the construction of a south tomb, were kept and became traditional, the true pyramid complex is a symbolic architectural shift clearly stating the deceased king's identification with the sun god. The shape of the pyramid is like that of the *ben-ben* (*bnbn*), the primaeval mound upon which the sun god alighted and created the world. The god's daily travel to the west, dying each night and traveling through the underworld to be born again in the east each morning, is copied in the axial arrangement of the pyramid complex structures, from the valley temple to the pyramid, of east to west. The true pyramid and its complex proclaimed the king's "absorption into the mystic symbol of the sun" (Kemp 2006, 109). It is also possible that the ancient Egyptians saw the smooth sides of the true pyramid as "a material representation of the sun's rays" (Edwards 1975, 291) by which the king could ascend, as reflected in the slightly later Old Kingdom Pyramid: "May the sky make the sunlight strong for you, may you rise up to the sky" (Faulkner 1969, 196). It is also notable that the burial chamber itself is moved up into the body of the pyramid and is no longer underground (Billing 2011, 55).

Sneferu, in fact, built three true pyramids, the first at Meydum and two more at Dahshur (Figure 9). His pyramid at Meydum is the earliest true pyramid

Figure 9 Sneferu's pyramid at Meydum. Photo: Lisa Sabbahy

complex with a valley temple and then a causeway leading from the valley temple to the funerary temple, which was set against the east face of the pyramid (Figure 10). The Meydum pyramid appeared to be part of his family's necropolis there, since at least two princes, Nefermaat, "eldest king's son," and Rahotep, "king's son," were buried in mastabas there. They are assumed to be Sneferu's sons based on the placement of their tombs at Meydum, as well as the fact that the name of Sneferu is found in the estate lists recorded in their tombs (Stadelmann 2008, 104).

Prince Nefermaat was his father's vizier and the only vizier known from Sneferu's reign. It was typical throughout the Fourth Dynasty that only a king's son served as vizier, although perhaps not for their own father. Lloyd has pointed out that "Ankhhaf, a son of Snofru, was the vizier of his nephew Khafre; Ankhmare, a son of Khafre, was vizier of his half-brother Menkaura; Babaef, a grandson of Khafre was vizier under Shepseskaf" (Lloyd 2014, 143). It is also typical that the vizier carried a second title, "Overseer of All Royal Works," and indeed Nefermaat held that position (Strudwick 1985, 110).

Figure 10 Small valley temple at the Meydum pyramid. Photo: Lisa Sabbahy

Along with those responsibilities were others that had no standardized titles in the early Fourth Dynasty, such as overseeing the granary and the treasury, and presumably they would have been "tasks of the vizier" (Strudwick 1985, 275; Nolan 2010, 335–336). Among Nefermaat's other titles were *iry-pat*, or "Elite." It has been pointed out that these eldest sons who were viziers, and also held the title of "Elite," never went on to become king. Stadelmann suggests that the "designated crown prince had no official function during the lifetime of his father. Therefore, we never find any hint, either name or depiction of the person to become king" (Stadelmann 2010a, 298).

Vizier Nefermaat had a religious title as well, "Priest of Bastet." Although the cult of Bastet goes back to the Early Dynastic Period, it seems to have been important and closely tied to the king beginning in the early Fourth Dynasty, and the priests of Bastet, with few exceptions, hold the rank of vizier at this time (Begelsbacher-Fischer 1981, 36; Strudwick 1985, 316). Sneferu's *heb sed* temple at the Bent Pyramid preserved remains of a scene of Bastet giving the king the "breath of life." Prince Rahotep held titles that were not as important as Nefermaat's, although he was "Greatest of the Seers," a title known from the time of King Netjerikhet and given to a high official at the royal court who also had responsibilities connected to the god Ra. Among other titles, Rahotep was also "Overseer of the Task Force" and "Overseer of the Bowmen" (Baud 1999b, 512).

At least four daughters are known from the family of King Sneferu (Sabbahy 1982, 121). Princess Hetepheres was the wife of her brother or half-brother, Ankhhaf, who served as the first vizier for his brother Khufu (Smith 1965, 24; Baud 1999b, 369). Hetepheres is the "Eldest King's Daughter, of His Body, Whom He Loves," making it clear she is the oldest and actual blood daughter of Sneferu and probably named after her mother, Queen Hetepheres. Princesses Nefertkau and Nefertnesu are only each known from one inscription giving their title of princess. Nefertnesu also holds the titles of "Priestess of Sneferu" and "Priestess of Hathor in All Her Places." A princess as priestess of her father is most common at the beginning of the Fourth Dynasty but rare later in the Old Kingdom (Sabbahy 1982, 129–131). Many princesses, and even more nonroyal women, were priestesses of Hathor in the Old Kingdom. Nefertkau is also called an eldest and actual daughter in her princess title.

Some scholars think that, since the kings seemed to have had many wives, each of the first children born to his wife would have used the title "Eldest" (Callender 2002, 143). This title applied to male royal children should be important because it would designate the successor to the throne, however, this does not seem to have been the case in the Old Kingdom. It is only much later in the New Kingdom that "Eldest Son" becomes a "'political' appellation of the heir to the throne" (Dodson and Hilton 2004, 33). A study of nonroyal ancient Egyptian families where there was more than one eldest child concluded that it indicated a premature death of the first eldest child, twins who were eldest children, or eldest children from more than one wife (McCorquodale 2013, 90–91). The same may not have applied to royalty, however, but it is not clear.

The last daughter of Sneferu, Wemtetka, is known from her limestone statue found in three pieces in the area of Sneferu's valley temple east of the Bent Pyramid (Fakhry 1961, 9). In front of her, on the statue base, is the title: "King's Daughter of His Body, Whom He Loves." Because of where the statue was found, it is assumed her father was Sneferu. Wemtetka is depicted seated on the ground in the same fashion as the woman seated by the leg of King Netjerikhet on the relief from Heliopolis and also like the queen of Djedefra sitting next to her husband's leg on a broken statue from Abu Roasch (Fay 1998, 172–173, figs. 3–4). However, Wemtetka sits on the statue base all by herself.

In regnal year 15, Sneferu begins the southern pyramid at Dahshur, best known in modern times as the Bent Pyramid. By regnal year 29, the Bent Pyramid was abandoned, as it was cracking badly from subsiding into the "clay rich substratum and sandy limestone" below it (Klemm and Klemm 2010, 48). The slope of the pyramid had been lessened to forty-three degrees, to relieve the weight, giving it a bent profile, but that did not seem to help (Lehner and Hawass 2017, 74).

Another pyramid was built slightly farther to the north, known as the Northern or Red Pyramid. A foundation block found at the pyramid records year 15 of the count, or regnal year 30. Stadelmann suggests that to have taken up to year 48 to complete the pyramid is a reasonable estimate, and the twenty-four-year reign for Sneferu mentioned in the Turin Papyrus has to have been based on the biannual cattle counts, as mentioned earlier in this section, not regnal years (Stadelmann 2008, 110). Sneferu appears to have been buried in the North Pyramid; skeletal remains of an older male adult, assumed to be his, were found in the debris in the burial chamber (Batrawi 1951, 435–444).

There was a funerary temple built against the east side of this pyramid, although nothing was left but the foundations. The front of the temple had been constructed with stone blocks but the rest of the building was finished with mud bricks, "perhaps even after Snofru's death" (Stadelmann 1997, 5). Fragments of unfinished relief showing the enthroned king wearing the *heb sed* cloak were found among the foundation blocks. There were also two blocks with *heb sed* scenes reused at the site of Lisht, to the south, which may have come from this temple (Arnold 1999a, 196–198). The plan of the temple has been reconstructed with a pillared court with a statue chapel on each side and based on the assumption of an offering place with a false door back against the pyramid. At both the north and the south of the temple, root holes were found, so there must have been a "sacred grove" (Stadelmann 1997, 7).

Along with these large-scale pyramids, Sneferu also built a small, solid pyramid at Seila, on the edge of the Fayum directly west of Meydum. This pyramid seems to be similar to seven other small pyramids at sites in Upper Egypt that are generally dated to the end of the Third Dynasty and the reign of King Huni, since a granite cone-shaped block with the cartouche of Huni was found near the small pyramid at Elephantine (see Stadelmann 2007, 426, figs. 1a–b). Attributing the one at Elephantine to Huni does not mean he built the others, however (Stadelmann 2007, 427). A date in the early Fourth Dynasty has also been suggested for these small pyramids, which would associate them, other than the one at Elephantine, with Sneferu. The Seila pyramid clearly dates to the reign of Sneferu, as a stela with both his Horus name and his prenomen was found on the east side of the pyramid (Edwards 1997, 89, fig. 1b).

These small pyramids have been found at the sites of Seila, Zawyet al-Meitin, Abydos (Sinki), Naqada, al-Kula, Edfu, and Elephantine. All these pyramids seem to be three-stepped solid structures, except for Seila, which has four steps. It has been suggested that these small structures are a "first attempt by the central government towards achieving an official religion (the solar doctrine) for the whole land" (Radwan 2003, 111). These small pyramids do seem to be a concerted effort to spread a statement of the king's rule and power throughout provincial Upper Egypt and perhaps they also served as the focus of a cult for his *ka* or soul. This function is probably the clearest at Seila, where an alabaster altar for libations was found within a small chapel on the north side of the pyramid, along with fragments from a small seated statue of the king (Muhlestein 2015, 244–245; Stadelmann 2010b, 32–34). The Seila pyramid also had a 15-meter-long causeway on the east, leading away from a small area probably used for offerings. The causeway had a "clear ending, with the bottommost blocks running perpendicular to the rest of the stones" and no structure of any kind (Muhlestein 2015, 256).

In their study, Dreyer and Kaiser (1980, 56) suggested a possible connection between the locations of the small pyramids and royal domains, which is somewhat similar to Seidlmayer's statement that these pyramids "could have served to make explicit and intelligible the ideological background of the economic demands of the state on a local level" (Seidlmayer 1996, 124). North of the small pyramid at Elephantine was an administrative center dated to the late Third to early Fourth Dynasties. Seidlmayer suggests, based on the archaeological evidence and written documents found, that this may have been the "administrative building of a royal domain or estate" (p. 121).

These small pyramids, therefore, might have been a symbolic expression of the cult of the king and placed in areas that supported the king's cult with produce from royal estates. The Palermo Stone gives Snefru credit for founding thirty-five estates, or *hwt*, in a single year, as well as cattle farms (Wilkinson 2000, 143). The autobiographical texts of Metjen at Saqqara, dating to the early Fourth Dynasty, describe the activities of an official who administered agricultural land in both the Delta and Upper Egypt and show the "dominance" of countryside royal estates in the time of Snefru (Moreno García 2007, 319).

It has also been suggested that the south tomb, or small pyramid found to the south of the king's pyramid, such as that at Meydum, the Bent Pyramid at Dahshur, and the Great Pyramid, were locations for the king's cult and appear "to be similar to the provincial pyramids in design and purpose" (Papazian 2008, 75). On the other hand, Kemp has suggested, based on his restudy of the monument at Zawyet al-Meitin, that it is characteristic of the Old Kingdom Egypt, where "large plain, solid architectural masses conveyed authority" and, possibly, provincial governors could have stated their own authority by building such a structure (Kemp 2014–2015, 246).

At the same time that Sneferu began the building of his Northern or Red Pyramid at Dahshur in year 15 of the cattle count, or regnal year 30, he also began the building of a temple, which has been referred to as a valley temple and a statue-cult temple but appears to have been built for his *heb sed*. The temple itself is east of the Bent Pyramid and was constructed in and on the southern end of an earlier enclosure that seems to have been contemporary with the building of the Bent Pyramid. This enclosure served as a space for rituals celebrated by the living king and there is archaeological evidence pointing to at least three different periods of use (Alexanian and Arnold 2016, 6–7). It consisted of a north–south enclosure, with an open court and a small, chambered structure in the middle. Around the inside of all four walls were pits from tree roots; "four rows of 26 tree pits" were found along the west wall alone (Alexanian and Arnold 2016, 5). The use of this enclosure stopped with the building of the *heb sed* temple. To build this temple, "the existing enclosure wall was demolished, but the interior brick building and parts of the garden remained intact" (F. Arnold 2016, p. 3).

East of the *heb sed* temple was a small harbor, and a brick-built causeway came up from the harbor to the east side of the temple. From the west side of the temple, a stone block causeway then continued up to the Bent Pyramid. A recent study of the ancient landscape of Dahshur suggests that the stone of the plateau had been cut and given a geometric shape during the construction of the Bent Pyramid, so that the pyramid would have seemed to be set on a square stone platform and clearly be the point of visual focus (Alexanian and Arnold 2016, 7).

The *heb sed* temple itself was rectangular and oriented north–south, with the entrance in the south. Out in front of each of the two southern corners stood a stela with the four names of the king (Fakhry 1961a, fig. 3) (Figure 11). Sneferu's Horus name was *neb maat* (*nb m3ᶜt*), Lord of *Maat*, which implies he is the sun god (Nuzzolo 2018, 39). The building entrance led through a corridor that passed parallel storage magazines on the left and right (Figure 12). Female bearers, from the king's estates in the various nomes, and each carrying a symbolic offering table and an *ankh*-sign (*ᶜnḫ*), were depicted along the lower part of the entrance corridor wall. Those from the nomes of Upper Egypt processed along the west wall, while those from Lower Egypt processed along the east. The name of the nome is written before each group of offering bearers, and the names of the estates are carried on their heads (Jacquet-Gordon 1962, 125–137). The king created these estates to support his funerary establishment, and thirty-five such estates, including cattle farms, were created by Sneferu during one year recorded in the Palermo Stone (Wilkinson 2000, 143; Friedman 2015b, 26). Most of Sneferu's estates were in the area of northern Upper Egypt, where the valley is widest (Lehner 1997, 228).

Much larger scenes of the king in rituals were in the register above the procession of the nomes, although these are all badly damaged or lost (Arnold 1999b, fig. 49). Remains of two scenes show the feet of the king. In the first, the feet can be recognized as the king's by the tip of the bull's tail he wears, and they face a deity with the king's cartouche between them. In the second, just a foot of the king pushing off from the ground while running is preserved (Fakhry 1961a, figs. 18, 25). In both cases, the feet of the king show he is facing or moving to the south, while the smaller figures of the offering bearers below are

Figure 11 Stela at Dahshur *heb sed* temple with titulary of Sneferu (JE 89289). Photo: Sally el-Sabbahy, Courtesy of the Egyptian Museum, Cairo

moving to the north. Oppenheim suggests that this difference in direction is based on the understanding that the bearers are bringing sustenance to the king, and this combined with the rituals shown in the reliefs on the pillars enabled the reanimated and restored king to come forth out of his temple (Oppenheim 2005, 461). Friedman depicts the king running south and passing through the door with the Twenty-Second Upper Egyptian nome on his right, and the First Lower Egyptian nome on his left. Placing these dual coordinates on a map would set the king at Memphis, "where in real life the Old Kingdom *heb sed* festival was celebrated" (Friedman 2011b, 107, fig. 20b).

The corridor led to an open court, at the back of which were two rows of rectangular pillars. The procession of offering bearers continues on the east and west walls of the temple parallel with the pillars, perhaps because these two areas were roofed and so the scenes would be protected. Behind were six niches with standing statues of the king cut into them. On both sides of each niche were relief depictions of the king, with his names above, facing toward the niche (Fakhry 1961a, figs. 119–120). The few fragments of statues preserved

Figure 12 Entrance into the *heb sed* temple of Sneferu, Dahshur. Photo: Lisa Sabbahy

from the niches show the king wearing the White Crown and a *shendjet* kilt, the royal kilt, although the fragments left of the kings' figures alongside the niches show both the White Crown and the Red.

All ten pillars in the temple had been cut down and quarried into blocks. The fragments that were not removed were smashed and scattered across the temple court. Although parts of scenes can be reconstructed, it is impossible to tell where they might have been located. The relief decoration showed the king either running or standing, and both Oppenheim (2005, 461) and Friedman (1995, 34) have pointed out that these depictions of the king are very similar to those of King Djoser in the panels underground in corridors under the pyramid and in the South Tomb, discussed in the section "The Third Dynasty: The Reign of King Netjerikhet (2667–2648)." There are some fragments depicting the king with a god or goddess. There are only three who can be identified: the god Min; the goddess Seshat, with whom the king is marking the corners for the building of a temple (Fakhry 1961a, figs. 84, 91, 144–116); and the goddess Sakhmet or Bastet, who embraces the king and gives him the breath of life

(Fakhry 1961a, fig. 141). These are the earliest securely dated scenes of a king and a deity from a royal pyramid complex (Oppenheim 2005, 460).

One other religious structure must have existed in the reign of Sneferu, the *meret* (*mrt*) sanctuary. In the Palermo Stone, the Fifth Dynasty king Neferirkara is stated as having given an electrum statue of the young god Ihy, son of Hathor of the Sycamore tree, to Sneferu's *meret* sanctuary (Urkunden I, 247.16). *Meret* sanctuaries are mentioned in texts but no such sanctuary has been discovered or identified archaeologically. It is not even clear where such a sanctuary would have been located, although it would probably have been within or near a royal cemetery (Verner 2015, 328). Wildung has suggested that the *meret* of Sneferu may have been at Meydum (Wildung, 1969a, 137; 1969b, 109). Seidel has stated that it cannot be proven but it could be assumed that the *meret* was connected with the valley temple and would have been a small chapel nearby (Seidel 1996, 47). From work with the archives from Abusir, Posener-Krieger has pointed out that the *meret* is associated with an area called the *ra-sha* (Posener-Krieger 1976, 618n2) and *meret* sanctuaries may have been in the same location (Verner 2014, 116). The *ra-sha* (*r-š*) is generally considered to have been an area out on the Nile River–side of the pyramid complex, possibly part of a harbor area where boats arrived, perhaps first with building materials and then with products for the royal cult. Just as a harbor for Sneferu has been located east of his *heb sed* temple, using core samples, archaeologists have also located harbors, or basins, out in front of the three Giza pyramids (Lehner 2013, 2014). In the discussion of Menkaura's valley temple in the section "The Reign of Menkaura (2532–2503)," Hathor and the king, his *heb sed*, and the provisions for it might all be connected in the *meret*.

A *meret* sanctuary is always linked to the name of a king and belonged to a cult of Hathor, seemingly focused on the relationship between Hathor and the king, in terms of Hathor as the wife of Horus. The name of the sanctuary might be based on the verb *mri*, "to love," and may have been the place where the ritual marriage of the king to the goddess Hathor was celebrated (Bárta 1983, 103). The *meret* sanctuary in the reign of Sneferu is the earliest known and also the only one known from the Fourth Dynasty. *Meret* sanctuaries and their priests are mentioned in the Fifth Dynasty, as well as the very early Sixth Dynasty, but they seem to disappear after that (Verner 2015, 329).

The goddess Hathor functioned "as the female element in relationship to the male role of the king," and, in creating "unity out of duality," Hathor establishes the "prerequisite conditions for generation and renewal" (Troy 1986, 57–58). Hathor and the queen, therefore, had identical positions. Much later, in the ancient Egyptian New Kingdom, when the king clearly deified himself as the sun god, such as Ramses II at the Temple of Abu Simbel (Habachi 1969, 43), the queen joins him, deified as the goddess Hathor. With Sneferu's pyramid complexes being a statement of the king's identification with the sun god, evidence of the importance of Hathor is to be expected.

There is a small field of mastabas at Dahshur between the Bent Pyramid and the North Pyramid called the "Lepsius mastaba field." The largest of these mastabas belongs to the king's son Netjeraperef, who probably dates to the last part of the reign of Sneferu. The ancient Egyptians did not separate terms for children and grandchildren, and the excavators of this tomb have suggested this man was probably Sneferu's grandson and son of the king's son Iynefer (Stadelmann and Alexanian 1998, 304; Stadelmann 2010a, 295). Netjeraperef's full list of titles appears on a stela that was found at Snefru's *heb sed* temple. It stood there in the Old Kingdom but in the Middle Kingdom was reused as a lintel (Fakhry 1961b, 4, fig. 283). His titles represent a lower echelon of titles than those held by royal male relatives at the level of vizier at the beginning of the Fourth Dynasty. Netjeraperef is known as the "Overseer of the Phyles of Upper Egypt" and "Great One of the Tens of Upper Egypt," and he also had titles that tied him to the administration of the king's household, which was kept within the royal family at that time and probably also overseen by the vizier. Netjeraperef was the "Master of Largess in the Mansion of Life," whom Gardiner suggests was the official presiding over the king's meals (Gardiner 1938, 89). He was also tied to the provincial administration. "Fourth Dynasty administrators seem to have controlled several nomes at once" (Nolan 2010, 340), and Netjeraperef was "Provincial Administrator" and overseer of the business of the 5th, 6th, and 7th nomes of Upper Egypt. He was also "Priest of Sneferu's Southern Shining Pyramid," the Bent Pyramid (Fakhry 1961b, fig. 283).

THE REIGN OF KHUFU (2589–2566)

Sneferu's son, Khnum-Khufwy, "Khnum, he protects me" (Leprohon 2013, 35), usually written in the short form Khufu, succeeded him to the throne. Khufu's reign is given as twenty-three years in the Turin Papyrus, although most scholars believe this is erroneous and his reign must have been longer. In 2003, an inscription was found in the desert near Dakhleh Oasis, left by an expedition King Khufu sent in the year following his thirteenth cattle count, which means regnal year 27 (Kuhlmann 2005, 247). In 2013, fragments of papyrus were found at the early Old Kingdom harbor of Wadi al-Jarf on the Red Sea coast, one of which also carried the date of Khufu's thirteenth cattle count. The papyrus was concerned with the transfer of casing blocks from Turah quarry to the king's pyramid construction site and mentions Khufu's brother and vizier, Ankhhaf, as in charge of the project (Tallet and Marouard 2014, 10). Khufu had picked out a site to the north of Dahshur, Giza, to construct his funerary complex. Outside of this king's pyramid complex at

Giza, which is extensive and includes small pyramids for his queens, a field of mastaba tombs to the east of his pyramid for his sons and daughters, and another in the west for his high officials (see Lehner and Hawass 2017, 172–184, 313–318), there is little other evidence with which to construct a history of Khufu's reign.

There are four fragments of alabaster statuettes, including two bases with Khufu's cartouche, and other fragments from two life-sized alabaster statues attributed to Khufu that were found at Giza (Smith 1946, 20). One completely preserved statuette depicting Khufu, carved in ivory, was found at the temple in Abydos and is now in the Cairo Museum, but other than the fact that the king's name is on the statuette, there is no proof that it dates to the Fourth Dynasty (Hawass, 1985). There are fragments of relief scenes that were scattered in the area at the top of the causeway, the mortuary temple and the queens' pyramids, but it is difficult to say where these scenes had been originally. Flentye has studied the Giza fragments found in the area of the queen's pyramids, the causeway, and the entrance into the mortuary temple (2011a, 77–84). She suggests that the relief decoration with figures of goats and cattle could have come from the causeway walls or from inside the mortuary temple (Flentye 2011a, fig. 3). Flentye also believes the boat scenes, depictions of family members, and any scenes tied to the *heb sed* also came from this temple. These include the blocks found in the area of the funerary temple, causeway, and boat pits found by Selim Hassan, who labels them in his publication as from the walls of the causeway (Hassan 1960). Blocks with *heb sed*–related scenes were found in the mortuary temple of Sneferu at the Northern Pyramid at Dahshur, and it is logical to assume that the Khufu blocks with *heb sed* scenes come from a mortuary temple as well. The fact that there is no relief decoration from either the mortuary temple of Khafra or that of Menkaura means there is no other comparable material from Giza.

One of these *heb sed*–related scenes shows Khufu in the Red Crown with a scarf or other similar material over his shoulder. This has been thought to be a scene of the king's ritual visit to Heliopolis during the *heb sed* (Hassan 1960, 21–22; Oppenheim 2005, 466–467) but it has also been suggested that the scene belongs to the "Feast of the White Hippopotamus" (Lauer 1949, 113–114; Behrmann, 1989, doc. 62; Cwiek, 2003:197; Flentye 2011a, 81), a little-known but clearly religious ritual (Troy 2006, 144; Altenmüller 1994). In another very long block with vertical lines of inscription at each end, two badly damaged figures of the king are back to back. On the left, only part of the king's head cloth with a Horus falcon on it is preserved, while on the right, the king, smaller in size, wearing a *heb sed* robe and holding the flail, sits on a throne (Hassan 1960, pls. 6B; Reisner and Smith 1955, figs. 6a, 6b). The head cloth with falcon could be mirrored by what may be fragments of an alabaster statue of Khufu showing the exact same thing. These statue fragments, now in the

Museum of Fine Arts in Boston, also came from the area of Khufu's mortuary temple (Roehrig 1999, 254).

Several complete blocks and a number of fragments that can be attributed to the pyramid complex of Khufu were discovered reused in the pyramid precinct and temple foundations of the Middle Kingdom king Amenemhat I at Lisht (see Jánosi 2016, 21n62). There were also a few found in a nearby nonroyal tomb at Lisht (Arnold 2007b, 67–68). All in all, there are twenty-seven blocks and pieces from Lisht that can be divided into the following types of decoration: texts, personifications of estates and produce, attendants, boats and sailors, the *heb sed*, and other ceremonial scenes. Goedicke suggests that a large block with the kings titulary (Goedicke 1971, 11) and three scenes of estates and animals (Goedicke 1971, 13–19) came from Khufu's valley temple. All of the ceremonial scenes, particularly those from the *heb sed*, Goedicke suggests, came from the mortuary temple (Goedicke 1971, 29–46). In terms of the king's relationship or interaction with deities, there is little evidence. One block from those belonging to the *heb sed* depicts Wepwawet. Goedicke thinks that this depiction is meant to show a priest with a Wepwawet mask, who would be at the front of the king's procession (Goedicke 1971, 29–30). A second block depicts the goddess Meret, who is also known in the *heb sed* scenes of later Old Kingdom kings Sahura and Pepy II (Goedicke 1971, 38).

Later, in the Middle Kingdom, there is evidence for a cult connection between King Khufu and a lion goddess, probably Bastet. Two pottery statues of the goddess were discovered in a rock-cut chamber in a hillside in northern Saqqara (Yoshimura and Kawai 2003, 38) (Figure 13). One of the pottery statues has two small figures of child kings standing on each side of its legs; the back pillar on the right side is inscribed with the Horus name of Khufu. The second lion goddess figure holds a lotus scepter and has one child king standing on its side; the name inscribed on the base is that of King Pepy I. The objects in the chamber show that it was used in the early Old Kingdom, and the lioness statues associated with an assemblage of Middle Kingdom pottery show that cult activity started up again then (Yoshimura, Kawai, and Kashiwagi 2005, 390–394). This would fit with other evidence for a revival of interest in Old Kingdom kings in the Twelfth Dynasty (Malek 2000).

There are only parts of the foundation walls and one part of the basalt floor of Khufu's mortuary temple remaining. Its plan has been reconstructed, but the back-most part in the west, which would have been the most important, was completely destroyed by the cutting of a large hole in either the Twenty-Sixth Dynasty or the Roman period (Lehner and Hawass 2017, 163). The temple was wider than deep, and the main internal space was an open court surrounded by red granite pillars. The interior walls of the court would have been limestone decorated with the relief scenes of the *heb sed*. Two smaller rows of pillars filled

Figure 13 Two pottery lion goddess statues from North Saqqara. Photo: Sally el-Sabbahy, Courtesy of the Egyptian Museum, Cairo

a niche in the west side, which led into a north–south chamber for five statues (Arnold 1997, fig. 13).

Five boat pits are associated with the pyramid of Khufu. Two pits were placed parallel to the east face of the pyramid, one north and one south of the funerary temple. A third pit was parallel to and north of the causeway. Two other pits were found south of the pyramid, parallel to the south face. These two pits were rectangular, not boat-shaped like the other three, and still had the remains of boats in them (Lehner 2017, 166). Lehner suggests that they were dismantled because they had been used in the funeral, while the other boat-shaped pits had held intact boats for the use of King Khufu in his afterlife (Lehner 2017, 168).

The upper part of Khufu's causeway is gone and the lower part, along with the valley temple, is buried under the modern settlement of Nazlet al-Saman (Goyon 1967). In digging done for sewer work in 1990, basalt blocks were found that must be the pavement of the valley temple, although its ruinous condition and the fact that it was covered over by a strata of Nile silt point to the fact that the temple had been destroyed in ancient times (Lehner and Hawass 2017, 186–187).

Certainly, the size of Khufu's pyramid and the layout of the surrounding complex are a statement of his power and control. Roth has suggested that the "kings no longer derived their power from their relationship to earlier kings" (1993, 50) but from their relationship to the sun god, and so they were free to place their funerary monument away from that of their ancestors. With Sneferu, Khufu, and his son Djedefra, we see different locations for their pyramids being picked. It might also be telling that, with Djedefra, the title "son of Ra" is added to his throne name, making a clear link to the sun god (Leprohon 2013, 19) and referring to his father as the sun god. The king's actual name, Djedefra, also included Ra. His brother and successor, Khafra, also used the word for the sun in his name and carried on the new tradition of having a "son of the sun" title. The pyramid of Khufu, named "the horizon of Khufu," must have been a statement about the king being Ra, as the horizon is where the sun appears.

Two queens are accepted as the wives of Khufu, Meritites I and Henutsen, although the evidence for both is not without questions. Meritites I has been thought to have been buried in the small queen's pyramid, GI-a, on the southeast front of the Great Pyramid. A now lost stela found by Auguste Mariette at Giza gave the titles of Meritites I, including that she was *weret hetes* (*wrt ḥts*), "great of affection" under Sneferu, *weret hetes* under Khufu, and *imahu* (*imꜣḫw*) "honored" under Khafra (Mariette 1976, 565; de Rouge 1877, pl. LXII). It has been suggested that Meritites I was a young wife of Sneferu, and when he died she married his son, Khufu, and by the time his grandson, Khafra, was king, she was elderly and therefore "honored" (Sabbahy 1982, 50–51). Early on, Reisner suggested Meritites I was a daughter of Sneferu and was married to her brother Khufu (Reisner 1955, 6–7), but since the title *weret hetes* was one only given to a queen, it must indicate that she was married to Sneferu and then later to his son, Khufu.

Fragments of the name Meritites, along with fragments of a queen's titles were found in the mastaba of Kawab (G7110–7120), Khufu's eldest son, so that Meritites I is assumed to have been Kawab's mother (Reisner 1955, 6, fig. 9). Some scholars point out the fact that Kawab's mastaba is right in front of the queen's pyramid GI-a, which is purposely planned to show royal family connections. Kawab held the title vizier as well as the honorific title *iry-pat* (Strudwick 1985, 146–147). Kawab must have died before his father, however, because it was his brother Djedefra (whose name can also be read as Radjedef), not Kawab, who ruled after Khufu. As Stadelmann has pointed out, however, none of the kings' sons with the high titles of vizier and *iry-pat* ever became king (Stadelmann 2010a, 297–298). Kawab was married to his sister Hetepheres II, who later became one of the queens of Djedefra.

Scholars do not yet have archaeological evidence for a palace or any other domestic structure for the royal family at this early period of Egyptian history. There is good archaeological evidence of both palaces and separate domestic structures, or harems, for queens from the New Kingdom but not before. In particular, the site of Medinet el-Gurob in the Fayum, which was occupied from the reign of Thutmose III in the Eighteenth Dynasty down through the Ramesside period, is a main source for information on the ancient Egyptian harem (see Picton 2016; Shaw 2011; Yoyotte 2008).

There is textual evidence for the word meaning "royal harem" in the Old Kingdom, *ipt nswt* (Reiser 1972, 1). The word *ipt* is first known from a clay sealing found in the First Dynasty tomb of King Semerkhet at Abydos (Petrie 1900, pl. 28). A title for the official who oversaw the harem, the "Overseer of the King's Harem," is first known from a fragment of a diorite vessel found at Djoser's Step Pyramid complex (Kahl et al. 1995, 56–57). After that, the title of harem overseer is found fairly regularly in the Old Kingdom (Roth 2012, 2) – for example, on the architrave of the official Khufuseneb I from his mastaba in the Western Cemetery at Giza, along with his titles of priest of Khufu and "One Who is Over the Secrets of His Lord" (Junker 1944, 143 fig. 46). Several scholars have interpreted the words *ipt nswt* (*ipt nswt*) as the "royal counting house" rather than harem (Lorten 1974; Ward 1986) but that translation does not seem to make sense in the contexts in which the phrase is used and, by and large, is not accepted (Callender 1994, 10). By the New Kingdom, the phrase *per khenret* (*pr ḫnrt*), "house of the harem," is used rather than *ipt nswt* (Reisner 1972, 11).

There is no evidence that the harem in ancient Egypt should be connected with more modern connotations of a secluded or forbidden place where the king's wives would be hidden away and kept out of sight. It appears to have been either part of the palace or a separate building from the palace that was lived in by female members of the royal family, their female attendants, their children, and sons of high officials who were raised and educated in the royal palace (Callender 1994, 11). Titles of harem officials always seem to have belonged to men, not women.

It is tempting to wonder if a king's wife always remained in the royal harem, even if her husband had passed away. Was the harem a place that royal women stayed a part of, perhaps changing their relationship to other members of the family, as the king on the throne changed? Such a situation might be expressed in the text of the stela of Meritites I that was discussed earlier in this section. She may have been a wife of Sneferu who later married Khufu and then lived on as an elderly woman in the reign of Khafra. There is some evidence of widowed queens marrying the successor of their husband and this will be discussed further in Chapter 3, which is concerned with the Sixth Dynasty.

Henutsen is presumed to have been buried in the small queen's pyramid GI-c, based on the fact that a later Twenty-First Dynasty temple of Isis, "Mistress of the Pyramid," was built in front of this small pyramid, containing what is called the "Inventory Stela," which names a Queen Henutsen (Hassan 1953, 113). She is also assumed to be the mother of Prince Khufukhaf and therefore the queen depicted in his tomb, G 7140, just east of her pyramid (Lehner and Hawass 2017, 174, fig. 8.36). She is not named but referred to as "his mother who bore him." She is only given one title, "The One Who Sees Horus and Seth." This is the first example of this complete title, as, in the Early Dynastic Period, it was written only as "The One Who Sees Horus." "The One Who Sees Horus and Seth" is a title held only by a queen and expresses her personal relationship with the king who embodied both of these two gods (Sabbahy 1982, 53–54). Henutsen wears a short wig set back on her head and a pointed cloak just over her left shoulder. Queen Hetephernebty, the wife of King Netjerikhet was shown in this same wig and cloak when she was depicted with her daughter on the block from Heliopolis, and there is one more example later from the reign of King Khafra discussed in the section "The Reign of Khafra (2558–2532)."

It is difficult to conclude what this particular iconography of the queen suggests other than the fact that she is perhaps somewhat old and for that reason wrapped in a cloak (Fay 1999, 108–109). Since the queen appears like this with a grown son or daughter of the king, this scene may well have depicted the queen as having successfully raised royal offspring and therefore reached a status within the royal family that might have been difficult with the short lifespans and high child mortality rates expected in an ancient population.

THE REIGN OF DJEDEFRA (2566–2558)

Khufu's son, Djedefra, chose to move to the northwest to Abu Roasch to build his pyramid. His reign was always thought to be fairly short, at eight to nine years, but more recent evidence points to a reign of twenty-three years, which would fit better with the fact that he seems to have completed the building of his pyramid (Valloggia 2011, 6–8). Abu Roasch was used as a quarry in Roman times and later, so there is little left of his pyramid complex. There is a descending corridor down to what was once a granite-lined burial chamber. On the east face of the pyramid is a small temple and along its east side a rectangular enclosure with rooms for priests to live in (Valloggia 2011, pl. 180) and, at the north end, a bakery and brewery (Valloggia 2017, pl. 183). Although it is not called this in the excavation report (Valloggia 2011, 58), this area for food production may have been the *per shena* (*pr šnᶜ*) of the pyramid complex. The earliest attestation of a *per shena* is in the Second Dynasty, and they are known to have been included in pyramid complexes and sun temples belonging to the Fifth Dynasty (Papazian 2005, 145, 168). A good example of a *per shena* is the one found in the Heit el-Ghurab workmen's village at Giza (Lehner and Hawass 2017, 378; AERAgram 1996, 6–7). At the south of the Abu Roasch enclosure is a boat-shaped pit like those found at Giza (Valloggia 2011, 59–60, figs. 216–227).

Broken statuary was found by the earliest excavations in 1901, including the famous quartzite head of Djedefra and the quartzite statuette of him and his wife, both now in the collection of the Louvre. It is interesting that quartzite was used for these pieces, as this rock comes from the Gebel Ahmar near Heliopolis, and red quartzite is the "most solar of all the stones of Egypt" (Quirke 2001, 30). In the statuette, the queen sits down next to the feet of the king, just like in the Heliopolis relief of King Djoser and his female family, discussed in the section "The Third Dynasty: The Reign of King Netjerikhet (2667–2648)" (Fay 1998, 161). There are at least thirteen fragments of various sizes from similar statues from the site that remain unpublished. Some preserve parts of titles belonging to a queen, and one has the name Khentetka (Baud 1999b, 559).

Djedefra seems to have had two queens, Khentetka and Hetepheres II. Hetepheres II was first married to Kawab, the brother of Djedefra, and they had a daughter, Meresankh III, who later is married to Khafra (Dunham and Simpson 1974, 7). In 2002, a small subsidiary pyramid on the southeast corner of Djedefra's pyramid was cleared and showed that the substructure had been converted into a burial chamber, undoubtedly for a royal female (Valloggia 2003, 230; 2011, fig. 277). A great deal of early Fourth Dynasty pottery, a canopic vessel, and an alabaster bowl with the Horus name of Khufu was found, and so the assumption was made that this was the burial of one of Khufu's daughters who had married their brother, Djedefra.

Brother–sister marriage among much later Ptolemaic rulers is well documented (Ager 2005; Buraselis 2008), and nonroyal brother–sister marriage in Roman Egypt has been the subject of many studies (Hopkins 1980; Strong 2005; Huebner 2007). Possible pharaonic precedents for sibling marriage at the nonroyal level have been studied (Černy 1954; Frandsen 2009, 36–9), and the evidence for it is decidedly slight. Černy could find no full brother–sister marriages among commoners and, in the more than 2,000 years of pharaonic history, only five possible marriages among step-siblings. A fairly recent study on the Old Kingdom concluded that there "is no definitive evidence of brother-sister marriages outside the royal family" (McCorquodale 2013, 120). Polygamy outside the royal family has also been studied for the pharaonic period, and the evidence is slight as well (Simpson 1974a; Kanawati 1976).

A marriage to a sister seems to have been a statement by a king that he was a god. In the Heliopolitan creation myth, the sun god Ra created the first male–female, brother–sister, god–goddess pair, who then married each other and created the next divine pair. So this type of marriage was a statement of being a god. Another way that brother–sister royal marriage can be explained is that the feminine counterpart to the sun god was Hathor, and she took on any feminine aspect needed by the sun god. Hathor provides the model for the royal woman. In other words, a royal female was part of a "multigenerational composition" (Troy 1986, 3) of the female element of kingship: "the royal women, as mortal representatives of the feminine prototype, complement Hathor's divinity" (Troy 1986, 54).

There were large amounts of smashed royal statuary at the site of Abu Roasch that showed various materials being used. The majority of the statues of the king himself were built out of quartzite and statues of his daughters out of limestone (Cwiek 2003, 97n390; Baud 1999a). A limestone statue base was found bearing the name of Princess Neferhetepes, and the lower part of a statuette of Princess Hetepheres was also found in a chapel of the pyramid's mortuary temple (Smith 1946, 33). The titles of Princess Neferhetepes show that she was a priestess of Hathor, in all her places, as well as a priestess in the funerary cult of her father (Sabbahy 1982, 122). There are at least five princesses in the Fourth Dynasty who have the title of priestess connected with the cult of their father, but the title becomes rare in the Fifth and Sixth Dynasties (Sabbahy 1982, 129–131).

Granite statuettes of Djedefra's sons as scribes were also found there. That of Prince Setka was intact, with the granite statuette set into a piece of wood in a limestone base (Smith 1946, 33; Ziegler 1999, 250–251). Setka's titles included "Eldest Son of the King," *iry-pat*, "Sole Companion of the King," "Controller of the Palace," and "One Who Is Over the Secrets of the King's Dressing Room." All of these titles stress his high position and closeness to the king. There were two statuette bases with the titles of Prince Hornet and one base for Prince Baka. These two princes were also called eldest son, which could mean they all had different mothers or, as Stadelmann suggests, the title of eldest son wasn't always just given to the firstborn son (Stadelmann 1984, 169). Hornet's other titles were *iry-pat* and "Sole Companion"; Baka was not an *iry-pat* but was "Controller of the Palace" and "Master of Largess in the Mansion of Life," as well as "Priest of Djedefra" (Römer 1977, 47). An offering table for the king's son, *iry-pat* Hornet, was found in Mastaba 13 in the "F Necropolis" at Abu Roasch, so it is assumed he must have been buried there (Baud 2003, 34). Another prince, Nikau-Djedefra was buried in Mastaba 15, as his false door was found there, which preserves his titles of king's son and sole companion (Gourdon 2006, 249; Baud 2003, 33–34). The "F Necropolis" was about a mile north of the pyramid complex of Djedefra and roughly divided into two parts, of which the northern part had three large mastabas with somewhat smaller ones clustered around them (Baud et al, 2003: 52, fig. 2; Baud and Moeller 2006, 18). The necropolis is quite different from those of earlier Fourth Dynasty kings, as it is quite far from the king's pyramid and not set out in such organized and parallel rows as Sneferu's mastaba field set between the Bent and

Northern pyramids at Dahshur or organized in "streets" like the mastabas east and west of the pyramid of Khufu at Giza (Baud et al 2003, 59, fig. 9).

The part of the Turin Canon for the Fourth Dynasty is badly damaged (Gundacker 2015, 137), so that scholars differ on who took the throne right after Djedefra. Possibly a son of Djedefra had a short reign after the death of his father or after the death of Khafra. The substructure of a largely unfinished pyramid at Zawyet al-Aryan is very much like that of Djedefra's, and there is some, although disputed, textual evidence that the king's son Baka followed him on the throne (Valloggia 2003, 231). After this, however, Khafra, whose name means "He appears as Ra" (Leprohon 2013, 31), another son of Khufu, takes the throne. The succession to the throne, therefore, reverted to the sons of Khufu instead of Djedefra. This should indicate to scholars to keep in mind that father-to-son succession was not "written in stone" because of the myth of Osiris. Some scholars accept that Baka ruled after Khafra, and before Menkaura, perhaps indicating that a son of Djedefra had become old enough to take back the throne (Hornung 1999, 29–30).

THE REIGN OF KHAFRA (2558–2532)

In the reign of Khafra, and his son Menkaura, royal funerary complexes were once again built at Giza. Khafra's pyramid complex is probably the best preserved in terms of architecture and completeness, but there is virtually no relief decoration preserved, although there is evidence for a great deal of statuary. Menkaura's complex was unfinished at his death, and the mortuary and valley temples were completed in mud brick and therefore without relief decoration. A number of triad statues were found in the valley temple, and these will be discussed in the section "The Reign of Menkaura (2532–2503)." One interesting fact about these Giza pyramids is that the southeast corner of the pyramids of Khafra and Khufu lie on a line directed straight toward Heliopolis, but the pyramid of Menkaura is off this line by several meters, perhaps because of changes to the original plan for the pyramid (Verner and Bruna 2011, 288).

The valley temple of Khafra is quite well preserved. It was built out of local limestone and then lined with red granite. The center T-shaped columned court also has granite pillars and an alabaster floor, with cuttings for the placement of twenty-three statues (Arnold 1997, 52, fig. 14). Most discussions of the meaning of these statues tie them to the funeral ceremony of the "Opening of the Mouth", the different statues symbolizing different parts of the king's body that had to be "activated" so that the king could live again in the afterlife. There were statues out of gneiss or diorite, of greywacke and others that were alabaster. Flentye suggests a possible reconstruction of the order of the statues within the temple, based on the type of stone used, with those of diorite facing north, alabaster facing south, and greywacke facing east (Figure 14). The greywacke statues were also the only ones with the inclusion of the name Ra in the inscriptions on them, such as "son of Ra" and the phrase "eternal life like Ra" (Flentye 2011a, 89).

There is an entrance to the temple on the north side, with a door 16 feet high inscribed with the titles of the king and ending with "beloved of Bastet, living forever" (Lehner and Hawass 2017, 209). The inscription on the sides of a similar doorway on the south side ended with "beloved of Hathor, [living forever]" (Hölscher 1912, 17, fig. 7–8). Up in the wall directly inside each of these two doors is a 2-meter-high niche. The northern niche is thought to have held a dyad of Khafra and Bastet, a large fragment of which was found in the valley temple and is now in the Cairo Museum (Borchardt 1911, 11–12; Flentye 2011a, 87, fig. 10), and it is assumed there was a similar dyad with Hathor in the southern niche (Seidel 1996, 20). Lehner suggests both niches held statues of baboons greeting the rising sun (Lehner and Hawass 2017, 209); fragments of a large granite statue of a baboon were found in the southern entrance, and other fragments were found out in front of the valley temple (Hölscher 1912, 42).

Figure 14 Diorite statue of Khafra from his valley temple (CG 9). Photo: Sally el-Sabbahy, Courtesy of the Egyptian Museum, Cairo

Bastet was known from the Second Dynasty as a lioness, not a cat, which is Bastet's form in later pharaonic times. Bastet's cult center was Per-Bastet in the northeast Delta, and she was the northern equivalent of Hathor, whose main cult place was Dendera in Upper Egypt. Hathor could also take the form of a lion, and it could be that these goddesses were the sphinxes that were originally placed outside the two doors of the valley temple (Hölscher 1912, 15, fig. 5). The cuttings for the bases of these statues show that they were 26 feet long (Hölscher 1912, 17; Lehner 1997, 126).

The valley temple, the Sphinx, and the Sphinx Temple "were all created as part of the same quarrying and construction process" (Lehner and Hawass 2017, 220). Like the valley temple, the Sphinx Temple would have been cased in red granite, with an alabaster floor; there were cuttings in the floor for ten large statues of Khafra (Lehner and Hawass 2017, 221; Hölscher 1912, 11, fig. 5). The temple may not have been completed in the Old Kingdom, and the building materials of the temple were later stripped away. Based on construction evidence, Lehner states that the Sphinx definitely dates to Khafra (Lehner and Hawass 2017, 241).

When built in the Fourth Dynasty, the Sphinx could have represented King Khafra as Horus, while at the same time representing the sun god, as "sphinxes in later times signified the pharaoh in the form of the primeval sun and creator god" (Lehner 2003, 179). When a name for the Great Sphinx is known in the New Kingdom, it was Horemakhet, "Horus-in-the-Horizon," a fusion of Horus and the sun god. Studies of solar alignment at Giza have shown that, at the summer solstice, the sunset would have been seen in the middle between the pyramids of Khufu and Khafra, and so the two pyramids with the ball of the sun would have been the hieroglyphic symbolic *akhet* (*ꜣḫt*), or horizon (Dash 2011, 8; Lehner 2011, 9).

The temple of the Sphinx is considered by some scholars as "a precursor of the Fifth Dynasty sun temples," as well as evidence that solar religion was penetrating the royal funerary cult (Verner 2006, 181). Ricke suggested that, although there is no evidence that the temple was completed in the Fourth Dynasty, or that a cult of the Great Sphinx functioned then, there were two small chapels opposite the two entrance doors that could have functioned as chapels for the goddesses Hathor and Neith. Priestesses for these two goddesses, "Hathor, Mistress of the Sycamore in the House of Khafra" and "Neith in the House of Khafra" are known from tombs at Giza, although no chapels for these goddesses are known (Schott 1950, 123). It is possible that the name of the sphinx temple was "The House of Khafra" (Ricke 1950, 38). It is interesting that, in the small temple built by King Amenhotep II in the Eighteenth Dynasty, just on the north side of the sphinx temple, votive material was found, similar to that at other Hathor temples (Pinch 1993, 79).

Although it is difficult to find much information about the cult of the goddess Neith before the Late Period, in the period of the Fourth and Fifth

Dynasties there were both royal and nonroyal priestesses of Hathor, who were also priestesses of Neith, all but one of whom are documented in the Giza–Saqqara area (Galvin 1981, 73; Sabbahy 1982, 129–131; Callender 2002, 148). If the Sphinx Temple was a sun temple it would make sense that Hathor would be present, as in the sun temples Hathor plays an important role as the partner of the sun god (Verner 2014/2015, 459).

The more than 1,600-foot causeway to the mortuary temple was lined with limestone but perhaps had no relief decoration (Arnold 1997, 58). Two decorated blocks possibly came from Khafra's causeway or mortuary temple but it is not clear (Flentye 2011a, 86–87; Oppenheim 2005, 469–470). A granite architrave block reused in the pyramid of Amenemhat I at Lisht is clearly Khafra's as it carries his cartouche. Goedicke suggests it originated from his mortuary temple (Goedicke 1971, 23n7), although others have suggested the valley temple or even an Old Kingdom temple of a deity may have been the source (Oppenheim 2005, 465n38).

Ricke accepted the block as one from the court of the mortuary temple and restored it as bridging a space between pillars around the center court that alternated with doorways and seated royal statues (Ricke 1950, 50, fig. 17, pl. 2). Hölscher had restored the court with Osiride statues of the king against the wall between all the doorways (Hölscher 1912, 27–28, fig. 16). Ricke's reconstruction has been questioned most recently by Jánosi, who does not think that the Lisht block came from this temple and that the statues may have been striding, not seated (Jánosi 2016). There must have been at least as many statues of Khafra in his mortuary temple as his valley temple, if not more; at least a hundred statues may have been part of his pyramid complex (Ziegler 1999, 252). All of this statuary was a statement of Khafra's power, kingship, and, perhaps most importantly, his relationship with the gods and goddesses.

A number of queens are suggested to have been the wives of King Khafra. There are no planned queens' pyramids as part of his funerary complex, however, and the queens' tombs known from his reign are either mastabas or rock-cut tombs. Jánosi has pointed out that each king was consistent in building a particular type of tomb for his queens but that the type of tomb "varied from reign to reign" (Jánosi 1992, 54). One of Khafra's queens, Meresankh III, was clearly a member of the royal family. She was the daughter of Prince Kawab and Princess Hetepheres. Her mother, Hetepheres II, became the wife of King Djedefra after Kawab died. Meresankh III, among her many other titles, was "King's Daughter," which she could have had as a title since she was the granddaughter of King Khufu or else because she was the stepdaughter of King Djedefra. She was also, through both her parents, related to her husband, King Khafra.

The ancient Egyptians did not use terms that made a distinction between descending generational relationships such as son and grandson, daughter and granddaughter (Franke 1983; Baud 1999b, 162–170; Campagno 2009, 2), so that a king's son or daughter might also have been his grandson or granddaughter. The actual son or daughter relationship could be stressed in royal titles, however, by adding "of his body," referring to the father. All the Fourth Dynasty queens who have the title "King's Daughter" in their titulary use the full title "King's Daughter of his body" to make clear they belong to the royal bloodline (Sabbahy 1982, 137). While it appears that "King's Daughter" can be given to both daughters and granddaughters, in both cases they are always members of the royal family (Sabbahy 1982, 133–139), which is not always true for the title "King's Son." By the end of the Fourth Dynasty, the title of "King's Son" could be only titular, that is, given to men who were not part of the royal family (Schmitz 1976, 166–171). The king granted this title to high officials from whom he expected the same loyalty as he would from one of his sons (Baud 1999b, 373–379).

The four main titles held by an Old Kingdom queen, almost always found together, were "King's Wife," "One Who Sees Horus and Seth," "Great of Affection," and "Great of Praise." These are the four titles Meresankh III has when she is shown in the tomb of her son, Nebemakhet. He was a vizier and also had titles such as *iry-pat*, "Sole Companion," and "Overseer of the Secrets." Meresankh III was buried in Mastaba G 7530–7540, one of the mastabas added into the Eastern Cemetery, south of the queens' pyramids, when King Khafra returned to the site of Giza to build his pyramid complex (Lehner and Hawass, 2017, 319). In the hall of her mastaba, Meresankh depicts her father, Kawab, and her mother Hetepheres II with her on the east wall (Dunham and Simpson, 1974, fig. 4). A large figure of Kawab stands at the north end of the wall, facing away from the register with Meresankh and her mother, who also face away from him. This back-to-back placement, along with the fact that Kawab faces left on the wall, means that he is deceased (Kanawati 1981b, 219). Meresankh stands behind her mother in a light skiff in the marsh, holding onto her with her left arm and pulling up a papyrus stalk with her right. The text behind her says "she pulls papyrus for Hathor in the marshland together with her mother." This pulling of the papyrus is the *sesh wadj* (*sš wꜣḏ*) ritual, which in the later Fourth Dynasty into the early part of the Fifth Dynasty was carried out only by royalty (Woods 2011, 317; Altenmüller 2002, 14–16). This ritual not only was to rustle the papyri, like shaking a sistrum to calm the goddess Hathor, but also had a funerary undertone of symbolizing rebirth in the afterlife (Bleeker 1973, 88).

Meresankh and her mother are shown again on the west wall, which has an offering formula in the large, top register. Her mother stands in front of her, wearing a wig set back on her head and a pointed cloak over her shoulders.

Queens Hetephernebty and Henutsen wore this same wig and cloak earlier when they were shown with their children. Parallel to the scene in the papyrus marsh, these two women may be shown together to stress two successive female generations, which "relates the royal family to the pattern of cosmic renewal" (Troy 1986, 3), a concept discussed in the context of Queen Hetephernebty and her daughter Intkaues in the section "The Third Dynasty: The Reign of King Netjerikhet (2667–2648)."

The texts associated with these two figures of Meresankh III and her mother, Hetepheres II, give their complete list of queenly titles. Meresankh displays a number of priestess titles. Two of these are "Priestess of Hathor," titles that are unique for a queen. At least six princesses were priestesses of Hathor in the Fourth Dynasty but not a single queen. Meresankh not only is "Priestess of Hathor" but also has a second title, "Priestess of Hathor, Mistress of Dendera," which is the earliest known example of this specific title (Dunham and Simpson 1974, Fig. 7, middle column; Fischer 1968, 23). Meresankh may have held these two titles when she was a princess and then included them again into her titulary, using it only in the main room of her tomb (Dunham and Simpson 1974, figs. 7, 9). Undoubtedly because of the *sesh wadj* scene, Meresankh III wanted to stress her devotion to Hathor.

Another priestess title states that Meresankh III is a "Priestess of Thoth," a god who was closely associated with Horus and thus to the king. Thoth "guarantees the legitimacy of the king," "proclaims the divine resolution that recognizes the newly-crowned king," and "establishes the titles of the king" (Bleeker 1973, 144). She was also "Priestess of Bapef," a deity about whom almost nothing is known but who appears to have been a ram god, perhaps an animal form in which the king could be worshipped (Sabbahy 1982, 67). Her mother, Hetepheres II, holds priestess titles for Thoth, Bapef, and another little-known animal deity, Tjasepef, whose name is written with a bull on a standard. Tjasepef is perhaps another kind of powerful animal in which the king could be worshipped (Sabbahy 1982, 66–67). The priestess titles for Bapef and Tjasepef are last known in the titles of Neferhetepes, the mother of King Sahura in the Fifth Dynasty. Their disappearance has to be tied to changes in the expression of kingship and that perhaps the animal forms of royal power, so important, for example, at a site like Hierakonpolis in Dynasty 0, were fading away or no longer considered appropriate.

A second queen of Khafra's, Queen Khamerernebty I, was the mother of Menkaura, who succeeded his father Khafra to the throne. She was also the mother of Khamerernebty II, who married Menkaura, so Khamerernebty II and Menkaura appear to have had a full brother–sister marriage. There is no evidence for Khamerernebty I's father, but logically it would have to have been Khufu, very late in his reign, or Djedefra. In any case, she and her husband, Khafra were related, but it is not clear how closely. Either they were siblings or Khamerernebty I was Khafra's niece.

There is no evidence of a tomb for Queen Khamerernebty I, but her titles as king's mother, king's daughter, and king's wife are given on the lintel over her daughter's tomb entrance (G8978), along with her daughter's titles. It is possible that the tomb originally started out as one for Khamerernebty I (Callender and Jánosi 1997, 18). The fact that a mother and daughter are associated with each other in the daughter's tomb, just like Khafra's other queen, Meresankh III, and her mother, may also be stressing the royal family and cosmic renewal. Was this particularly necessary at this time because a brother-to-brother succession had taken place? In this case, the association was with titulary, not depictions, but the point was to stress generational stability within the royal line. It is also interesting that this mother and daughter also shared similar titles of priestess. Khamerernebty I was a priestess of Thoth and a priestess of Tjasepef, and her daughter Khamerernebty II held these same two titles (Sabbahy 1982, 62, 73). A larger-than-life-size limestone seated statue of Khamerernebty II, now in the Cairo Museum, was found in the tomb, along with five other statues (Figure 15). The titles of queen and king's daughter are

Figure 15 Limestone statue of Khamerernebty II from Giza (JE 48856). Photo: Sally el-Sabbahy, Courtesy of the Egyptian Museum, Cairo

carved on each side of her throne. There were no symbols held or worn by a queen in the Old Kingdom, so her titles, throne, and the large size of the statue state her royal status (Fay 1998, 164).

Hekenuhedjet, the third wife of Khafra, is depicted in the tomb of her son Prince Sekhemra, and parts of the inscription preserved above her and her son give the queen's title "Who Sees Horus and Seth" and her name (Hassan 1943, 117, fig. 62). Her son, Sekhemra, was born during the reign of Khafra and had a long career, probably dying in the reign of Sahura in the Fifth Dynasty, when his tomb was decorated (Studwick 1985, 136). Sekhemra seems to start out with titles of the highest level in the palace administration – "Controller of the Palace," "The One Over the Secrets of the Morning House" – but by the end of his career is *iry-pat* and "Vizier" (Hassan 1943, 107). Sekhemra was the last vizier "who was certainly of royal descent" (Bárta 2019).

Tomb LG 88, in the cliff southeast of Khafra's pyramid, belongs to the fourth wife of Khafra, queen and king's daughter, Persenet. This tomb is connected to the adjacent tomb LG 87, which belongs to Prince Nikaura. Khafra is thought to have been his father, and Persenet is accepted as his mother (Strudwick, 1985, 106). Nikaura holds the titles of "Vizier," *iry-pat*, "Sole Companion," and "Eldest Son of the King."

THE REIGN OF MENKAURA (2532–2503) AND THE END OF THE FOURTH DYNASTY

Menkaura's pyramid complex was unfinished at his death, which, based on the Turin King List, might have occurred after a reign of eighteen or possibly twenty-eight years (Verner 2006, 134). It has generally been accepted that Shepseskaf was the son of Menkaura, and he was the one who finished both the mortuary and the valley temples, although in mud brick, as well as completing the chapels of the three smaller pyramids to the south of the main pyramid. Workers under Shepseskaf must have finished some of Menkaura's statuary as well, as the triad of the king, Hathor, and the Cynopolis nome personification did not have the king's Horus name or serekh. Beginning with the Fourth Dynasty, not using the king's Horus name indicated that the king was no longer living (Friedman 2011b, 95; Nolan 2010, 32–40).

Reisner found fragments of a stela in two areas of the mortuary temple, the largest of which was a piece of the bottom, preserving the ends of eight vertical lines of inscription (Reisner 1931, 13, 15, pl. 19). The stela (Sethe 1933, 160) clearly carries the name of Shepseskaf, and in the first vertical line dates the inscription to: "year after the first cattle count," which should be his regnal year 3. It gives the name of the pyramid complex of Menkaura in three places and also has the broken statement: "He has made as his monument for ////." One fragment refers to offerings for Menkaura. There were also fragments from two Sixth Dynasty decrees found in the mortuary temple, giving evidence for a continued cult for Menkaura (Reisner 1933, 15; Lehner 2015, 229). The occupation layers in Menkaura's valley temple, dating to the Fifth and Sixth Dynasties, also give evidence for his ongoing cult at those times (Lehner 2015, 238). Shepseskaf is usually given a reign of four years (Verner 2006, 135), perhaps barely enough time to have finished his father's pyramid complex, even in brick, and built his own mastaba-style tomb in south Saqqara.

The mortuary temple of Menkaura had two basic parts, an open court on the eastern half and then the western half with a central chapel with a larger-than-life-size seated alabaster statue of Menkaura, now reconstructed in the Museum of Fine Arts in Boston (Lehner and Hawass 2017, 255). This may have been the first colossal statue at Giza and perhaps the influence behind the colossal seated statue of Userkaf in the court of his funerary temple at Saqqara at the beginning of the Fifth Dynasty (Flentye 2017, 136). As noted, Queen Khamerernebty II, his wife, had a large limestone, seated statue of herself in her mastaba, measuring more than 2 meters high (CM 48856) (Lesko 1998, 152–155).

At some later time, a small offering area was built between the west wall of the mortuary temple and the pyramid behind. Menkaura's pyramid was being cased in red granite, but the casing was left with only sixteen courses done and granite blocks are still lying around the pyramid (Figure 16). Three smaller, subsidiary pyramids, G3a, G3b, and G3c, are on the south side of the king's

Figure 16 Menkaura's pyramid at Giza with granite casing blocks still on the ground. Photo: Lisa Sabbahy

pyramid, and there is evidence suggesting that they might have been used later for the burials of queens (Lehner and Hawass 2017, 260–269). There is only evidence for one queen of King Menkaura, Queen Khamerernebty II, so it would be logical to assume she had been buried in one of them. However, she had a mastaba at Giza in the Central Field East (Lehner and Hawass 2017, 328–331).

Blocks of the main pyramid's causeway foundation can be seen on the east of the mortuary temple and west of the valley temple, but it is not clear that the causeway was ever completed, roofed, or decorated. When Reisner's team began the search for the valley temple, the causeway "could be followed about half the way down" where all traces of the rest of the causeway had been washed away down to bedrock (Reisner 1931, 34). Menkaura's valley temple was square-shaped and divided into two halves, somewhat similar to the mortuary temple, with an entrance hall and storage magazines on each side leading to an open rectangular court on the east and a central niche with storage magazines on each side in the western half. From the archaeological evidence, it appears that the open court was used for housing during the Fifth Dynasty and that the area for the offering cult for the king was refurbished as well; from the evidence of seal impressions, this happened in the reign of Niuserra. There was further reuse in the Sixth Dynasty, and at this time the antechamber in front of the sanctuary in the middle of the west wall had four columns added making a portico, behind which were four seated alabaster statues of Menkaura (Kemp 2006, 208).

The greywacke dyad of the king and queen, or possibly the queen mother, and four complete and one broken triads of the king, the goddess Hathor, and nome personifications were discovered southwest of this antechamber in an area that had filled with flood debris and rubble from decayed houses. The dyad does not have any titles inscribed on the base, so the identification of the female figure is not certain. She does not wear the vulture headdress of the queen mother or the horns and disk of Hathor. Friedman has made a compelling argument that this figure is Khamerernebty I, shown with the king in a role connected with the *heb sed* (Friedman 2008).

Friedman, who has studied the triads in depth, suggests that there were probably more originally, perhaps ten, and that each triad was associated with a nome where there would have been a cult of the goddess Hathor, as suggested somewhat earlier by Wood (1974, 86). The nomes represented by these triads are all Upper Egyptian nomes: 4th nome, Thebes; 7th nome, Diospolis Parva; 15th nome, Hermopolis; 17th nome, Cynopolis (Friedman 2011a, 2) (Figure 17). All of these nomes had in them cults of Hathor, as well as royal estates, or *hwt*, that supported these cults, and in return Hathor provisioned the king for his *heb sed* (Friedman 2015b, 39). One of the triads has the personification of the 17th nome, where there was a provincial temple of Hathor at Tehne to which Menkaura

Figure 17 Triad with Menkaura and Hathor from Giza (JE 40679). Photo: Sally el-Sabbahy, Courtesy of Egyptian Museum, Cairo

donated land. This was made clear in the slightly later Fifth Dynasty text of an official named Nikaankh, who was not only an administrator in the *hwt*, or estate of the king there, but also overseer of the priests in the Tehne cult of Hathor (Sethe 1933, 12–13).

Reisner mentions in his publication of the valley temple material that he found other fragments "of alabaster statues which seem to be parts of triads similar to the slate triads" and suggested that these alabaster triads would have been the ones representing Lower Egypt (Reisner 1931, 110n16). Both Cwiek and Friedman accept this as a possibility, as greywacke symbolized Hathor and alabaster, Bastet (Friedman 2015b, 21n5; Cwiek 2003, 311), and it is possible that an alabaster fragment of a cat goddess statue in Hildesheim came from one of these triads (Seidel 1996, 10–12). The inclusion of both Hathor and Bastet in the valley temple parallel the dyads of Khafra, one with Hathor and one with Bastet set in the large niches above the two entrances of his valley temple. In a more recent publication, however, Friedman has suggested that alabaster ties Menkaura to a "solar sphere with Re" and the greywacke connects him to "Heb Seds through Hathor" (Friedman 2018, 132).

These triads were originally placed in the open court of Menkaura's valley temple, and the "overarching theme of the triads is the *heb sed* festival" (Friedman 2011a, 19). Like the estate figures walking into the *heb sed* temple of Sneferu at Dahshur, these triads represent economic support for Menkaura's *heb sed*, provided for him through his divine mother Hathor (Friedman 2011a, 13–14). Above all else, these statues stress the relationship of the goddess Hathor with the living and eternal king. The important relationship of king as son of Hathor, and therefore the son of the sun god, Ra, will be one clearly restated by Mentuhotep II of the late Eleventh Dynasty as he reunites Egypt.

These triads are statements of the king's power throughout Egypt, specifically in the four nomes represented in the preserved triads. The statement made by these triads is very much like the statement of royal power made by the building of small pyramids in the provinces in the late Third and early Fourth Dynasties (Friedman 2015a). The triads bring the goddess Hathor and her different cults into the king's own cult "and make it look like she is provisioning his" (Friedman 2011a, 37). These triads also make an important statement about the king's, and also the queen's, divinity. The queen in her role of king's wife is Hathor, as the king is Ra. It has been suggested, because of the importance of the goddess Hathor in the valley temple, particularly in Menkaura's, that the valley temple could be identified with the *meret* (Arnold 1977, 13).

Further evidence of a functioning cult of the living king Menkaura in his valley or mortuary temple comes from area AA in the western town of Heit el-Ghurab. Seals were discovered with the name of Menkaura, with nine of the seals also having the title "Assistant Royal Purification Priest" and three others with titles associated with the "Royal Funerary Workshop," indicating the "mortuary cult of the king was active during his lifetime" (Nolan 2012, 2–3). It is fair to assume that Shepseskaf would have finished building the burial complex of Menkaura if he was Menkaura's son or if he was the son of one of Menkaura's close family members and reigned after him if Menkaura had no son. Khuenra, "eldest son of the king," is known to have been a son of Menkaura and Khamerernebty II. Khuenra is depicted with his mother in his tomb, MQ1 in the Menkaura cemetery (Reisner 1934, fig. 10). He is shown as a young boy, nude and wearing a sidelock of hair, so he might well have died before his father. There is no evidence of another son for Menkaura.

The tomb of Khentkaues, a queen of the late Fourth Dynasty, is just to the northwest of Menkaura's valley temple. It appears that the final mud-brick construction around Queen Khentkaues's tomb and the attached priestly settlement took place when the valley temple of Menkaura was being finished (Lehner and all 2011, 190–191; Lehner 2015, 268–273). Lehner makes a point of saying that Shepseskaf's work there, finishing both the tomb of Khentkaues and the valley temple of Menkaura, was "after the cessation at Giza of large scale stone work in the Fourth Dynasty Giza tradition" (Lehner 2015, 268). Based on the proximity of the two structures, the settlement stretching between them, and the basin used as a harbor, there was clearly some type of relationship between the pyramid town of Khentkaues and the valley temple of Menkaura. Shepseskaf did not build himself a pyramid but a very large mastaba-like structure, cased in limestone with red granite for the bottommost course, at South Saqqara (Jéquier 1928a). Lehner gives it a height of about 60 feet (Lehner 1997, 139). It had a mortuary temple on the east side as well as a causeway leading up to it. Nothing is known about a valley temple. It has been pointed out that the arrangement of the substructure of the pyramid of Menkaura, the tomb of Khentkaues, and the mastaba of Shepseskaf are all very similar and that the substructure plan of Khentkaues "appears transitional" between Menkaura's and Shepseskaf's (Lehner and Hawass 2017, 300; Bárta 2016, 58, fig. 3) (Figure 18).

Figure 18 The tomb of the queen mother, Khentkaues I, Giza. Photo: Lisa Sabbahy

An important point, so far still debated, is what was the family relationship between Khentkaues I, Menkaura, and Shepseskaf. A fragment in the chapel of the tomb of Khentkaues preserves the title "King's Daughter" (Hassan 1943, 22). On a fragment from her north false door she is called "Mother of Two Kings of Upper and Lower Egypt" (Hassan 1943, 24), a title that could also be translated as "King of Upper and Lower Egypt and Mother of the King of Upper and Lower Egypt," meaning that Khentkaues I may have served as king and also been the mother of one. For the most part, scholars seem to have moved away from that interpretation and accept her as a mother of two sons who both became kings of Egypt (Verner 2015, 87). On the granite door jambs of the chapel, the titles of Khentkaues are more complete and she is: "Mother of Two Kings of Upper and Lower Egypt," "God's Daughter," and "Anything Good That She Orders Is Done for Her" (Hassan 1943, 17). In fact, these three titles are the basic ones of the titulary of the king's mother. "God's Daughter," or *sat-netjer*, is a parallel title to "King's Daughter" and refers to the fact that the woman is the daughter of a deceased king. The fact that whatever she orders is done reflects her stature and the respect due to her (Sabbahy 1998).

There is a small figure of the queen seated on a throne under her titles. She appears to wear a vulture headdress, the symbol of the king's mother, because what might be a vulture head protrudes from her forehead (Hassan 1943, fig. 2). Because the object on her forehead is not that clear, it has also been called a uraeus, which could support her possible title of king (Lehner 1997, 138). Lehner's latest comment on her depiction is that: "A tick at her forehead conveyed the projecting vulture head rather than a uraeus – if it is not simply a natural fleck in the granite surface" (Lehner and Hawass 2017, 297).

Who were the two sons of Khentkaues I who became kings? Lehner states that "I know of no evidence that anyone etched or re-carved the titles of Khentkawes I into the granite of her false doors or the jambs flanking the entrance to her chapel at some time long after the monument was complete" (Lehner 2015, 238). This would seem to mean that Khentkaues could have been the mother of Khafra and Menkaura, or Menkaura and Shepseskaf (Lehner 2015, 268). Since objects with the name of Khafra, such as a mace fragment and statue base, were found in or near her tomb, Verner suggests that Khentkaues was probably the daughter of Khafra (Verner 2014, 24), the sister of Menkaura, and the mother of Shepseskaf and Userkaf (Verner 2015, 87). This family relationship seems the most logical, although there is no evidence yet known to establish who her husband was.

It is odd that, even after a reign of eighteen years, Menkaura had not finished his pyramid, or its complex, especially since it was considerably smaller in size than his predecessors' pyramids. Was there a situation that caused a delay in beginning the construction of his funerary complex and therefore its size was reduced in order to finish it more quickly? The king was also casing a good part of his pyramid with granite, which is unusual because it is only the lowest course of the casing that is sometimes completed in granite, such as in the pyramid of Khafra (Lehner and Hawass 2017, 193). Menkaura's pyramid had sixteen courses finished in granite and then limestone for the rest of the casing above that (Lehner and Hawass 2017, 245).

According to the family tree put together by Harpur (1987, 244), Menkaura had eleven brothers. Such a large family could well have led to disputes over the succession to the throne, although we have no proof of that. Who Shepseskaf was is another unanswered question for the late Fourth Dynasty, as well as the fact that the Turin King List, which is badly damaged for the Fourth Dynasty "unquestionably lists an additional king at the very end of the Fourth Dynasty, who followed Shepseskaf," but there is no trace of the name left (Gundacker 2015, 138).

At the end of the Fourth Dynasty, changes took place in the structure of the state administration and the status of the officials that filled it, as well as in the relationship of the royal family to families of the nonroyal elite. Bárta has suggested that the changeover from the Fourth Dynasty to the Fifth shows the development from a period of the display of massive power by royalty to a "standard state phase" (Bárta 2013a, 166). The administration had to expand and, to do so, this meant offering positions to men who were not members of the royal family and, more and more often, to men who ruled in their provinces and remained there to be buried rather than being buried in one of the Memphite royal cemeteries.

Perhaps the clearest sign of change is that the position of vizier was given to nonroyal men. In the period of the very late Fourth Dynasty to the reign of Sahure in the Fifth Dynasty, Dulíková (2011) has pointed out that there were two groups of viziers: kings' sons and nonroyal men. During this time, which ends with only nonroyal men serving as vizier, the title of vizier, when written with the addition of the hieroglyphic sign of the phallus, marks a king's son (Dulíková 2011, 333–335). It appears that the nonroyal vizier was more important in the running of the country, while the royal vizier "was perhaps concerned only with the ceremonial and courtly functions of the office" (Strudwick 1985, 338), although this interpretation of the situation has been questioned (Nolan 2010, 352). By the time of the reign of King Sahure, it appears that the sons of the king did not hold any administrative titles at all but only titles of elite status, such as the old title *iry-pat* and the title of king's son (Strudwick 1985, 321; El-Awady 2009, fig. 83; Dulíková 2011, 335). These nonroyal viziers also held specific titles showing what administrative offices they had control over, such as the granaries, treasuries, scribes, and courts, which was not common in the Fourth Dynasty (Bárta 2013a, 166).

CHAPTER THREE

THE LATER OLD KINGDOM

THE FIFTH DYNASTY

Traditionally, the beginning of the Fifth Dynasty has been tied to a story in the Westcar Papyrus, in which the wife of a priest of the sun god gives birth to triplets. Goddesses appeared to help with the birth, and, as each male child was born, Meskhenet, the divine midwife, said: "A king who will assume the kingship in this whole land" (Lichtheim 1973, 220). Many books about the history of ancient Egypt interpret this story quite literally, stating that the first three kings of the Fifth Dynasty, Userkaf, Sahura, and Neferirkara, were brothers who were born as triplets. This situation is no longer accepted as history, although it is possible that the story may reflect the situation of Queen Khentkaues I, who appears to have been the mother of two kings.

Recent archaeological work at Abusir has produced evidence that the wife of King Sahura also had two sons, possibly twins, and one of them, taking the crown name Neferirkara, succeeded his father (Verner 2015, 89, 200, 595). Neferirkara's wife was named Khentkaues, and she is now referred to as Khentkaues II. Further excavation at Abusir has turned up the badly damaged mastaba tomb of a third queen with that name, now called Khentkaues III, who Verner suggests was the daughter of Neferirkara and Khentkaues II (Verner 2015, 90).

The Fifth Dynasty lasted roughly 150 years, from 2494 to 2345 BCE, and consisted of the reigns of nine kings. The most striking characteristic of the Fifth Dynasty is that the majority of the kings built their funerary complexes at the site of Abusir, just north of Saqqara, and also built sun temple complexes at Abu Ghurab, just north of Abusir. Although only two sun temples have been located and excavated, the names of six sun temples are known. It has been suggested that more than one king might have named and used a particular sun temple structure, so there may not have been six different ones (Stadelmann 2000, 241–242).

THE REIGN OF USERKAF (2494–2487)

The first king of the Fifth Dynasty was Userkaf, who may well have been the brother of Shepseskaf. Scholars have commented on the fact that Shepseskaf and Userkaf have the same name pattern and do not include the name of Ra in their names, as the Fourth Dynasty kings just before them, Khafra and Menkaura, did. This, along with the fact that Shepseskaf did not build a pyramid, is taken as evidence that their father was not a king and perhaps not even of royal blood (Verner 2014, 18–19; Bárta 2016, 57). It has also been suggested that Shepseskaf's mastaba was planned to reflect the old tradition of the mastaba tombs of the first kings at Abydos (Allen 2003a, 24).

Userkaf returned to the tradition of building a pyramid in which to be buried, although it was not large at 160 feet in height (Lehner 1997, 17). Userkaf had it built at Saqqara in the northeast corner of Netjerikhet's Step Pyramid complex within the space created by the Dry Moat, a trench that goes completely around the Step Pyramid complex (Myśliwiec 2006, 233) (Figure 19). By the placement of his pyramid, Userkaf may have wanted to associate himself with Netjerikhet, another king who began a new era (Goedicke 2000, 406; Verner 2014–2015, 458). Following the practice of Netjerikhet in his titulary, Userkaf also used the same name for both his Horus name and his Two Ladies name; it was *ir maat* (*ir mꜣꜥt*) "The One Who Carries Out *Maat*" (Leprohon 2013, 37–38). It is interesting that Userkaf is beginning a dynasty and, perhaps to reinforce his position, uses names including the word *Maat* like Sneferu did at the beginning of the Fourth Dynasty (Bárta and Dulíková 2017, 28).

His pyramid was named "Pure are the Places of Userkaf" (Lehner, 1997, 17). Scholars who are interested in the alignments of Old Kingdom pyramids point out that Userkaf's pyramid aligns exactly with Shepseskaf's large mastaba to the south and beyond that to Sneferu's Bent Pyramid even farther to the south (Bárta 2016, 63, fig. 6). Because of the limited space between the wall of the Step Pyramid complex and the Dry Moat, Userkaf's pyramid complex was aligned north–south rather than east–west. The pyramid, even smaller than Menkaura's was on the north, and the mortuary temple and south tomb were arranged in a rectangle on the south (Labrousse and Lauer 2000, vol. 2, figs. 39-40). When found, the complex was in very poor shape, since stone had been

Figure 19 The pyramid of Userkaf, with Netjerikhet's Pyramid in the background. Photo: Lisa Sabbahy

quarried from it and a number of large tomb shafts cut into the mortuary temple in the Twenty-Sixth Dynasty (Fakhry 1961, 169). The floors of the causeway, the open court, and the offering chapel were all paved with basalt. The pillars of the open court were red granite and a three-times-life-size granite head of the king was found, which originally belonged to a statue that sat on the south side of the open court (Labbé-Toutée and Ziegler 1999, 314–315).

Some pieces of the decorated limestone walls of the court remained, giving evidence of finely carved scenes, in particular those of birds in the swamp and the king with diadem, horns, and feathers (Labrousse and Lauer 2000, 2:figs. 102, 104; Smith 1946, pl. 52). Two other blocks from this pyramid were found reused in the pyramid of Amenemhat I at Lisht (Oppenheim 1999, 318–321). Just south of the king's complex was a small pyramid and adjoining mortuary temple for Queen Neferhetepes. The stone blocks from her complex had all been removed, so little of its plan can be discerned (Labrousse and Lauer 2000, 2: fig. 341).

Fragments of a block found in the entry hall of the funerary temple of the queen show female offering bearers. Some of the estate names labeling them are also preserved, including one mentioning the queen herself (Labousse 1997, 270; Labrousse and Lauer 2000, 2: pl. 115). This queen mother was also mentioned in the mastaba of an official named Persen, from the reign of Sahura, who mentions offerings reverting to him from the queen's cult, which had received them from the Temple of Ptah at Memphis (Papazian 2010, 137–138; Mariette 1976, 299–300).

That Neferhetepes is the only known wife of Userkaf, and was mother of his son and successor, Sahura, has been proven by the discovery of two new scenes on blocks from Sahura's causeway in 2002 (El-Awady 2006, 192). Neferhetepes had been considered the daughter of Djedefra of the Fourth Dynasty by some scholars (Dodson and Hilton 2004, 52–53), but others have pointed out that this would give her an impossibly long lifespan (Roth 2001, 99–102; Callender 2011b, 158–159). With the new evidence from Abusir, her historical position is clear but not necessarily who her parents were. Was Neferhetepes a daughter of Menkaura and married to Userkaf to help secure his right to the throne (El-Awady 2006, 198)?

One scene depicts the king with his mother and wife behind him when he greets the expedition arriving from Punt with incense trees (El-Awady 2009, pl. 5). The mother wears a vulture cap, which in the Old Kingdom was only worn by a king's mother (Sabbahy 1998, 308). Above her is her complete titulary, beginning with two titles stating her family relationships: "King's Mother" and "God's Daughter." This second title means that her father had been king (Sabbahy 1998, 305–306). A second scene shows King Sahura on a throne in front of his family and court officials celebrating the bringing of these incense trees from Punt. His mother sits in the top register wearing the vulture cap. Her name, somewhat damaged, is written above her (El-Awady 2009, pl. 6).

One other daughter of King Userkaf and Queen Neferhetepes is known as well, Princess Khamaat. She is important because she married an official named Ptahshepses and is the first known royal woman to have been married to someone outside the royal family (Dorman 2002). The biographical inscription of Ptahshepses came from his mastaba at Saqqara and is now in the collection of the British Museum (EA 682). The text explains that Ptahshepses was born in the reign of King Menkaura and grew up in the royal harem. He was a youth in the time of King Shepseskaf, and then King Userkaf gave him his oldest daughter, Khamaat, to be his wife (Strudwick 2005, 304). By the reign of King Sahura, Ptahshepses was the High Priest of the god Ptah, and he apparently lived on into the reign of Nyuserra, since he held the title of priest in that king's sun temple (Dorman 2002, 107).

Userkaf started another new tradition by building a sun temple, called "Ra's Nekhen," on a hill in the north of Abusir, right where the area now referred to as Abu Ghurab begins. Alignment between monuments has also been found here, as Userkaf's sun temple is on a line from Sneferu's Northern Pyramid in the south to Khufu's pyramid in the north. This certainly must have been planned: Was this Userkaf ushering in "a new solar era" or making a statement "by precise use of the sacred space" (Nuzzolo 2015b, 301) left between Saqqara and Giza? Was the idea behind the building of a sun temple another way for Userkaf to claim legitimacy for his kingship?

The word Nekhen in the sun temple's name has two different possible translations, the first being the ancient Egyptian name of Hierakonpolis, which was "Nekhen" (Janák, Vymazalová, and Coppens 2011, 432). Not only was the early temple at Hierakonpolis the findspot of early expressions of power and control such as Narmer's palette and mace-head but the mound of the early temple provided an "arena" for royal appearances and rituals (McNamara 2008, 931). The other meaning of the word Nekhen could be "fortress" (Nuzzolo 2016, 182), referring to the Early Dynastic funerary fortresses at Abydos, which were used for royal rituals and ceremonies. Regardless of the translation, it appears that "Nekhen of Ra" provided a ritual space for the king associated with the sun god.

The second register on the back of the Palermo Stone preserves partial entries from the end of Userkaf's fifth regnal year to the beginning of his seventh (Wilkinson 2000, 152). The Turin Canon lists seven years as the total for Userkaf's reign, so perhaps the Palermo Stone would not have had information beyond the seventh year (Verner 2006, 136). In his seventh year, Userkaf endows the gods of Nekhen of Ra with two oxen and two geese every day, coming from "24 arouras" of land from one of the king's estates. The king also grants both Ra and Hathor "44 arouras" of land in Lower Egypt (Wilkinson 2000, 153). Ra and Hathor were the two main deities in the sun temple and worshipped as the parents of the king (Helck 1984, 70; Voss 2004, 162–164). In the sun temple, "the cult of Re, a specific form of the sun god, and of Hathor, Re's partner, comes to the fore" (Verner 2014–2015, 459).

The plan of Userkaf's sun temple apparently went through four stages, the first of which was in the time of Userkaf, and the others under later kings, changing the structure. It began as a square mud-wall enclosure with a mound or possibly mastaba-like structure with a wooden pole with a disk on top (Krejčí 2010, 102, fig. 9.2; Nuzzolo 2007, 1403). A solar disk cult implement is mentioned in the Abusir Papyri (Posener-Krieger 1976, 77). The final form was a rectangular east–west enclosure with a *ben-ben*, a stone representing the mound of earth on which the sun god Ra, in the form of a great gray heron, landed and created the world (Quirke 2001, 27–28). In ancient Egyptian art, the *ben-ben* could have a rounded top or a pointed top (Kemp 2006, 139).

In front of Userkaf's *ben-ben* structure was an altar as well as subsidiary structures for priests and storage (Ricke 1965, 4–31; Nuzzolo 2007, 1402). There were also two diorite statue shrines on the front side of the *ben-ben*, probably for statues of Ra and Hathor (Stadelmann 1985, 164). The second stage of the structure may well have been done under Userkaf's son, Sahura, who possibly even had his own cult at the Nekhen of Ra (Verner 2017a, 242), as titles of priests of Sahura were found on clay sealings there (Voss 2004, 29–30; Verner 2014, 202), and there is no evidence Sahura completed the building of his own sun temple, "Ra's Field" (Verner 2014, 207–209).

East of the enclosure of the sun temple, and connected to it by a causeway, was a lower temple, or valley temple. This made the final form of the sun temple complex similar to the plan of a pyramid complex, which had a valley temple and causeway leading up to the mortuary temple on the east face of the pyramid. It has been pointed out the lower, or eastern, temple of Userkaf's sun temple resembles the *heb sed* temple of Sneferu at the Bent Pyramid, as well as the mortuary temple at Khafra's Giza pyramid (Nuzzolo 2016, 164; Nuzzolo 2007, 221). Although very badly destroyed, it is clear there was an open court with "16 rectangular granite pillars" with five to seven statue niches at the back of it (Lehner 1997,151). This similarity with the *heb sed* temple of Sneferu reflects what is now understood as the purpose of sun temples, which was not only for a solar cult but also where the king's *heb sed* would be celebrated eternally (Verner, 2017b, 14; Nuzzolo 2015a). There is no evidence that a *heb sed* was depicted in Userkaf's valley temple, and in the later sun temple of King Nyuserra, *heb sed* scenes were placed in the corridor and chapel in the upper temple (Verner 2017a, 240–241; Nuzzolo 2018, 94).

One other institution of Userkaf's is known, his *meret*. There are two priests with titles connecting them to the *meret* of Userkaf (Bárta 1983, 99). One, a *wab*-priest of the *meret* named Ptahhotep, possibly contemporary with Userkaf, was also a *hem-netjer*, (*ḥm- nṯr*), or priest, of not only the king but also his sun temple (Porter and Moss 1981, 581; Mariette 1976, 314). The second priest, possibly from the end of the Fifth Dynasty, named Khnumhotep, was the inspector of the *wab*-priests at Nekhen-Ra, a *hem-netjer*-priest of Userkaf, a *hem-netjer* of Hathor in "Front of the Pyramid" complex, and the overseer of priests of "Hathor of the Sycamore" in Userkaf's *meret* (Mariette 1976, 312; Verner 2015b, 325). This second example shows clearly how the same official served the three ritual institutions of the king: the pyramid complex, sun temple, and *meret* sanctuary.

THE REIGN OF SAHURA (2487–2475)

Based on the Turin King List, Sahura reigned for twelve years and, based on contemporary cattle count dates, the longest duration given for his reign is thirteen years (Verner 2006, 137). Although there is no absolutely clear evidence that Userkaf was his father, as discussed in the previous section, Sahura's mother was Neferhetepes, the wife of Userkaf. Sahura's wife was Meret-Nebty. In one of the newly discovered scenes from the Sahura causeway, Queen Meret-Nebty is shown sitting at her husband's feet as he pulls the rope of a net trapping birds (El-Awady 2009, pl. 13). Meret-Nebty does not have the title *sat-nsw* (*s3t- nsw*), "Daughter of the King," in either scene, which would prove her royalty, but queens in the Fifth Dynasty do not seem to use that title, although it was very common in the Fourth Dynasty (Sabbahy 1982, 115–116).

In another scene from the causeway, the king's mother stands behind Sahura as the king greets an expedition returning from Punt (El-Awady 2009, pl. 5). She holds hands with a younger woman who is behind her and depicted on a smaller scale. This second woman has the titulary of a king's wife written above her figure, including the basic title of "King's Wife Whom He Loves," and her name, Meret-Nebty. Borchardt unearthed a damaged block of relief from Sahura's mortuary temple with queens' titles and only the word Nebty left in the name and, after discussing the female names compounded with *nebty*, decided the queen's name must have been Nefret-ha-nebty (Borchardt 1913, 2:117, pl. 48). This assumption was corrected with the discovery of the new blocks (El-Awady 2009). The way in which the king's mother holds the younger woman's hand, and their difference in size, suggests that the king's mother is her mother as well, and, if so, this would show that Sahura married his sister. There is no evidence known for any other wife of Sahura.

It would appear that Meret-Nebty was the mother of twins, since there are two sons of Sahura who are portrayed together and called eldest king's son (El-Awady 2009, fig. 106). Evidence of two eldest sons who are twins has also been found in a nonroyal context (Kanawati 1976, 248). This study concluded, however, that, for the most part, more than one eldest child pointed to polygamy rather than twins or successive marriages (Kanawati 1976, 251). El-Awady has proposed that the eldest son shown first in the scene, Renefer, took the throne after the death of his father, using the name Neferirkara.

The reign of Sahura is outstanding for the canonization of the architecture and decoration of the king's pyramid complex, particularly the funerary temple that was followed with little change throughout the rest of the Fifth Dynasty and the following Sixth. It is estimated that "only 1–2 percent of the original wall surface" of the Sahura funerary temple has survived (Arnold 1997, 73), although when it was completed the temple had 370 meters of wall space for relief decoration (D. Arnold 1999, 98). A discussion of the decoration plan of the temple, then, is based on a limited amount of evidence.

The valley temple and causeway led up to an entry hall known as the *per weru* (*pr wrw*), which led into the central court, or broad court, paved with basalt, that was the only unroofed part of the temple. This was the "central feature" of the outer portion of the funerary temple, as it was a "stage" (D. Arnold 1999, 94, 96) for the king to display his upholding of *Maat* and bringing prosperity to Egypt. Billing describes the outer part of the temple as "focused on the king and his control of the world as divine ruler" while the inner part of the temple was concerned with the "cult of the transfigured spirit of the king-god" (Billing 2018, 548).

Sixteen red granite palm columns held up lintels forming a portico around the broad court, and on the walls of the north and south sides the king is shown defeating the Libyans and the Asiatics (Borchardt 1913, 2:pls. 1–3). Right in the center of the court was an alabaster offering table, decorated with the *sema-tawy* motif as well as Nile gods bringing offerings (Borchardt 1910, 1:48–50). Arnold thinks that this courtyard symbolizes an island emerging from the primaeval waters "analogous to the first created land" (D. Arnold 1999, 95).

There was also a corridor that went around this entire court, and its wall against the court on the east and west was decorated with ships, which supported the idea that the court it surrounded was an island (Borchardt 1913, 2:pls. 11–14; D. Arnold 1999, 94–95). The king is also depicted hunting in both desert and marsh land (Borchardt 1913, 2:pl. 16). At the back, on the west side, the corridor led off to storerooms and other spaces on the north, and more extensive storerooms and the small south pyramid enclosure on the south side. Going straight ahead out of the broad court a staircase led up and into the inner portion of the funerary temple. First there is a five-niched statue chamber with alabaster floor and then off the south of this chamber two further rectangular antechambers before the sanctuary against the east face of the pyramid. In the reign of Nyuseera, the second of these antechambers becomes a small square room with a central column that is decorated with scenes associated with the *heb sed*. This is the space scholars refer to as the *antechambre carrée* (El-Awady 2009, 44). Daily rituals took place for the king in the sanctuary, while the five-niched statue chamber seems to have been associated with monthly rituals (Posener-Krieger 1976, 52–57).

One last scene used in royal funerary complexes, and known first from the reign of Sneferu, is a goddess, Nekhbet, Bastet, or Sakhmet, embracing or suckling the king. This scene is found in niched central doorways in both valley and funerary temples and proclaims the king's "eternal rebirth" (D. Arnold 1999, 97). In Sahura's complex, this type of niched entrance was found where the valley temple leads to the causeway; a scene of Nekhbet suckling Sahura was found by Borchardt in the valley temple (Borchardt 1913, 2:pl. 18). There was a secondary entrance into the back portion of Sahura's funerary temple on the south side of the temple by the small south pyramid. Inside this entrance, the king is shown offering to the goddess Bastet (Borchardt 1913, 2:pls. 35–36).

THE REIGN OF NYUSERRA (2445–2421)

Nyuserra, a grandson of Sahura, took the throne after his brother, possibly twin brother, Raneferef, who seems to have died as a young man after two years on the throne (Verner 2017b, 115). Their mother, Khentkaues II held the title of

"Mother of two Kings of Upper and Lower Egypt," which seems to express this situation (Verner 2014, 58–59), and it is interesting because this unusual title was also held by Khentkaues I at the end of the Fourth Dynasty, as discussed in Chapter 2 in the section on the reign of King Menkaura. It is not clear, however, if, in either case, the two sons were twins or simply brothers. As seen in the Fourth Dynasty, Khafra, brother of Djedefra, ruled after Djedefra's death, therefore following his brother, and not his father, on the throne, so brother-to-brother succession was not unknown. Nyuserra reigned for at least eleven years (Verner 2006, 139) and possibly for as many as twenty-eight or thirty-one (Bárta and Dulíková 2015, 31; Bárta 2015, 5).

Nyuserra's reign has been described as "a major break between the previous and subsequent developments" in the Old Kingdom (Bárta and Dulíková 2015, 32), and the characteristics of his reign that stand out as changes will be reviewed. Nyuserra carried out the completion of his father's pyramid complex, placing his own pyramid, named "The Places of Nyuserra Endure" (Lehner 1997, 17), directly next to his father's pyramid on the north side and taking over his father's valley temple and causeway, perhaps to stress his relationship to his father in order to bolster his legitimacy to rule (Verner 2017a, 72–73) since he succeeded his brother on the throne.

Nyuserra also completed the pyramid for his brother, Raneferef, although it was not completed as a pyramid but as a hill or primeval mound in a square shape (Verner 1997, 306). On papyrus documents found in the funerary temple, the tomb is actually referred to as an *iat* (*i3t*) or a hill (Posener-Krieger, Verner, and Vymasalová 2006, 337). The funerary temple was finished in mud brick on a north–south axis across the east face of the square mound. The focus of the temple was on a hypostyle hall in the south half, which was a space for the cult of the king's statues (Verner 2017b, 10–11, fig. 2) and referred to in contemporary documents as the "abode of the statue" (Verner 2016, 325). Large numbers of faience fragments were found, which had been used for decoration, most probably on wooden naoi for the statues of Raneferef (Landgráfová 2006a, 49–52). The fragments show that the faience decoration supplied all the scenes a king needed in his funerary temple but in a simplified way and more easily produced and cheaper than carved stone relief.

Landgráfová's study of the fragments shows that the motifs corresponded with the standard depictions found in an Old Kingdom royal funerary temple. Therefore, these depictions are a statement of the required essentials for kingship, legitimacy, and eternal life. They identify the king, in terms of name, epithets, and symbols. They depict his acceptance by the deities, in terms of being embraced, suckled, and given life. They grant the king legitimization through his coronation by Horus and Seth and his *heb sed*. They prove his upholding of *Maat* with offerings to the gods, visits to their chapels, and the *sema-tawy* symbol. They provide the sustenance for the king's afterlife with offering bearers and offerings (Landgráfová 2006a, 16–23). The only motif not present was the apotropaic one, in terms of scenes of hunting, slaughtering, and smiting, although Landgráfová points out that statuettes of bound captives were found, and these served as a substitute for scenes on a wall (Landgráfová 2006a, 51).

As well as Raneferef's burial and temple, Nyuserra finished the small pyramid complex for their mother, Khentkaues II, which was located on the south side of her husband's pyramid. There is firm evidence for this marriage since a block from the funerary temple of King Neferirkara names his wife, "One Who Sees Horus and Seth, Great of Affection and Great of Praise, Khentkaues" (Verner 2017a, 101; Sabbahy 1982, 84). Excavation has shown that the pyramid and its funerary temple were built in three different stages, having been begun by her husband, Neferirkara. A mason's mark on the foundation platform gives her title as "King's Wife," and in smaller writing "King's Mother" was added in front, which must have been in the time of her son, Raneferef, who was responsible for the next stage of construction (Verner 2017a, 102; Verner 1995, 43, inscription 1; 47, inscription 13). Nyuserra finished it; there are fragments of Khentkaues II's red granite false door with Nyuserra's throne and Horus names and the title of "Mother of the Two Kings" with a portion of the top of her head, wearing the vulture headdress, below (Verner 2017a, 102; Verner 1995, 84, frag. 200/A/78). Papyri from the funerary temple of Khentkaues II refer to "16 wooden shrines with the statues of the royal mother placed in the temple" (Verner 2016, 327). Her shrines were also decorated with faience; in fact, all the complexes finished by Nyuserra used faience for the decoration, which might explain how he was able to complete so many monuments (Landgráfová 2006b, 207).

Slightly to the south and east is another small pyramid in this area, known as Lepsius Pyramid 24 (Krejčí et al. 2008; Krejčí 2008, 126, 130–133). It has been suggested that Reputnebu, the wife of Nyuserra was buried here, although there is no evidence to prove that. The pyramid is not that close to Nyuserra's, which is a bit odd, and sits closer to the tomb of Raneferef. Krejčí conjectures that Reputnebu may have been the widow of Raneferef, who Nyuserra married (Krejčí 2008, 131–132). This entire cluster of royal burials was the focus of a cult of Nyuserra and his parents lasting into the Middle Kingdom (Morales 2006, 315).

North of Userkaf's sun temple, Nyuserra built his sun temple, "Ra's Delight," the second sun temple that has been found and excavated. It is in a much better state of preservation than the sun temple of Userkaf. It is very possible that Nyuserra took over the unfinished sun temple of his brother Raneferef and completed it for himself (Krejčí 2010, 162–163). There are two building stages clear at "Ra's Delight," and it could be that the first stage belonged to "Ra is Satisfied," the sun temple of Raneferef, mentioned in inscriptions (Verner 2014, 211) but so far unknown archaeologically.

Nyuserra's sun temple had a lower valley temple, but it only served as an entrance building to the causeway and did not have a court area or niches like the valley temple of Userkaf's sun temple. The valley temple had a large door and portico on the front and smaller porticos on the north and south sides. On the left and right sides of the main door, hieroglyphic texts, of which only fragments were found, listed festivals, and the offerings, including large amounts of food, given by King Nyuserra (Helck 1977; Strudwick 2005, 86–91). The inscription starts out stating that the king "has ordered the establishment of divine offerings specifically for his father Ra" (Strudwick 2005, 87). This was the first time a king stated Ra was his father, although Djedefra's adding of "son of Ra" into his royal titulary was similar (see Chapter 2 and the section on the reign of Djedefra). There is a mention of electrum statues of Ra and Hathor placed in the House of Gold in the more fragmentary section (Helck 1977, 70; Strudwick 2005, 90), which is interesting since the sun temple of Userkaf, as described in the section "The Reign of Userkaf (2494–2487)," had two small chapels in front of the central *ben-ben* that probably held similar statues. The titles of a priest from the reign of Nyuserra are given on the architrave of his Giza tomb (Mariette 1976, D48), now in the British Museum (EA 1275). Nyka-ankh is a priest of the solar temples of both Userkaf and Nyuserra, as well as a priest of Hathor. The triad of Ra, Hathor, and the king "is well established in the double titles of the priesthood" who serve both Ra and Hathor (Troy 1986, 55).

The causeway led up to a rectangular enclosure with a large base (Borchardt 1905, fig. 20) topped by a squat obelisk, or *ben-ben*, as the dominant structure in the middle. Along the south inner wall of the enclosure was a corridor decorated with scenes from the *heb sed* festival, leading to a north–south chapel also associated with the *heb sed* festival (Bissing and Kees 1923; Kees 1928, fig. 42) that may have been the king's robing room. This chapel also had an entrance from the court in the east wall. Parallel to this chapel was a north–south passageway decorated with scenes of the two ancient Egyptian seasons of summer and inundation, now in the Egyptian Museum in Berlin (Edel and Wenig 1974) (Figure 20). The third season, winter, may not have been shown or has not been preserved. These scenes, for the most part showing plant and animal life throughout the year, were intended "to praise the beneficial influence of the sun on the earth" (von Lieven 2010, 31). The passageway then continued up onto the base of the obelisk.

The scenes in the corridor, and particularly the chapel because they are better preserved, offer the most extensive pictorial evidence of the *heb sed* known from the Old Kingdom (Nuzzolo 2015a, 369). The most complete scenes show the king's ritual run, counting the cattle, a procession of offerings, offering of

Figure 20 Summer scene from depictions of the seasons, Sun Temple of Nyuserra, Abu Ghurab (Berlin 20038). Photo: Lisa Sabbahy, Courtesy of the Neues Museum, Berlin

sacrificial animals, priests and others paying homage in front of the king's throne, and the king leaving his throne for a litter and being carried in procession (Bissing and Kees 1923, pls. 9–20). Fragments from the south corridor seem to belong to these same types of scenes but also add a scene of slaughtering (Kees 1928, pl. 23).

Out in front of the obelisk structure was a large alabaster offering table (Borchardt 1905, figs. 33–34), with a slaughtering area on its north side, complete with alabaster basins (Borchardt 1905, fig. 38). No entrance into the complex seems to have been planned for cattle, and no flakes of flint butchering knives have been found in the slaughtering area. There also does not seem to be a system for draining liquids from the basins or from the slaughtering area. Rather than slaughtering, the area may have been used to prepare cuts of meat for offering (Verner 2014, 214). This latter interpretation is supported by a recent study by Nuzzolo, who suggests that both the small and the large so-called slaughtering areas were for the "ritual purification of offerings" (Nuzzolo 2016, 63). Borchardt noted but did not excavate the settlement around the valley temple, where the actual slaughtering and other preparations of food offerings must have been carried out (Borchardt 1905, 7–8; Nuzzolo 2016, 57). Although it is not known whether or not this settlement had a slaughterhouse, it is certainly possible (Vymazalová 2011, 303).

Along the north wall, there were a series of ten parallel storage rooms, with quartzite door frames carrying the king's name. There is still evidence in two door posts of bolts to seal the door, hinting that expensive objects perhaps cult implements were being kept there, and not food products (Nuzzolo and Pirelli 2011, 677–678). On the south, outside the wall of the sun temple complex, was a large brick "sun boat" (Borchardt 1905, 52–54), almost 100 feet long (Lehner 1997, 152), which must have been decorated, or the upper part done in wood, as fragments of gilded and painted wood were found as well as copper nails (Nuzzolo 2018, 130; Verner 2014, 215).

The papyrus archives found in the funerary temple of Neferirkara, Nyuserra's father, reveal evidence concerning the economic relationship of the king's pyramid complex and his sun temple complex. All the produce originates in the estates belonging to the king, which were spread all over Egypt. For Nyuserra, for example, twenty-eight estates are known (Khalid 2008a, 62). From the estates, the produce was sent on to the king's palace in the Memphite area. From there, a portion was sent to the sun temple, which, in turn, sent part of it on to the funerary temple (Vymazalová 2011, 296; Posener-Krieger 1976, 631–634).

Another connection between the sun temple and the king's funerary temple is the fact that the majority of the priests serving in the sun temple also seem to have a position in the funerary temple. Nuzzolo has shown that almost 80 percent of the *hem-netjer*, who are priests, and the *wab*-priests, who are of a lower rank, belonging to the sun temple "were involved in the same cult functions" in the king's funerary temple (Nuzzolo 2010, 93). Even more of these men, about 90 percent, had a position in the royal palace where they were involved not so much with administration but in "caring for . . . the person of the king" (Nuzzolo 2010, 294).

Understanding the purpose of the sun temple and why they were built beginning with the Fifth Dynasty has changed over time. Clearly, sun temples are tied to the sun god Ra and the king's connection to him, as well as the king's *heb sed*, and therefore confirmation of the king's rule. Why, when in the Fourth Dynasty the king proclaims his rule as Horus and as the sun god in one complex, the pyramid complex, does the next dynasty choose to erect two separate complexes? Did Userkaf feel the need to stress his legitimacy and relationship to the sun god? Userkaf's architect may have based the plan of his lower, or valley, temple on that of King Sneferu, celebrating his eternal *heb sed* with that building, while the upper complex reflected "a contemporary building of the solar cult in Heliopolis" (Verner 2014/2015, 469). Unfortunately, there is no evidence for what, if any, sun temple would have been in Heliopolis at that time and what form it would have taken.

Nuzzolo suggests that: "In the Fifth Dynasty, the situation seems to evolve toward a reconciliation of the older cultic traditions with the new solar expectations" (Nuzzolo 2016, 177). He sees a division that parallels the Early Dynastic royal burials at Abydos, when there was a tomb complex separate from the ritual space offered by the so-called funerary fort. The Fifth Dynasty pyramid complex served the "king as the living Horus," while the sun temple offered the space for his eternal regeneration through the *heb sed*, as well as "the final merging, of the king with the sun god Ra" (Nuzzolo 2016, 179).

Nyuserra's successor, Menkauhor, was the last king of the Fifth Dynasty to have a sun temple, "Ra's Horizon," which is known only from textual evidence, none dating later than the beginning of the Sixth Dynasty (Verner 2017a, 252). It has been argued that the disappearance of sun temples must be connected to the rise in importance of the god Osiris. The name of Osiris first appears in a private tomb dating to the reign of King Nyuserra.

Despite possibly having a reign of more than thirty years, there is scant evidence for the female family of Nyuserra. A fragmentary alabaster statue from the valley temple of the king's pyramid complex carries the inscription "The One Who Is Joined to the One Beloved of the Two Ladies," "The King's Wife Whom He Loves, Reput-nub" (Borchardt 1907, 109, fig. 88; Sabbahy 1982, 86). This is the only evidence known for a wife of Nyuserra. There is also evidence for a daughter, Khamerernebty, who held the titles of "Princess," "Priestess of Hathor," and "Sole Ornament of the king" (Sabbahy 1982, 125). Her last title, "Sole Ornament of the King," seems to have been a title unique to her, although "Ornament of the King" was held by a Fourth Dynasty princess named Nysederkay (Sabbahy 1982, 123). Princess Khamerernebty was the wife of her father's vizier, Ptahshepses, who constructed his mastaba just to the northeast of the king's pyramid complex (Verner 2017a). Ptahshepses held the title "King's Son," which, although he was not a physical son of Nyuserra, makes his high status clear.

Only one actual son of Nyuserra is known, and he was not discovered until excavations at Abusir between 2006 and 2009 (Verner 2017a, 189). A small hill, named Lepsius Pyramid 23, in front and slightly south of the pyramid of Queen Khentkaues II turned out to be a badly destroyed and reused mastaba. One of the mason's marks on blocks within the serdab of the mastaba read: "the Eldest Son of the King, Werkaura" (Krejčí et al. 2014, 275–276). The only other evidence for Werkaura is a fragment of relief decoration from the funerary temple of Nyuserra, which shows a man sitting in front of the bottom of a cartouche, and the hieroglyphic signs for *wer* (*wr*) and *kau* (*k3w*) are preserved in front of him (Verner 2017a, 190, fig. 111; Borchardt 1907, 84, fig. 60c).

A study by Dulíková pointed out that at least thirteen women who carried the title "King's Daughter" in the reign of Nyuserra, or possibly just before or after his reign, married men who were not members of the royal family (Bárta and Dulíková 2015, 37; Dulíková 2016, 19). These women are identified by the title "King's Daughter" in their tombs, which also provide evidence for the name and titles of their husbands. This is the first evidence of widespread marriage between the royal family and the elite, but it coincides with the fact that the administration is now run by officials who are not from the royal family. By bringing these men into the royal family as sons-in-law, the king secured their loyalty and perhaps had more control over them, which would have been particularly important in terms of the viziers (Bárta 2013a, 170). In fact, the viziers under Nyuserra held the title "King's Son," although there was no blood relationship.

At much the same time, there was an expansion of titles among officials of low rank. Some of these titles were administrative, and some of them reflected the king's favor. The "One Who Is Over the Secrets," was a title given to officials in the royal court who were physically close to the king. It was a relatively rare title in the Fourth Dynasty, with fifteen title holders known, but by the mid-Fifth Dynasty there were ninety-six (Rydström 1994, 86–89). It has been suggested that this title was needed in order to make clear that the nonroyal men who took over positions that had formerly been held by members of the royal family had to be discreet and keep royal business secret (Bárta 2005, 119; Rydström 1994, 65).

Another title that had always been held by one of the king's sons, but by the mid-Fifth Dynasty was held by officials from outside the royal family, was "Inspector of the Palace" (Bárta 1999). When these titles and the officials who held them are studied through time, such as was done by Dulíková for the Fourth through the Sixth Dynasties, it becomes apparent that both the high-ranking and the lower-ranking officials of the Fifth Dynasty were handing newly acquired titles down to sons or other members of their families, creating positions that became hereditary, not bestowed by the king (Dulíková 2017). From the time of Nyuserra on, kinship became the most important element in obtaining jobs and promotions.

One of the most important new titles that appeared in the reign of Nyuserra may be that of "Overseer of Upper Egypt," because it clearly stated a royal interest in controlling the provinces of Upper Egypt. The creation of this position may have come about from changes in the position of nomarchs, who switched "from responsibility for multiple nomes, to responsibility for one nome" (Clarke 2009, 172). The Overseer of Upper Egypt's main responsibility seems to have been to collect taxes (Brovarski 2013, 98; Kanawati 1980, 71) but, as taxes could be in the form of produce, particularly grain, as well as physical labor on state projects, the responsibilities of the position probably also involved managing the supply of corvée laborers, as well as protecting any religious institution, such as a temple or chapel, that had been granted exemption from taxes. The Overseer of Upper Egypt reported directly to the vizier, and possibly a better job description for the Overseer of Upper Egypt is that he was in charge of "resource management" for Upper Egypt (Clarke 2009, 127–128).

The official Kai, who later became a vizier, appears to have been the earliest Overseer of Upper Egypt (Dulíková 2016, 60; Strudwick 1985, 143), although some scholars place Kai later in the reign of Djedkara rather than Nyuserra. Kai's tomb was in North Saqqara, and so he probably lived and worked in Memphis; he certainly did later as vizier. Later overseers, such as Weni in the Sixth Dynasty, discussed in the section "The Reign of King Pepy I (2321–2287)," were buried in their towns in Upper Egypt. The position of Overseer of Upper Egypt continued throughout the rest of the Old Kingdom, the following First Intermediate Period, and into the Twelfth Dynasty of the Middle Kingdom (Brovarski 2013).

Other changes during the rule of King Nyuserra that have been noted by archaeologists are that high officials began to make changes in the structure of their mastaba tombs, enlarging them and adding spaces and details normally found in royal complexes, such as columned courts, statue niches, and spaces for a boat burial as well as expanded relief decoration highlighting the tomb owner's official activities (Bárta 1998). This trend seems to have started with Ptahshepses, Nyuserra's son-in-law, who, as he was promoted to higher and higher positions, added to his mastaba, placed just northeast of the pyramid complex of Nyuserra, until it reached the size of 80 by 107 meters, dominating the royal necropolis of Abusir (Wilkinson 2007, 55).

These elite officials also held titles that state their physical closeness to the king and their part in carrying out the daily ritual of the king's washing, dressing, and eating. Such titles were found in the Fourth Dynasty but all belonged to the sons of the king, whereas by the Fifth Dynasty they belong to some of the highest officials of the land, such as the vizier of King Nyuserra, Ptahshepses. He held the title *a'a dua* (ꜥ3-dw3), (Strudwick 1985, 308), which some scholars read as *wn dua* (wn-dw3) (Helck 1954, 37), a priestly title of the god Dua, known in the Pyramid Texts. Dua is the god of morning light and also the god of the king's morning toilette ritual (Kees 1980, 109). The king's divinity was expressed in, and dependent on, such ritual: "the daily rituals of the king, no matter how mundane, took on a ritualized charge" (Shaw 2012, 74), as the "king's toilette at sunrise was thus a religious re-enactment of the sun god, his father's, daily birth where he washed his face in the waters of Nun" (Tassie 2017, 264). Royal hairdressers, manicurists, and barbers are also known; in fact, Ptahshepses at one point was the king's hairdresser and manicurist. Ptahshepses also held a number of epithets that reflect not only his close relationship to the king but his discretion as well: "Privy to the Secret of the House of Morning," "Privy to the Secret of the God's Word," and "Privy to His Lord's Secret in All His Places" (Wilkinson 2007, 530; Verner 2002, 162). Baud summed this situation up by saying: "The solar world of the Fifth Dynasty was a universe of courtiers entitled 'Sole Companions' in which the monarch, in his

Memphite Versailles, kept in closest proximity to himself a large political society fixated on his splendor and dedicated to his person" (Baud 2014, 76).

This preoccupation with the person of the king might be reflected in the Old Kingdom phrase *setep-sa* (*stp-s3*) that often appears in Old Kingdom biographical inscriptions when an official is describing an interaction with the king. It appears to mean a "form of court service" (Shaw 2010, 180) or "attendance on the monarch's person" (Goelet 1986, 95). In the Middle Kingdom, the meaning of this word changed to "palace." Another possible hint at the relationship of officials to the divine king they served is an incident described in the biography of the official Rawer, who seems to have touched or tripped over the scepter of the king during a ritual (Allen 1992). Apparently, the king immediately said: "It is the desire of my majesty that he be very well, and that no blow be struck against him" (Strudwick 2005, 306). It is not clear whether without the king's interception Rawer might have been punished for making a misstep in an important religious ritual or because it was forbidden for him to have physical contact with the king.

One last, and what would become very important, change that occurred in the reign of Nyuserra was the appearance of the god Osiris whose name occurs in offering formulae in nonroyal tombs. The first evidence of the name Osiris is in the *hetep-di-nsw* (*ḥtp-di-nsw*), "offerings that the king gives," formula on the top line of the false door lintel in the Saqqara mastaba of the priest Ptahshepses, who was born during the reign of Menkaura of the Fourth Dynasty and married the daughter of Userkaf at the beginning of the Fifth. His false door, now in the British Museum (EA 682), dates to the reign of Nyuserra. The first line of the architrave begins: "an offering which the king gives, and an offering which Osiris gives, great god, lord of Truth (*maat*)." In all, from the reign of King Nyuserra to the end of the Fifth Dynasty, there are approximately sixty mentions of the god Osiris in elite, but nonroyal, tomb offering formula inscriptions (Begelsbacher-Fischer 1981, 124–125).

THE END OF THE FIFTH DYNASTY

Three last kings of the Fifth Dynasty ruled after Nyuserra for a total of a little more than sixty years. Menkauhor, whose origins are unknown, followed Nyuserra with a short reign of eight years. Menkauhor built the last known sun temple, and although there is written evidence for it, it has never been found. The temple was named the "Horizon of Ra" and a priest and overseer of priests belonging to it are known (Verner 2014, 218–219). There is also no known tomb of Menkauhor, although Lepsius Pyramid 29, at the edge of the plateau at North Saqqara, has been attributed to him (Verner 2017a, 27; Verner 2014, 176–177).

Menkauhor was succeeded on the throne by Djedkara Isesi, who is sometimes called the son of Menkauhor, although there is no evidence of Djedkara's family origins. He may have ruled as long as forty-four years, as the twenty-second occasion of his cattle count is recorded (Verner 2017a, 214). He continued the administrative reforms started by Nyuserra to have more royal control in Upper Egypt. Djedkara kept two viziers in Memphis, while a third vizier was based at Akhmim, and he also established three administrative centers, in the 10th, 15th, and 20th Upper Egyptian nomes (Kanawati 1980, 128).

Djedkara built his pyramid complex in southern Saqqara, although the reasons for his move to this location are not understood (Verner and Callender 2002, 105–108). An adjacent similar, but smaller, complex was built for his queen. It is interesting that the queen's complex contains a square room with one pillar, referred to as the *antichambre carrée*, which previously has only ever been found in the pyramid complex of a king (Megahed 2016, 255). The latest interpretation of this room and its wall scenes is that it is "a place where the king is rejuvenated as *immortal*" as well as "given life and millions of *sed*-festivals by the gods" (Megahed 2016, 254–255).

The queen's name was finally discovered in further excavations of her complex in 2019. On a fallen red granite pillar from the portico of her funerary temple is an inscription with her titles and name: "One Who Sees Horus and Seth," "Great of Affection," "Great of Praise" "King's Wife Whom He Loves," Setibhor (Ahram Online 2019). Other family members of King Djedkara, a son, "Eldest King's Son of His Body Whom He Loves" Neserkauhor, and two daughters, "King's Daughter of His Body Whom He Loves" Khekeretnebty and "King's Daughter of His Body" Hedjetnebu, were not buried at Saqqara but in mastabas at Abusir, in the southeast part of the Fifth Dynasty royal necropolis (Verner and Callender 2002).

THE REIGN OF UNAS (2375–2345) AND THE PYRAMID TEXTS

Unas, the last king of the dynasty, does not seem to have been related to either of his predecessors; there is no evidence yet known that indicates who his parents were. The scribe of the Turin King List made a division after Unas and tabulated the regnal years from the First to Fifth Dynasties. Scholars are not certain what that division indicates, other than the fact that Unas was followed by his son-in-law and not by a son of his own. Possibly the placement of Unas's pyramid just southwest of Djoser's Step Pyramid complex was designed to associate him with this earlier king and therefore legitimize his rule (Figure 21). Placement near the earlier monument of a famous king has been suggested as the reason that Userkaf, the first king of the Fifth Dynasty, placed his pyramid complex inside the northeast corner of Djoser's complex (Verner 2003, 259).

Figure 21 A view across the causeway of Unas to the Step Pyramid, Saqqara. Photo: Lisa Sabbahy

Part of the pyramid and the mortuary temple of Unas are also on top of a royal tomb of Hetepsekhemwy and/or Raneb of the Second Dynasty (Dreyer 2003a, 74), perhaps also for legitimation.

It has been shown that the north and south walls of Unas's burial chamber are alabaster blocks decorated with scenes of a king hippopotamus hunting that had been removed from another king's mortuary temple, "most likely Djedkara's in South Sakkara" (Youssef 2011, 822). According to the Turin King List, Unas had a fairly long reign of thirty years (Verner 2006, 142), although the highest known date from a contemporary source is the eighth cattle count (Posener-Krieger 1976, 491). For a king with a relatively long rule, almost nothing is known about Unas historically. Two of his wives are known, Henut and Nebet, who have adjoining mastabas just east of Unas's pyramid, alongside his causeway (Munro 1993; Sabbahy 1981). A daughter of King Unas, Iput, became the wife of Teti, his successor to the throne, although Teti does not appear to have been related to Unas. The mother of Teti is known to have been a woman named Sesheshet, and she carries the title of "King's Mother" but does not have any other titles indicating that she was part of the royal family (Stasser 2013) (Figure 22).

Unas is best known for the Pyramid Texts that cover the walls of his pyramid's inner chambers. He is the first king to have these texts, and although the location of his pyramid might have been picked to express ties with his predecessors, these texts are a clear change in religious expression. They are a "new systematization of ritual practice" (Morales 2015b, 174) and, from now until the end of the Sixth Dynasty, kings, and in the later Sixth Dynasty, queens, have these texts inside their pyramids. Ankhenespepy II, the mother

Figure 22 A view of the east side of the pyramid of Unas, Saqqara. Photo: Lisa Sabbahy

of King Pepy II, seems to have been the first queen to have Pyramid Texts in her burial chamber, perhaps a reflection of the fact that she ruled as regent while Pepy was a young boy and so, in fact, had been king in his name.

Two gods are important in the Pyramid Texts, Osiris and Ra, who "both belong to a single concept of the deceased's eternal existence after death" (Allen 2005, 7). Like Ra, who merged with Osiris in the underworld, and was born again each morning, the *ba* (*b3*) of the deceased king merged with its own Osiris, its mummified body lying in the tomb, which empowered it "to become an akh, a being capable of renewed life" (Allen 2005, 8). The Pyramid Texts contained the spells needed to enable this merging and successful rebirth every day.

Allen has distinguished different sets of spells within Unas's pyramid chambers. In the burial chamber, Protection and Personal Spells are up in the gables, while on the chamber walls the Offering Ritual is on the north wall and the Resurrection Ritual is on the south (Allen 1994, 13, fig. 3). Out in the antechamber and the pyramid corridor are the spells "meant for the personal use of the king's spirit as it makes its way to the next world" (Allen 1994, 18) (Figure 23).

Figure 23 Pyramid Texts on the west wall of the entrance into the antechamber, pyramid of Unas, Saqqara. Photo: Lisa Sabbahy

It has been suggested that the appearance and importance of Osiris ended the building of sun temples, but Smith has argued that there is no reason "why an increased emphasis on Osiris should have resulted in a diminution of Re's importance" (Smith 2017, 129). Since Ra and Osiris are both part of the rebirth expressed in the Pyramid Texts, and equally important in the afterlife, a loss of the sun god's importance seems unlikely. A more convincing explanation is that the rituals and importance of Ra shifted to the state temple at Heliopolis. In fact, in the Pyramid Texts of Unas is the first "explicit textual reference associating Ra with Heliopolis" (Nuzzolo and Krejčí 2017, 375)."There is a Heliopolitan in Unis, god: your Heliopolitan is in Unis, god. There is a Heliopolitan in Unas, Sun: Your Heliopolitan is in Unas, Sun" (Allen 2005, 58).

With the ending of the solar temples in Abusir came "the elevation of the cult of Re in Iunu," or Heliopolis (Vymazalová 2011, 300). From the later Fifth Dynasty into the Sixth, the importance of the cult of Ra at Heliopolis had been growing. The Palermo Stone records that King Neferirkara gave land to the "souls of Heliopolis," under the control of two "Great of Seers," or High Priests of Ra (Strudwick 2005, 73). By the Sixth Dynasty, these high priests began to be buried at Heliopolis rather than in the royal necropolis near the king's pyramid complex, as four of their tombs were found there (Daressy 1916; Moursi 1972, 32–36). It has also been suggested that at this time the title of high priest of the temple at Heliopolis had shifted from a title belonging to an official at the king's court to one belonging to the temple itself (Quirke 2001, 106). King Teti, the Sixth Dynasty successor of Unas, erected an obelisk at

Heliopolis, "the oldest object which directly documents the existence of the solar cult in Heliopolis" (Nuzzolo and Krejčí 2017, 363).

As pointed out, the name Osiris is first known in a nonroyal tomb dating to the reign of King Nyuserra, in which it appears in the offering formula for the deceased. The name of Osiris continues to be used in these offering formulae from then on. Another, possibly related, change is found in the "table of bread" scenes on the false doors of the tombs in this period. The loaves of bread on the offering tables change into the shape of reeds (Kahlbächer 2013). These reeds could point to an association with the god Osiris (Bárta 2005, 120; Bárta 1995, 33), as the *Sekhet Iaru*, or Field of Reeds, was the idyllic setting of the afterlife.

If these kinds of changes in the expression of the afterlife and the importance of Osiris were being made in elite tombs, there is no reason why the priesthood could not have compiled ritual texts expressing similar beliefs just for royal use in royal tombs. Lloyd suggests that the texts that became the Pyramid Texts in the time of Unas "are clearly considerably older and were probably in use as ritual texts as part of the royal funeral long before they were recorded in royal monuments" (Lloyd 2014, 71). Morales makes the point that Fourth Dynasty offering lists suggest that the "canonization had begun by the reign of Khufu and took definitive shape by the Fifth Dynasty" (Morales 2015b, 184; see also Morales 2015a, 61).

For Morales, the important change made by the priests at Memphis was "the recontextualization of discursive and scriptural materials into the architecture of the pyramid" (Morales 2016, 173). Hays argues that this "entextualization" of the Pyramid Texts changed them from ritual script used in action to "an object of knowledge" and that this, in turn, affected the tomb design of both elite and royalty, shifting interest away from the ritual areas of tomb superstructures and into the tombs' substructures (Hayes 2015, 221–222). As pointed out by Bárta, early in the Sixth Dynasty, "it was the burial chamber and the underground parts of the tomb that gained in importance" (Bárta 2005, 121).

After a discussion of the themes in the Pyramid Texts and the formulaic wishes in private tombs, Smith concludes that there is significant agreement between the royal and the nonroyal texts, and "the spells inscribed inside royal pyramids and the offering formulas inscribed in private tombs, reflect the same basic conception of the afterlife" (Smith 2017, 154). One important difference is that in the private tomb inscriptions "the god and the deceased are regarded as distinct beings," while in the Pyramid Texts "we also find the dead identified with the deity" (Smith 2014, 88). Bárta described how, in the later Fifth Dynasty, high officials began expanding their tombs with architectural features copied from those found in royal mortuary temples. The same sort of entitlement that allowed these officials to copy certain parts of royal funerary architecture may have brought about the copying of royal funerary ritual by adding the name Osiris into elite tomb texts of offerings for the afterlife as well as possibly changing offering scene symbolism. The king, or his priests, may have decided it was necessary to have a body of specifically royal expression of Osirian belief just for use in royal tombs, resulting in the writing of Pyramid Texts on the walls of the king's pyramid chambers.

THE SIXTH DYNASTY

The Sixth Dynasty lasts approximately 160 years, with the rule of six kings, the last of whom may have been Nitiqret, or Nitocris, who was female, and little is known of her life and reign (Callender 2011a). However, the existence of this king at all has been questioned (Ryholt 2000). This section will concentrate on the reigns of the four Sixth Dynasty kings best known through textual and archaeological evidence: Teti, Pepy I, Merenra I, and Pepy II. In terms of a discussion revolving around kingship and power, these Sixth Dynasty rulers continued the state structure that had evolved by the time of the late Fifth Dynasty and, even though they seem much more concerned with their hold over the provinces, steadily lost central control. There was a continual drain on the king's resources with the number of decrees granted to religious institutions, particularly in Upper Egypt, not only giving them land and people but protecting them from taxation. By the end of the Sixth Dynasty, the continued drying-up of the climate of Egypt, the end of the Neolithic wet phase, was probably complete, which may well have taken a toll on agricultural production, although water for agriculture was tied to Nile levels, not rainfall. There is evidence, however, that Nile levels were falling, and inundation levels may have been more erratic.

Royal marriages proliferate, and the different families of the king must have brought about power struggles, seemingly manifested in new threats to kingship: harem conspiracy and assassination, both of which seem to have occurred in the Sixth Dynasty. It is concievable that, men not related to the royal family taking the throne, such as King Teti, and the large numbers of royal wives, such as appear in the reign of Pepy I, produced unstable and competitive conditions between royal wives and their sons and perhaps also among royal relatives and in-law elite families.

THE REIGN OF KING TETI (2345–2323)

The Sixth Dynasty begins with the rule of King Teti, who does not seem to have been related to his predecessor, King Unas. The names picked for his titulary might possibly hint at political problems. Teti's Horus name and Two Ladies name are both "The One Who Has Satisfied the Two Lands," and his Golden Horus name is "The Uniter" (Leprohon 2013, 42). The name of his mother, Sesheshet, is known from a number of inscriptions. A small pyramid was found northeast of Teti's pyramid in 2008 and, although it can't be proven, some scholars say it is Sesheshet's (Hawass 2011, 182) (Figure 24). Teti marries Unas's daughter, Iput I, which may have helped his claim to the throne, although he also had another wife, Khuit II, whom he might have married first. Khuit II's pyramid was excavated in 1996, and it is clear that her pyramid was built before that of Iput, which was first a mastaba and later changed into a pyramid by her son Pepy I when he was king (Hawass 2000). Khuit II has the titles of "King's Wife" and "King's Daughter," so she must have been Unas's daughter as well.

Also found by the pyramids of these two queens was the tomb of Tetiankh-kem, the eldest son of Teti who held various administrative and religious titles, including the titles of "Overseer of Upper Egypt" and "Overseer of the Two Granaries." His mummy, although in poor condition, was of a young man of twenty to twenty-five years of age. Although there does not seem to be any evidence that proves this, Hawass accepts that Tetiankh-kem, as the eldest son of Teti, was the son of Queen Khuit II (Hawass 2000, 433). If Khuit II was the first of Teti's queens, it would be logical to assume the oldest son was hers.

King Teti may have had as many as four to five daughters; two of them are best documented and were married to viziers. Nub-khet-nbty had the title "King's Daughter of His Body Whom He Loves." She was the wife of the vizier Kagemni, who had served under King Unas. She was not buried with her

Figure 24 The pyramid of Teti, Saqqara. Photo: Lisa Sabbahy

husband, and her tomb is unknown (Verner and Callender 2002, 153). Watethathor was a king's daughter, priestess of Hathor, and priestess of Neit (Sabbahy 1982, 127) and married to the vizier Mereruka, whose mastaba she and their son, Mery-Teti, shared. In Mereruka's mastaba, Watethathor had the "only known completely separate chapel for a wife in her husband's tomb" (Kanawati 2007, 78).

Teti left behind a number of small monuments. He was the first king known to place an obelisk at Heliopolis. The upper portion of this quartzite obelisk is inscribed with the beginning of his titulary, including his prenomen in a cartouche with the phase "Son of Ra" (Quirke 2001, 84, fig. 36). Teti built a *ka*-chapel at Bubastis. The brick walls of the enclosure were still more than a meter high when they were discovered in the early 1970s. Inside a rectangular area of more than 100 by 50 meters, badly damaged by fire and later burials, were remains of storage magazines as well as one limestone pillar on a base with hieroglyphs giving the name of Teti followed by *hwt-ka*, "*ka*-chapel" (el Sawi 1979, 76, pls. 165, 167).

King Teti set up a stela in the temple of Osiris at Abydos, now in the British Museum (626), with a decree stating protection for the fields and the workers belonging to the temple of Khentimentiu (Goedicke 1967, 37–39; see also Papazian 2012, 131). This type of decree was used to protect the laborers and produce that had been assigned to this temple, so that they could not be requisitioned for any other use. The most famous small object belonging to the reign of King Teti is an alabaster sistrum, found possibly at Memphis and now in the Metropolitan Museum of Art (26.7 1450). The sistrum is inscribed with the titulary of Teti and states that he is "beloved of the goddess Hathor of Dendera."

King Teti appears to have had a reign of possibly twenty-two to thirty years, after which, Manetho, in his *Aegyptiaca* according to Africanus, says "he was murdered by his bodyguard" (Manetho trans. Waddell 1971, 53). Kanawati sees no reason to doubt the validity of Manetho's claim (Kanawati 2003, 12), as the only other king Manetho states was assassinated was "Ammanemes" the second (Manetho trans. Waddell 1971, 67). While Manetho gets which Ammanemes incorrect, the assassination is substantiated by references in other ancient Egyptian texts. Kanawati, in fact, suggests that there may have been problems during the change of reign from Unas to Teti, and a later assassination of Teti was followed by a short and possibly problematic reign of a king named Userkara. Then, in the early reign of Pepy I, the queen's conspiracy mentioned in the autobiography of Weni occurred, followed by a second seemingly more involved conspiracy against the king in or after Pepy I's regnal year 21 (Kanawati 2003, 183–185).

Two particular points in Kanawati's argument are quite interesting. There is a substantial increase in the number of men holding the title *henty-sha* (*ḫnty – š*) in the late Fifth to Sixth Dynasty. The title *henty-sha* has been traditionally translated as "tenant" or tenant-landholder, although Roth suggested a translation of "attendant," which "suggests the relationship of personal service to the king that seems to be the distinguishing feature of the title" (Roth 1995, 42). Kanawati believes that "guard" is an even better translation, even though these men did other tasks besides guarding the king (Kanawati 2003, 16–21). King Teti apparently "drastically increased" the number of *henty-sha* attached to both his palace and his pyramid's mortuary temple (Kanawati 2003, 152).

The second point of Kanawati's argument is that there are a number of tombs from this period in the Unas and Teti cemeteries at Saqqara that had the tomb owner's image and titles damaged, the tomb decoration changed for another owner, or the tombs were simply left unused. For example, at least ten of the tombs in the Teti cemetery never had a burial, two were reused, and others had their figures erased or damaged (Kanawati 2003, 48–137). Kanawati interprets this reuse and abandonment as punishment of the tomb owners for their part in a conspiracy against the king.

THE REIGN OF KING PEPY I (2321–2287)

The son of Teti and Iput I, Pepy, followed his father on the throne as Pepy I, seemingly after a short two- to four-year reign of the king named Userkara. This king appears in the Sixth Dynasty Royal Annals found in South Saqqara as well as in the Abydos King List and the Turin King List. Nothing is really known about him, except that his name is in the king lists (Stadelmann 1994, 335) and also found on three small objects, a copper blade and two seal cylinders (Altenmüller 2001, 602). For scholars who accept that Teti was assassinated, Userkara becomes the usurper who took the throne, until Teti's son, Pepy, was able to regain it (Kanawati 2003, 4).

The conspiracy against Pepy I is known from the autobiographical text of his high official Weni, which was inscribed on a large, rectangular limestone slab set into the wall of a chapel at Weni's tomb at Abydos and now in the Cairo Museum (1435) (Figure 25). Weni explains that he was first at the royal court as a young man in the time of King Teti. Later, under King Pepy I, he became a companion and inspector of priests of the king's pyramid town. His majesty also made Weni *sab-ra-Nekhen* (*s3b – r* – *nḥn*), which has been translated as a "Speaker of Nekhen," an official title that is always in a judicial context (Bárta 2013b, 27). In this position, Weni says that, when "there was a secret charge in the royal harem against 'the king's wife, great of affection', his majesty made me go in to hear it alone" and that Weni "heard things being alone with the judge and the vizier, concerning all the secrets" (translated from hieroglyphs in Sethe 1933, 100, lines 13–16).

Figure 25 The Inscription of Weni from Abydos (CG 1435). Photo: Sally el-Sabbahy Courtesy of the Egyptian Museum, Cairo

Weni did not name the queen but used two titles, "King's Wife," and "Great of Affection," to refer to her. It would certainly seem from the circumstances that a conspiracy had been discovered – perhaps planned by one of Pepy's wives in order to have her son take the throne. Kanawati suggests that Pepy I could not have been very old at that time and unlikely to have had sons old enough that they could be part of a conspiracy to succeed him (Kanawati 2003, 172). It has even been suggested that Pepy I's early reign was actually a regency by his mother, Iput I (Altenmüller 2001, 602). It is somewhat unusual, however, for the queen being charged to be referred to with the title "King's Wife" followed by the title *weret hetes*, "Great of Affection." Why add that second title? It is also unusual because *weret hetes* is almost always found in combination with *weret heset*, "Great of Praise." Meritites I of the early Fourth Dynasty, discussed in Chapter 2, was also referred to as *weret hetes* under two kings, Sneferu and Khufu, seeming to indicate that she had been married first to Sneferu and then to Khufu. Was this queen of Pepy I a widow from the harem of Teti? If so, she may have had a son, half-brother of Pepy, whom she wanted to place on the throne. This is, of course, speculative, as scholars still do not have much evidence on which to base an understanding of the makeup of the Old Kingdom harem, but later, in the reign of King Merenra, there is clear evidence of one of his father's queens becoming his queen. So, a widowed queen might just stay in the harem and be inherited, so to speak, by the new king.

It is generally stated that, by regnal year 10, Pepy I changed his prenomen from Nefersahor to Meryra. Spalinger suggests that the change "can be dated to the latter part of his reign although an exact time frame is lacking" (Spalinger 1994, 304). Kanawati, in particular, sees the change of name as making peace with the priesthood of Ra, as the problems with Teti had been brought about by a "continuing struggle between the monarchy and the priesthood" (Kanawati 2007, 26). Nefersahor, "Perfect Is the Protection of Horus," is somewhat unusual, as it is not a solar name (Leprohon 2013, 42n77; Dobrev 1993, 196n57), although no prenomen is known for Unas or Teti, so there is not really contemporary evidence for comparison. Long ago, Sethe noticed that Pepy I's Pyramid Texts had been reworked and his prenomen changed (Sethe 1922, 5). The Pyramid Texts in his pyramid had almost been completely finished when they were reworked and changed, perhaps "as the reaction to the harem conspiracy" (Gundacker 2016, 238).

Certain texts were replaced and then the body of texts was extended. The texts with the king's original crown name were changed to his new name Meryra, and other texts had "changes in grammatical structure, through which the king went from speaking himself to being spoken of" (Billing 2018, 83). The sarcophagus of Pepy I was also replaced, undoubtedly because of the change in his name (Billing 2018, 85). Then, when finally finished, the texts covered "the entire horizontal corridor, the vestibule and the ascending passage" (Billing 2018, 82). The number of Pyramid Texts in the pyramid of Pepy I is "approximately 740," while those in the pyramid of Unas were "around 230" (Smith 2017, 182).

The Turin Canon gives Pepy I a twenty-year reign, but the Sixth Dynasty Annals record a twenty-fifth time of the count, which would be fifty years (Altenmüller 2001, 602), closer to Manetho who gives him fifty-three years (Kanawati 2000, 30). Spalinger, however, believes that the biennial system failed "to hold for Pepy I" and the evidence from his reign "must be placed aside" (Spalinger 1994, 306). Kanawati suggests that it makes sense to accept that the count was annual at this time, "as was the case in later periods," since a much more realistic reign for Pepy I cannot be "for much longer than 25 years" (Kanawati 2000, 31).

Pepy I was responsible for a number of *ka*-chapels, like the one belonging to King Teti at Bubastis. These were religious foundations for the living king, and therefore not part of the necropolis but associated with temples of deities. Papazian suggests that in this way not only was the cult of the king spread throughout the country but having the royal cult added into the temples was a "royal investment" that helped the temples expand and become more important economic centers (Papazian 2008a, 79–80). The king also issued decrees protecting the people, animals, and fields belonging to the *ka*-foundations, and such decrees "aimed as much at preserving the integrity of the royal cults with the divine temples, as at safeguarding the god's property" (Papazian 2005, 299).

The decree King Pepy I issued for the protection of his mother's *ka*-chapel, within the temple of the god Min at Coptos, is a good example of this type of text (Figure 26). The king states that the chapel along with its workers and animals are exempt from any kind of taxes. No official traveling south for any reason, not even those in the "following of Horus," in other words, not even a royal entourage, is allowed to demand anything from this chapel (Sethe 1933, 214; Goedicke 1967, 41–54).

A damaged tomb inscription from Giza describes that an "overseer of all the works of the king" named Nekabu was sent to sites in Lower Egypt to construct *ka*-foundations for Pepy I (Dunham 1938). The locations of the chapels are not mentioned, but Nekabu states that he returned having completed all the building that the king had ordered. *Ka*-chapels for King Pepy I are known to have existed in a number of sites, although the evidence for these chapels is the title of the official in charge of them, particularly the office of "Inspector of the priests of the *ka*- chapel of Pepy I" (Jones 2000, 940). There are titles for Pepy I *ka*-chapel inspectors from Akhmim, El Kab, Naqada, Asyut, Zawiyet al-Meitin, and Saqqara (Lange 2006, 133). The only *ka*-chapel that has been located archaeologically is the one at Bubastis.

The chapel at Bubastis was first excavated in 1939 by Labib Habachi and has recently been further excavated and restudied (Lange-Athinodorou and es-Senussi 2018). It is located just to the southwest of the earlier *ka*-chapel of King

Figure 26 Decree of Pepy I from Coptos, for his mother, Queen Iput (JE 41890). Photo: Sally el-Sabbahy, Courtesy Egyptian Museum, Cairo

Teti and within a similar large mud-brick enclosure. The lintel of the exterior of the southern entrance into the enclosure depicts the king being offered life by the goddess Bastet who stands in front of him, while Hathor, mistress of Dendera, stands behind him (Habachi 1957, fig. 2, pl. 2). The interior of the lintel has three large lines of inscription; the bottommost line of which gives the name "Ka-chapel of Pepy in Bubastis" (Habachi 1957, fig. 3A, pl. 3).

Edouard Naville claimed to have found two fragments of an obelisk of Pepy I reused at Bubastis (Naville 1891, 5–6, pl. 32C–D), although Habachi refers to them as "red granite, perhaps from door jambs" and at the end of the king's titulary is "son of Atum, lord of Heliopolis and Hathor, lady of Denderah" (Habachi 1957, 110; Morenz 1999, 62, figs. Ia–b). Because of Atum and Hathor being mentioned on the same object, the obelisk was probably originally set up in Heliopolis and taken to Bubastis in the Late Period during the building activity of the Bastet temple under Nectanebo II (Morenz 1999, 64).

A shrine of Pepy I for the god Khentimentiu in the side of the desert escarpment in South Abydos was discovered in 2010 (Kraemer 2017). Two chambers with pillars were cut roughly into the rock, the northern one of which still had damaged but readable short, vertical inscriptions. One, repeated three times, says: "King Pepy, son of Hathor of Denderah, beloved of Khentimentiu, living forever." The second, repeated twice, says: "King Pepy, the shrine which he made as his monument" (Kraemer 2017, figs. 6–10). Kraemer suggests that the southern chamber may have been produced by the quarrying of limestone blocks for the Pepy I temple of Khentimentiu Flinders Petrie found at Abydos (Petrie 1903, 10–11, pl. 59; Kemp 1968, 150, fig. 3), and the northern shrine was a later hasty addition, redefining "the site as a 'shrine' before it was abandoned" (Kraemer 2017, 32).

The names of seven queens of Pepy I are known, and there may well be further queens discovered in the ongoing excavation work at South Saqqara. Perhaps the most famous of his queens were the two sisters from Abydos, whom Pepy probably married in the latter part of his reign. They were the daughters of Khui and Nebet, seemingly an elite provincial couple. The marriage has been described as an attempt by Pepy I "to regain control over Upper Egypt" (Bárta 2013a, 172), as well as a marriage to cousins, possibly from the line of Unas (Kanawati 2010, 119, 123), since after one, or possibly two, conspiracies, Pepy I did not have a large number of people he trusted. Pepy I may have been purposefully seeking out relationships and a new base of power with provincial dignitaries who were not from the traditional elite families of the Memphite area. Weni, Pepy I's trusted and devoted official, was from Abydos, and perhaps his father, Iuu, who was a vizier during the middle of Pepy's reign, helped with all of this. Certainly, Weni and his father were in a position to be the first allowed to have tombs in the Middle Cemetery, directly across from the Second Dynasty enclosure of King Khasekhemwy and visibly in line with the royal tombs of the First and Second Dynasties. Iuu's tomb was the first one, in a square shape, more than 26 meters per side, resembling the bottom of a pyramid; Weni's tomb was even larger. Richards refers to the monumental landscape developed by these two tombs as a "spatial rhetoric of power" (Richards 2010, 342).

Papazian suggests that the "enmeshing of the royal house with influential Upper Egyptian families" (Papazian 2015, 407) may not have had any immediate impact on the king's power but may have helped the "entrenchment of provincial family bases leading up to, and during The First Intermediate Period" (p. 408). There is some evidence from stelae and similarity of names that the descendants of Khui and Nebet's family "may have preserved their powerbase and relevance for nearly a century and constituted the backbone of the Eighth Dynasty presence in the south" (p. 409).

Both of the daughters of Khui and Nebet had the name Ankhenespepy, "May Pepy Live for You," although the name Ankhenesmeryra, "May Meryra Live for You," using the prenomen instead of the king's nomen, is also found (Gourdon, 2006), although not often. Egyptologists refer to the two women as Ankhenespepy I and II. It is often assumed that their names were given to them at the time of their marriage, but there are several examples of nonroyal women with the same name (Sabbahy 2007, 157n71), so it is possible they were birth-names. It is also not clear if the king married them at the same time or separately. The situation of the two sisters married to Pepy I, and that they each had a son from him who became king, is explained in an inscription from Abydos belonging to their brother, Djau, who was a vizier in the middle of Pepy II's reign. Although found in a well, the tall vertical stela, or possibly door jamb, with the inscription might have come from, or was set up near, Building H southwest of the Khentymentiu Temple (Kemp 1968, 150).

Four vertical columns give the complete titulary for each of his sisters (Fischer 1977, fig. 58). Ankhenespepy I's titles are "King's Wife of Meryra Abides and Is Beautiful," "Great of Affection and Great of Praise," "Follower of the Great One," "Friend of Horus," "Companion of Horus," "Mother of the King of Upper and Lower Egypt Merenra Abides and Is Beautiful," Ankhenesmeryra. Ankhenespepy II's titles are "King's Wife of Meryra Abides and Is Beautiful," "Great of Affection and Great of Praise," "God's Daughter," "Follower of the Great One," "Friend of Horus," "Companion of Horus," "Mother of the King of Upper and Lower Egypt Neferkara Abides and Lives" (Sethe 1933, 117).

The only difference in their titles as queen and king's mother, other than the names of their sons, is that Ankhenespepy II has the title *sat-netjer*, "God's Daughter." A king's mother held the title "God's Daughter" because it is a statement of royal descent and passes legitimacy onto her son (Sabbahy

1998, 308). Her son, Pepy II, is the reigning king at this time. Her older sister is not given this title as her son, King Merenra, is deceased, and so it is the legitimacy of the living king that matters in this text, thus his mother holds that title. Ankhenespepy II is not the daughter of a king but uses the title because it is one that belongs to a king's mother. Kanawati has stated that there is evidence "that the provincial viziers and many high officials of the Sixth Dynasty had direct links to the royal family" (Kanawati 2010, 117) and that Nebet, the mother of Ankhenesmeryra I and II, descended from the line of King Unas. It might back up the queen mother's use of this title, if she was, for example, a royal granddaughter. Both of the queens express their spouse and mother relationship by giving the name of the pyramid of their husband and son. This kind of family affiliation, naming the pyramid rather than the king, only appears in inscriptions of the Sixth Dynasty (Labrousse and Leclant 1998, 96n15; Málek 1980, 237).

Pepy I most likely married Ankhenespepy I first, as she gave birth to the son who became the next king, King Merenra. He seems to have had a somewhat short rule, with rock inscriptions at Hatnub giving him the year after the fifth count, which, if biannual, would be ten years (Baud 2006, 152; Smith 1965, 50–51). Murnane states that it is possible that Merenra was very young and ruled in a co-regency with his father, although the evidence is "ambiguous" (Murnane 1977, 111–112, 227). The evidence is a gold pendant in the Cairo Museum (87193), perhaps from the king's kilt or that of a statue, which "bears the names and titles of the two kings" (Smith 1965, 50; see also Drioton, 1947). Two sets of cartouches on the pendant give cartouches with names of the two kings: one set gives "King of Upper and Lower Egypt, Son of Hathor, Mistress of Denderah, Pepy" and "King of Upper and Lower Egypt, Merenra," while the second set gives "King of Upper and Lower Egypt, Meryra" and "The Good God Merenra" (Drioton 1947, 55, fig. 3). Drioton's opinion was that this object was not evidence enough on which to base a co-regency (Drioton 1947, 56).

Other possible evidence for a co-regency of these two kings are two copper statues of Pepy and a second figure, who is assumed to be his young son, Merenra (Figure 27). They were found were found at Hierakonpolis (Quibell and Green 1902, 27–28, pl. 50), taken apart and buried under the floor of a chapel in the Horus Temple (Stadelmann 2005a, 125). There was a sheet of copper giving the titles of Pepy I and also mentioning the *heb sed* attached to the chest of the larger figure, but no identification was found for the smaller statue (Quibell and Green 1902, 45). There is another possible interpretation of these statues and that is that they are both Pepy I, one showing him as a young boy when he became king and the other showing him as an adult king having had a *heb sed* (Stadelmann 2005a, 129). In this case, the statues would not be co-regency evidence.

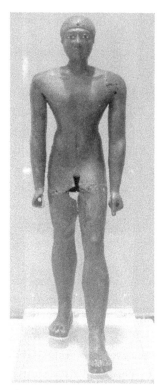

Figure 27 Copper statue of Pepy's son, Merenra, from Hierakonpolis (JE 23034). Photo: Sally el-Sabbahy, Courtesy of the Egyptian Museum, Cairo

If these two kings had a co-regency, that is, that they ruled together as king, then this is the oldest known co-regency in ancient Egypt. An attempted assassination would be a good impetus to institute a solution like this to protect the succession of power. With two kings ruling as one, if one dies or is killed, there is still a ruling king. Co-regencies were used again later in the Twelfth Dynasty, as discussed in Chapter 5, and they may have been reinstated by the royal house in connection with an assassination.

Kanawati suggested Pepy I started a co-regency with his son because of a plot against him late in his reign, led by his vizier Rawer (Kanawati 1981a). The evidence is somewhat indirect, but Rawer's mastaba at Saqqara had his names chiseled out on the two false doors belonging to him in the west wall (el-Fikey 1980, pl. 21), as well as the fact that his face was chiseled off in the only two complete figures of him preserved in the entrance into the tomb (el-Fikey 1980, pls. 1–2). Rawer must have been punished for something quite serious in order to have his existence in the afterlife destroyed like this. There is also no evidence that there was ever a burial in the tomb's burial chamber, which was originally cleared by Cecil Firth in the early 1920s, although there are no records of what Firth might have found (El-Fikey 1980, 2, 8). El-Fikey re-cleared the shaft and chambers at the bottom, but "there were no traces of a sarcophagus nor any blocks or objects" (el-Fikey 1980, 8).

There was a decree of King Pepy I found at Dahshur, dating to year 21 of the count, that stated protection from taxation for the workers, animals, and land that had been granted to the two pyramids of Sneferu. In the top horizontal line of inscription, the vizier's name had been removed (Goedicke 1967, fig. 5). It has been suggested that the name could have been that of Rawer and therefore removed, like the occurrence of his name in his tomb, although the evidence for the name on the decree being that of Rawer is "inconclusive" (el-Fikey 1980, 46).

The pyramid complex of Pepy I, named "The Perfection of Pepi Is Established," is situated in South Saqqara, just northwest of the pyramid of Djedkara Isesi (Lehner 1997, 17). The plan of Pepy I's mortuary temple and its decoration follows one that was developed in the reign of Sahura and followed afterward throughout the Fifth and Sixth Dynasties (Arnold 1997, 63).

The excavations over several decades at the South Saqqara site of the pyramid complex of Pepy I have revealed pyramids for both his queens and his daughters as well as several from the later reign of his son, Pepy II. The queen whose pyramid is still missing is Ankhenespepy I, whose tomb has not yet been discovered. There is actually little evidence of Ankhenespepy I, other than her titles in her brother's inscription and reference to her in two different decrees. In a decree of Pepy II at Abydos, relating to the endowment of her statue there, along with statues of the king himself, her sister, and her brother, the vizier (Goedicke 1967, fig. 7), she is referred to as the mother of Merenra. There is archaeological evidence of this queen's statue cult at Abydos preserved in door lintel fragments (Bussmann 2010).

In another decree found at the pyramid of Queen Neith, at the pyramid complex of Pepy II, Queen Ankhenespepy is referred to as "the oldest" and therefore must be Ankhenespepy I, the older sister with that name, and also the one who was mother of Neith. This decree was set up by an unknown king later than Pepy II and protects the priests, property, and produce necessary for the monthly festivals and offerings for these two royal women (Jéquier 1933, 5; Goedicke 1967, fig. 15). Labrousse has tentatively identified a fragment of decoration showing a royal woman smelling a lotus from the north wall of Pepy's offering hall as a figure of Ankhenespepy I, which would make sense since she appears to have been the principal queen (Labrousse 2010, 304; 2015, 167–168). He suggests the fragment came from a scene of the king at an offering table, with a very diminutive figure of Ankhenespepy I seated below it (Labrousse 2015, 172, fig. 2).

Four of the pyramids around the complex of King Pepy I can be identified as belonging to his queens. The largest of these pyramids, that of Pepy I's wife, the mother of Pepy II, Ankhenespepy II, was discovered in 2000 in the southwest corner of the king's complex. A massive, 17-ton, red granite lintel from a doorway into the pillared court of her mortuary temple had already been found in 1997 (Leclant and Clere 1998, pl. 28; Labrousse and Leclant 1998, 96) (Figure 28). The inscription on the lintel gives her name and title of king's mother on the left side, and the name of Pepy II's pyramid on the right. Damaged blocks from her mortuary temple have been reassembled into a scene of Ankhenespepy II pulling on papyrus stalks in the *sesh wadj* ritual, discussed in Chapter 2 with Meresankh III and her mother Hetepheres II, in her Fourth Dynasty mastaba at Giza. A large figure of Ankhenespepy II stands in a skiff with a tiny figure of another female in front of her; they are both pulling on papyri (Leclant and Minault-Gout 2000, pl. 17). The small figure is not named, but the name "Neith" was apparently added next to the figure at a later time (Callender 2017, 45). Ankhenespepy I had a daughter named Neith, so Neith, who married Pepy II, after being married to her brother Merenra, would have been the niece and daughter-in-law of Ankhenespepy II, but it is not possible to say for certain that she is the small figure in the scene.

Like the pyramid complex of the wife of King Djedkara at the end of the Fifth Dynasty, Ankhenespepy II's complex has an *antichambre carrée* (Labrousse 2010, 301), normally a space found only in kings' complexes. This square chamber with one central pillar appears to have always been decorated with

Figure 28 Granite lintel from the mortuary temple of Queen Ankhenespepy II, South Saqqara. Photo: © MAFS Mission archéologique franco-suisse de Saqqara

divinities or scenes of divine processions greeting the king. A dark stone sarcophagus was found in the burial chamber with some bones and linen wrapping still in it. The walls of the burial chamber are covered with Pyramid Texts, with the hieroglyphs retaining traces of green color.

In the area between the pyramids of Pepy I and Ankhenespepy II and in the area west of the Pepy I pyramid are other, somewhat smaller, pyramids belonging to other queens, including some of Pepy II, along with tombs of a royal son and two nonroyal individuals. Nebuwenet, Mahaa, and Inenek or Inti are three more queens of Pepy I. Nebuwenet's pyramid is on the south side of Pepy's, and her name and titles were found on the limestone door jambs of the gateway into her complex. The titles of Pepy I were on the lintel, along with mention of his *heb sed* (Leclant 1992, 218, fig. D). Nebuwenet's titles as queen on the well-preserved east jamb were typical for the Old Kingdom: "One Who Sees Horus and Seth," "Great of Affection," "Great of Praise," "Friend of Horus," "King's Wife Whom He Loves." Other fragments from the complex also supplied the title "*iry-pat*," or "elite" (Labrousse 2010, 300), a title held by royal princes in the earlier Old Kingdom. It becomes a queen's title in the Sixth Dynasty, and in the reign of Pepy II all his queens hold this title. The title is also used later in the Middle Kingdom by queens, princesses, and nonroyal elite women (Sabbahy 1982, 106).

Mahaa's pyramid complex was at the southwest corner of Pepy's complex and is unusual because, instead of a mortuary temple on the east side, there is a mastaba that belongs to her son, the "Count" and "King's Oldest Son of His Body Whom He Loves," Netjerkhethor. The mother and son are depicted on the east door jamb of the mastaba, where their titles are also inscribed (Leclant and Clere 1997, pl. 18, fig. 25; Labrousse 2012, 303, fig. 4.). The prince, depicted as smaller than his mother, holds a scepter and staff, while she holds a lotus to her nose. Mahaa's titles are the same as Nebuwenet's but with the addition of "One Joined to the Two Ladies," a title known once from the Fourth Dynasty (Sabbahy 1982, 115), and "Companion of Horus," "Follower of the Great One" and "Follower of Horus" are all rather common Old Kingdom titles for a queen, but before the Sixth Dynasty they are not found used all together. Mahaa's pyramid had not been finished, and there are no Pyramid Texts.

The pyramid complex of Inenek, also called Inti, is north of Nebuwenet's complex and much larger, with a pillared courtyard, two rows of storage magazines, and a small subsidiary pyramid in the southeast corner. It has been called "the most accomplished" queen's pyramid complex of the Old Kingdom (Labrousse 2010, 298). Inenek's titles were found on fragments of obelisks, pillars, and door jambs, and she holds many of the titles already listed for Nebuwenet and Mahaa, as well as a few others that are somewhat unusual. These titles are "Countess," "Chief Justice," "Vizier," "Daughter of Geb," "Daughter of Thoth," and "Daughter of Merhet," who was a bull god.

Titles of divine filiation, that is, naming someone the son or daughter of a god or goddess, are known from ancient Egypt, and they seem to indicate a position of rank or importance. A line of inscription across the top of Ankhenespepy II's sarcophagus gave her the titles "Daughter of Geb" and "Daughter of Nut," although in this case the titles might have a purely funerary meaning. In the Middle Kingdom, royal females in the families of Senusret II and Amenemhat III had the titles of "Daughter of Geb" and "Daughter of Thoth" (Sabbahy 1982, 211). These same unusual filiation titles, along with the title of vizier, were found on a stela (CG 1578; Fischer 2000, p.36, fig. 27) at Abydos, belonging to a nonroyal woman named Nebet, who some scholars accept as the same Nebet as the mother of Ankhenespepy I and II (Kanawati 2010). Whether or not the two Nebets are the same, the fact is that titles reflecting high rank, such as vizier and judge, along with titles of divine filiation, were given to a few women, royal and nonroyal, at this time. Did these women function as administrative officials? Were the titles given to these women a reflection of their importance or are they all to be interpreted as titles of status and rank and not reflective of actual administrative positions? In the Twenty-Fifth Dynasty of the Late Period and the Twenty-Sixth Dynasty respectively, the sister-spouse of King Piye and the god's wife of Amun, Ankhnesneferibra had the same divine filiation titles (Payraudeau 2015, 214–215). In Ptolemaic times, two queens, Arsinoe II and Cleopatra III, held divine filiation titles as well as the title of vizier, written with a female ending (Payraudeau 2015, 215–217). These titles must have been given to these particular women to stress their high rank, and, in the later cases, applying "old" titles may well have made them even more authoritative (Sabbahy 1982, 211–212).

Several block fragments inscribed with the name of Nedjeftet and typical Old Kingdom queen's titles, such as "King's Wife Whom He Loves," and "Great of Affection," were found on the south side of the complex of Inenek/ Inti (Dobrev and Leclant 1997, 154, figs. 1–2). No trace of a tomb for Nedjeftet has been found yet, and it is not clear which king would have been this woman's husband.

On the north side of Ankhenespepy II's pyramid are two rows of storage magazines and then a smaller complex belonging to Ankhenespepy III, a daughter of King Merenra and wife of Pepy II. Ankhenespepy II married her nephew Merenra after the death of her husband, Pepy I, and because Ankhenespepy III's pyramid was fit in next to Ankhenespepy II's, it is thought that Ankhenespepy II was probably her mother. Ankhenespepy III does not have Pyramid Texts inside her pyramid, but a band of inscription in black gives her titles as "King's Daughter," "King's Wife," and, added in later, "King's Mother."

On the east side of Ankhenespepy II's pyramid is the pyramid of Queen Meritites II, also called Merut, another queen of Pepy II. The complex was constructed out of limestone pieces, mud brick, and mortar and faced with limestone rather than solid limestone blocks. The complexes of Ankhenespepy III and Wedjebten, another queen of Pepy II, who were buried by the pyramid of Pepy II, were constructed in the same manner, and Labrousse suggests that they all should be dated to the middle of Pepy II's reign (Labrousse 2005). A large granite false door belonging to Queen Inenek/Inty was found, reused for Meritites II (Leclant and Clere 1997, 269, pl. 16, fig. 22) (Figure 29). The queen's titles on the false door that can be read from the photograph are quite standard, but there must be additional titles that are difficult to see, since in a recent article (Labrousse 2012, 305) states that "Meretites II held the title of vizier," although gives no further information. Dobrev makes reference to an inscription in the queen's mortuary temple that mentions a block with "at least twenty titles of Queen Meretites II/Merut" (Dobrev 2000, 394–395). Callender gives a long list of titles from a photograph of a "reconstruction drawing" that must show this block of inscription, but the internet link to the photograph no longer exists (Callender 2011b, 291). Based on Callender's list, Meritites II seems to have held every Sixth Dynasty queen's title known and a few new epithets as well, but it is hard for this author to comment without seeing the actual inscription. The burial chamber of Meritites II does not have Pyramid Texts but, like some of the other queens, has an inscription written in black around the upper wall of the chamber with titles. There were Pyramid

Figure 29 Granite false door reused for Queen Meritites II, South Saqqara. Photo: © MAFS Mission archéologique franco-suisse de Saqqara

Texts, however, on thirteen fragments of wood from some type of chest, perhaps a coffin, that was found in the chamber.

Yet another queen's pyramid complex, complete with a small subsidiary pyramid, was found on the southwest corner of Pepy I's complex. It belongs to a woman named Behenu, and, because of the Pyramid Texts in her burial chamber, she, or at least her tomb, probably belongs to the reign of Pepy II rather than that of Pepy I. A fragmented block of relief decoration from her sanctuary shows the queen seated under a protective falcon, smelling a jar of perfume (Labrousse 2012, 306). A damaged vertical inscription in front of her says she is "beloved of Pepy," which could be either king with that name, and preserves a fragment of the queen's title "One Who Sees Horus and Seth." On another small fragment is "Great of Affection" (Berger-el Naggar and Fraisse 2008, 3).

The last queen's name found in association with the pyramid complex of Pepy I is Sebutet, who is known only from a damaged lintel that was reused in a small pyramid belonging to a Twelfth Dynasty official named Raheryshefnahkt, located between the pyramid of Behenu and that of Ankhenespepy III. There are three lines of inscription and a figure of the queen sitting and smelling a lotus at the left end. She is called "King's Wife" in association with the name of the pyramid of Pepy I, and parts of the following queens' titles can be read: "One Who Sees Horus and Seth," "Great of Affection," "Great of Praise," "Follower of Horus," "Friend of Horus." In front of her figure is a vertical line of inscription, damaged at the top but clearly stating "whom he loves, Sebutet" (Labrousse 2010, 303).

Not all the excavated material at the pyramid complex of Pepy I and these queens has been published yet, and the cemetery area of South Saqqara is large and has by no means been completely excavated. Clearly, Pepy I must have had a substantial harem based on the fact that there are five of his queens accounted for here. Only one prince and one princess are known from this royal cemetery complex so far. Where are all the royal children?

Except for Ankhenespepy I and II, who were from an elite family at Abydos, the background of these other wives is unknown. Were they political marriages? None of these wives hold the title "King's Daughter," so there is no proof of marriage to royal daughters, but the women could have been related to the royal family in some way. Clearly the divine filiation and administrative titles given to Inenek/Inti seem to point to a special status for her.

After a reign of twenty to twenty-five years, and possibly including a co-regency with his son, Merenra, at the end, King Pepy I passed away. There is now evidence showing that Ankhenespepy II married her nephew Merenra after the death of her husband. In 1998, Labrousse discovered a block of relief decoration in the mortuary temple of Ankhenespepy II that stated she was mother in association with the name of the pyramid of King Pepy II, wife in association with the name of the pyramid of King Pepy I, and also wife in association with the name of King Merenra (Labrousse 2000, 486, fig. 1). This provides evidence for a widowed queen staying in the harem and marrying the new king, which seems to have happened at least twice in the Fourth Dynasty as well.

Further evidence of a royal widow staying in the harem, and that brother–sister marriages continued, is shown by the fact that Neith, the daughter of Pepy I and Ankhenespepy I, married her brother Merenra first and then her half-brother Pepy II when he took the throne after Merenra. On one side of an obelisk from the pyramid complex of Queen Neith, she is named "Eldest Daughter of His Body," in association with the pyramid of Pepy I, and also "King's Wife Whom He Loves," in association with the name of the pyramid of Pepy II. On another side, which is partially damaged, Neith is once again named as wife in association with the pyramid of Pepy II and then also wife in association with the pyramid of Merenra (Jéquier 1933, 4, fig. 1) The same relationship to Pepy I and II is found on part of a relief scene from Neith's mortuary temple (Jéquier 1933, pl. IV).

Merenra, the son of Ankhenespepy I, was older than his half-brother, the son of Ankhenespepy II, who became King Pepy II after the death of Merenra. Not much is known of Merenra's reign, which seems to have lasted at most ten years (Spalinger 1994, 306–307; Baud 2006, 151–152). One important document for information on the reign of Merenra is the abovementioned autobiography of Weni, as Weni started his career under King Teti and was the official who investigated the queen's conspiracy against Pepy I. Weni explains that King Merenra made him "Count" and "Overseer of Upper Egypt" (Sethe 1933, 105, 12). He then says that the king sent him to the First Cataract area to get stone for a sarcophagus and for the pyramidium of the king's pyramid as well as a granite false door, altar, doorways, and offering tables, and he delivered them to the pyramid of the king on six barges (Sethe 1933, 106, 14–107, 8). Weni also brought the king an alabaster altar from Hatnub and went to Nubia, had boats made, and loaded them with granite blocks for the king's pyramid (Sethe 1933, 10, 16–108, 90). In the fifth year of the count, King Merenra went to Elephantine and received the adoration (literally, the "kissing of the ground") from three Nubian chieftains (Sethe 1933, 110) in what seems to have been the last year of his reign.

THE REIGN OF KING PEPY II (2278–2184)

King Pepy II was six years old when he took the throne, and so his mother, Ankhenespepy II, ruled for him as regent. She ruled in his name, but she was the one making the decisions. A visual statement of her position as regent can be seen in the alabaster statuette in the Brooklyn Museum (39.119), which portrays the queen sitting on a throne with her young son, the king, sitting sideways on her lap with his feet on a second, perpendicular throne.

Ankhenespepy II wears a vulture headdress, which in the Old Kingdom signified the queen mother (Sabbahy 1998, 308). A small hole above her forehead once held a vulture's head, undoubtedly done in metal, perhaps gold, and traces of the vulture's wings can be seen going down her hair. The throne block on which the king has his feet carries a vertical inscription with his throne name, followed by "beloved of Khnum"; this same phrase is placed right before the name of his mother (James 1974, pl. 25). The reference to the god Khnum would seem to suggest that the piece came from a temple or chapel at Elephantine, although the provenance of the piece is not known.

More evidence for the regency of Pepy II's mother comes from an inscription at Maghara in the Sinai, dating to the second year of the count. The complete titulary of the king is given, along with the titles of his mother, who is named as both a king's mother and a king's wife. Her name uses the form of Ankhenesmeryra here, not Ankhenespepy, and is followed by a small figure of the queen.

Four queens of King Pepy II are buried at his pyramid complex at South Saqqara: Neith, Iput II, Ankhenespepy IV, and Wedjebten. All of them but Ankhenespepy IV have small pyramid complexes of their own around the king's complex. The complex of Queen Neith was at the northeast corner of Pepy II's complex. At the entrance to her complex were the two obelisks that give the name of her father, Pepy I, and two husbands, Merenra and Pepy II. The complete titulary of Neith is given in a band of inscription on the bottom of the west, north, and south walls of her burial chamber, underneath the Pyramid Texts that cover the walls (Jéquier 1933, pls. 8, 14–18). She is *iry-pat*, "King's Wife Whom He Loves," "Eldest King's Daughter of His Body," "One Who Sees Horus and Seth," "Great of Affection," "Great of Praise," "Friend of Horus," "Companion of Horus," "Follower of Horus," "One Who Is Joined to the Beloved of the Two Ladies." In the Pepy II decree at Abydos Neith is given the title "King's Mother." Neith's Pyramid Texts, unlike those of Iput II and Wedjebten, are well preserved. Because the wall space in a queen's tomb is smaller and differently shaped than a king's burial chambers, the layout of Neith's Pyramid Texts had to be adjusted accordingly (Allen 2005, 309–310).

Queen Iput II's complex is just behind and west of that of Neith. The titles of Iput II, given on a door lintel and two obelisks at the entrance into her complex, are similar to Neith's but simpler (Jéquier 1933, 42–43). She is *iry-pat*, "King's Wife," "Eldest King's Daughter," "One Who Sees Horus and Seth." Queen Iput II also had Pyramid Texts in her burial chamber, but the walls are badly broken up.

At some point, perhaps even after the death of Pepy II, an intrusive burial, one of five found in Iput II's complex, was made in the storage magazines south

THE REIGN OF KING PEPY II (2278–2184)   117

of the pyramid for Queen Ankhenespepy IV. Her sarcophagus had originally belonged to Queen Ankhenespepy I, and her names and titles were on the sarcophagus, along with the titulary of her husband, King Pepy I (Dobrev 2000, 391, fig. 2). The sarcophagus was covered with a lid that did not fit; originally it had been a block on which Sixth Dynasty Royal Annals were carved (Dobrev 2000). Also placed in the magazine was a false door constructed out of broken-up blocks and carrying the titles of a Queen Ankhenespepy, who was wife of Pepy II and mother of a king named Neferkara (Jéquier 1933, 53, fig. 31), but as there are a number of kings with that name in the period that followed the Sixth Dynasty, it is hard to say which king (Shaw 2000, 483). The titles on the sarcophagus and the false door do not match, so clearly funerary objects from two queens are involved.

The pyramid complex of Wedjebten is on the southeast corner of Pepy II's complex. The queen's titles have been preserved on fragments of door lintels, wall relief, and on a large alabaster offering table found in a chapel against the east face of her pyramid (Jéquier 1928b, figs. 3, 7, and 8). Much like Iput II, but even more so, Wedjebten's titulary is very limited: *iry-pat*, "King's Wife Whom He Loves," "Great of Affection." She does not have the title "King's Daughter" like both Neith and Iput II. A stela fragment may have the remains of the bottom of the title of "Follower of Horus" (Jéquier 1928b, fig. 6). Wedjebten had Pyramid Texts in her burial chamber, but it has been greatly damaged and the texts are in fragmented pieces (Jéquier 1928b, pl. 3). There is a second enclosure wall around Wedjebten's pyramid complex wall and in the space between, men and women, perhaps all from one priestly family line, have set up funerary stelae and altars to share in the distribution of offerings from the queen's cult (Jéquier 1928b, pls. 1, 24–31).

Jéquier found six fragments of a decree Pepy II issued at Wedjebten's pyramid complex (Jéquier 1928b, fig. 17; Goedicke 1967, 154–155). Undoubtedly the point of the decree was to protect and keep up her cult, but there is so little left of the text, it can't be reconstructed. The date of the decree is preserved but damaged and appears to give a date of thirty-three years of the count, although this has been questioned and a reading of possibly twenty-four suggested (Baud 2006, 153). There is still the unresolved problem of whether or not the count was annual or biannual in the Sixth Dynasty.

Manetho stated that Pepy II "began to reign at the age of six, and continued until his hundredth year" (Manetho trans. Waddell 1971, 55). The Turin Canon lists ninety years plus something for Pepy II (Gardiner 1959, pl. 2), which seems to confirm this, and a ninety-four-year reign for this king has long been accepted. If one accepts the count as biannual, however, there is still no contemporary date known for him greater than year 62 or 63 (Baud 2006, 156), which leaves thirty more years of reign with no evidence whatsoever (Goedicke 1988, 112). The problem of Pepy II's long reign can't be solved without more evidence, although some scholars have accepted a shorter reign for him (Gozzoli 2006, 208n77).

In the beginning of the Sixth Dynasty, and still in the time when Pepy II began to rule, there was a vizier in Memphis, another in Upper Egypt, and also an "Overseer of Upper Egypt," whose responsibility was the collecting of taxes. By years 25–35 of Pepy II, the title "Overseer of Upper Egypt" had been given to each of the nomarchs in Upper Egypt, who then were in charge of collecting taxes in their province, probably under the overall supervision of the southern vizier (Kanawati 1980, 129). The taxes collected as grain went to two granaries at Thebes and at Meir, and the nomarchs of these nomes held the title "Overseer of the Granaries" (Kanawati 1980, 130). Nomarchs often also held the title of "Overseer of the Priests," meaning that they had control over the local temple. Beginning with the Sixth Dynasty, in particular, the kings built at and added to provincial temples, and so the position of "Overseer of Priests" served as an "important foundation for the relationship of the provincial elite and the central state" (Moreno García 2013a, 199).

Along with temples, a second way that the king spread royal connections and control in the Upper Egyptian provinces was the establishment of *hwt*, which are basically agricultural domains. As pointed out in Chapter 1, *hwt* were known in Egypt from the First Dynasty and having *hwt* throughout the country was a way for the king to organize administrative rule over the provinces as well as the countryside (Moreno García 1999, 151). *Hwt*s were "islands of authority" that made "royal domination of a region effective" (Moreno García 2013, 198). This same system of controls did not seem to be used in the Delta or in the provinces in the most northern part of Upper Egypt, perhaps because they were closer to Memphis and could be more easily reached (Moreno García 2013, 203). It is also possible with the Sixth Dynasty's increasing amount of trade with Nubia and further south that the royal house wanted a strong and loyal southern Upper Egypt. The reigns of Merenra and Pepy II were a time of expeditions to the south, particularly under the "Overseer of Upper Egypt" and "Overseer of the Scouts" Harkuf, whose last expedition in the early reign of Pepy II brought back a dancing dwarf for the boy king (Sethe 1933, 120–131).

THE END OF THE SIXTH DYNASTY

After the death of Pepy II, his son from Queen Neith, Merenra II takes the throne and was possibly followed by another son, Neferkara, whose mother was Ankhenespepy III. Manetho, according to Eusebius, describes the Seventh Dynasty as consisting of "seventy kings of Memphis who ruled for seventy days" (Manetho trans. Waddell 1971, 57), so some Egyptologists "disregard the Seventh Dynasty based on its lacking any basis in historical fact" (Papazian

2015, 395). The Abydos King List gives the names of seventeen kings of the Eighth Dynasty. Most are only known by name, although Qakara-Ibi has a pyramid at South Saqqara, and other kings are known from decrees at Coptos and from cartouches found in the Wadi Hammamat (Papazian 2015, 398–403). At some point this line of rule stops, and the Ninth Dynasty at Heracleopolis claims the kingship; for Egyptologists, at this point the Old Kingdom ends and the First Intermediate Period begins.

Several factors could have brought about the end of the Old Kingdom, which basically means that there was an end to central control over Egypt by one king ruling from Memphis. This author doubts that any kind of "collapse" could be tied to the long, and therefore believed to be ineffective, reign of Pepy II in his later years, as the administration itself could have continued to function. It would seem much more realistic that, rather than collapse, there was an ongoing breaking away of provinces from Memphite rule. It was not collapse but decentralization. Nomarchs and other high officials, backed by a long family history of power and control, began to function more and more independently of the royal house. It is also quite possible that any number of these high officials might have been related to the royal family. As pointed out in the discussion of the many wives of Pepy I, and relevant to the many wives of Pepy II, there is just not enough evidence for the royal children who must have existed. Where are they all? Were many of them in the provinces but have not been recognized since they did not use royal titles in their tombs? There certainly could have been numerous royal sons who wanted to break away from the control of their sibling king in Memphis. Both members of the royal family and high officials may have purposely moved away from the king's center of control. Kaufman's statement is very apt here: "Throughout history, keeping administrative field officials loyal and obedient to central authorities has been one of the persistent problems of government" (Kaufman 1988, 228).

Perhaps the effects of climate change, which saw the drying up of the Neolithic wet phase over a period of time in the later Old Kingdom, hastened this decentralization of control. By the time of King Teti in the early Sixth Dynasty "the desert encroached quite closely on the Nile Valley" (Bárta 2015, 183), at least along the area of Abusir. There was also sand dune invasion of the valley's flood plain at Dahshur and the area to the south (Moeller 2005, 158). Lower Nile floods seem to have been the case at times in the Sixth Dynasty (Moeller 2005, 156). A recent study of Nile sediments at Saqqara concluded that at the end of the Old Kingdom there were "low Nile floods and arid conditions" (Hamdan et al. 2019, 286). A slightly earlier study came up with the same conclusions but also added that, along with low Nile levels and aridification, northern Egypt suffered from "intensive and repeated rainfalls" that caused "wide-spread sheet-flood accumulations" (Welc and Marks 2014, 132). Problems caused by low Nile levels did not only happen in the First

Intermediate Period. There is a stela (UC 143331) dating to regnal year 25 of Senusret I in the Twelfth Dynasty, belonging to Mentuhotep, the overseer of the priests, that states: "A low Nile came to pass ... and I did not allow my nome to hunger ... I did not permit misery to take place" (Simpson 2001, 8).

In a time of famine and low inundations, late Old Kingdom provincial centers may well have decided to fend for themselves to protect their fields and people. This certainly seems to have happened in the far south, for example, when Ankhtify of Mo'alla takes over control of the second and third nomes. Ankhtify took over authority and power that previously had only come from the king. The king, Neferkara, the name of a number of Eighth Dynasty kings, is mentioned once in Ankhtify's tomb, when he calls on the god Horus to grant the king a good Nile flood (Vandier 1950, 263), indicating that the king's religious role had not changed, however, just his political one (Seidelmayer 2000, 120).

Scholars seem to agree that not one single factor brought about the loss of centralized rule from Memphis (Müller-Wollenman 2014). Two main factors, stand out, however. First of all, there was loss of central control over Egypt's administration, although the political changes and power shifts that caused it are "poorly understood" (Moreno García 2013c, 151). Secondly, there was climate change throughout the later Old Kingdom. Evidence from drill cores show that, by the beginning of the First Intermediate Period, there was an onset of arid conditions as well as low Nile inundations (Hamdan 2019, 286).

CHAPTER FOUR

THE EARLY MIDDLE KINGDOM REUNIFIES EGYPT

BY THE THIRTIETH YEAR OF THE REIGN OF NEBHEPETRA Mentuhotep II, Egypt was once again a united country under the rule of one king. As a king who united the Egyptian state, Mentuhotep II was remembered later on a par with Menes of the First Dynasty and Ahmose of the Eighteenth (Habachi 1963, 50; Kemp 2006, 63). Mentuhotep II descended from a line of nomarchs, beginning with Intef the Great, who ruled Thebes during the First Intermediate Period. These local rulers used Horus names, beginning with Intef I, the third ruler in this dynastic line, and by the reign of Mentuhotep II's grandfather, Wa'ankh Intef II, the fourth ruler, these men are calling themselves: "King of Upper and Lower Egypt, Son of Ra." Their legitimacy and claim to the throne came from "a new deity of obvious solar origin" to whom they had built a temple on the East Bank, "Ra-Amun" (Gabolde 2018, 579). The evidence for the title of king comes from a stela in the tomb of a treasurer named Tjetji, who served both Intef II and III, and refers to both of them with these two titles (Clère and Vandier 1948, 15–16). Tjetji states that King Wa'ankh Intef II has control of Egypt from Elephantine to the town of This, indicating that, from the southern border of Egypt at the First Cataract, north to the capital city of the nome of Abydos, the southernmost eight nomes of Upper Egypt were under central Theban control, and the title of nomarch "gradually stops" in this area (Willems 2014, 84). Tjetji also mentions that the king received tribute from the chiefs of the desert lands, probably referring to the Western Desert, and the oases on the route going south into Nubia. An inscription in the tomb of the nomarch Itibi at Asyut mentions the Theban king Wa'ankh Intef II attacking Asyut, so conflict with the Heracleopolitan sovereignty to reunite Egypt was ongoing in his reign. Very little is known of Nakhtnebtepnefer Intef III, who followed him with a short reign of three to possibly eight years (Postel 2004, 121–130). Then his son, Mentuhotep II, succeeded him.

THE REIGN OF MENTUHOTEP II (2055–2004)

The Turin King List gives Mentuhotep II's a reign of fifty-one years, while contemporary documents supply evidence until regnal year 46 (Willems 2014, 87). He appears to have spent his first fourteen years in Thebes, during which time his Horus name was *Seankh-ib-tawy*, "The One Who Causes the Heart of the Two Lands to Live." Between regnal years 14 and 30, Mentuhotep II changed his Horus name to *Netjery- hedjet*, "The One Whose White Crown Is Divine," and in or around year 39 he took yet another Horus name, *Sema-tawy*, "Uniter of the Two Lands" (Leprohon 2013, 54–55). Scholars assume that at this point Mentuhotep II had defeated the Heracleopolitans and Egypt was reunited under his rule, bringing about the period Egyptologists refer to as the Middle Kingdom. Mentuhotep ruled for another twelve years, for a total of fifty-one years (Seidelmayer 2006, 160).

After ensuring his control over Lower Nubia (Postel 2008; Darnell 2008), Mentuhotep II moved north to take over those nomes loyal to Heracleopolis. Although the nomarchs ruling the nomes south of Thebes had been eliminated before the move north, the nomarchs of Middle Egypt, except for possibly Asyut, were left in place to rule by Mentuhotep II. These nomarchs may well have remained in power by shifting their allegiance from Heracleopolis to Thebes, once they realized they faced the same fate as Asyut (Seidlmayer 2000, 134), although, based on more recent excavations, "it is likely this ruling family remained in charge despite the Theban conquest" (Willems 2013, 385n134). It has been suggested that Mentuhotep II pursued a "conciliatory policy" not only to stop hostility but perhaps even more so to "adopt the style of traditional, northern Egyptian royalty" (Willems 2014, 89). It is not until the reign of Senusret III of the Twelfth Dynasty that the last of these nomarchs in Middle Egypt disappear, as their sons are absorbed into the central administration rather than inheriting their father's position in the nomes.

The ancestors of Mentuhotep II constructed *saff*, or row tombs, cut back into the rock at el-Tarif on the west bank of Thebes (Arnold 1976). These tombs are characterized by a long, open rectangular space with pillared façades at the west end, behind which are the burial chambers of the king and his family. Cut into the two, long east–west walls of the rectangular space were the tombs of his

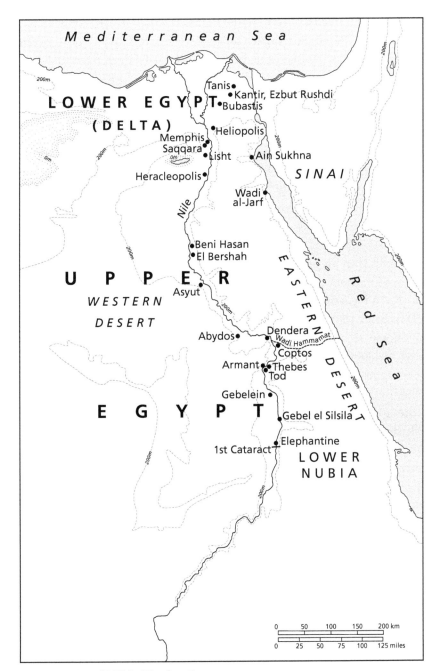

Figure 30 Map of Middle Kingdom Egypt

officials. It is interesting that the "disappearance of the nomarchs in southern Egypt coincides with the emergence of the large cemetery at al-Tarif" and this shift to a royal and elite cemetery must have been part of the "centralist policy of the Theban king" (Willems 2008, 37–38).

Mentuhotep II moved to an area to the south at Deir el-Bahari, constructing his tomb as part of his temple complex set against the cliff. This place was sacred to the goddess Hathor by that time; perhaps earlier it had belonged to a cow goddess who assimilated to Hathor by the end of the Old Kingdom (Allam 1963, 58; Pinch 1993, 4). There are a few Sixth Dynasty graffiti up in the rocks of northeast Deir el-Bahari that might be related to the presence of a shrine or chapel to Hathor (Rzepka 2003).

By the Sixth Dynasty, there is evidence for a Hathor cult at Thebes. The tomb of Unis-ankh has a scene of Hathoric dancers and harp players (TT 413) (Morris 2011, 75; Saleh 1977, pl. 3). Two women, a mother, Imy, wife of Ihy (TT 186), and her daughter, Meritites, wife of the nomarch Khenty (TT 405), both have the title "Priestess of Hathor" inscribed in their tombs (Saleh 1977, 18, 19, 25). Devotion to Hathor is clearly stated by Mentuhotep II's grandfather Wa'ankh Intef II in his prayer for protection day and night by Ra-Atum and Hathor on a limestone stela thought to have come from his *saff* tomb. Intef II refers to Ra as his father, and to Hathor he says that he is "Horus who loves you" (Lichtheim 1973, 95).

Mentuhotep II's mortuary complex was named "Most Excellent of the Places of Nebhepetra." When completed, a valley temple and large open causeway, 120 meters long and 46 meters wide (Arnold 2009, 149) led to the temple. An early version of the Festival of the Valley, the annual celebration when the god Amen left Karnak and crossed over to the West Bank, was probably being celebrated here in the reign of Mentuhotep II. Ullmann states that the procession of Amen from Karnak to Deir el-Bahari "can be dated the third part of his reign" when a statue of Amen was added into the king's cult chapel at his Deir el-Bahari tomb complex, and there must have been a "functional enlargement" of Karnak temple at that same time (Ullmann 2007, 8). There also may have been a *ka*-chapel for Mentuhotep II at Karnak, like the one he had at Dendera (Ullmann 2007, 7).

Mentuhotep II's founding of the procession of Amen would seem to be supported by a reconstructed scene on the south wall of the sanctuary in his temple, where the king is shown "steering the skiff of Amun" (Arnold and Arnold 2015, 40, fig. 43). The king might have been making a statement about his religious intentions in establishing this procession when he took the prenomen of Nebhepetra, which translates as "Possessor of the steering oar of Ra" (Leprohon 2013, 55). The word for "steering oar" was first spelled in his prenomen with the sign Aa "unclassified" but then became P8 "oar" (Gardiner 2001, 540, 499). Postel has pointed out the solar significance of this word and how it was important in the ideology being developed by Mentuhotep II (Postel 2004, 204–207). Darnell suggests that Mentuhotep II "transferred a Heliopolitan navigation to Thebes, and continued the creation of a Heliopolitan cult-scape centered at Thebes" (Darnell 2008, 105). In the damaged royal inscription from Ballas, which undoubtedly belongs to Mentuhotep II, it states: "That I did these things was when I was king, that I carried out the navigation for Thebes" (Darnell 2008, 92, pl. 9; Fischer 1964, pl. 37). It is possible that this navigation was for a religious purpose or perhaps both military and religious, as the text concerns the king's return from forcefully subduing Lower Nubia and then going to Edfu and Thebes (Darnell 2008, 104–105). Fischer pointed out that this text is an early example of a "Königsnovelle," a royal narrative that always includes a discussion between the king and his courtiers and then the king's decision on action. This form of literature will appear again in the reign of Senusret I in the early Twelfth Dynasty (Fischer 1964, 105–106).

There are remains below the Eighteenth Dynasty temple at Medinet Habu that might be Eleventh Dynasty (Hölscher 1939, 5, fig. 2). It is possible, although there is no proof so far, that a temple may have existed at Luxor in the early Middle Kingdom as well as at Karnak (Ullmann 2007, 11). Mentuhotep II may have been "the one who instituted the ceremonial link between the eastern and western halves of Amen's capital" (Darnell 2008, 105; see also Gundlach 1998, 296). Roth has suggested that later "Hatshepsut may have borrowed her entire program of ritual processions from Mentuhotep II" (Roth 2015, 540).

There was already some form of an Amen temple at Karnak in the reign of Mentuhotep II's father, as the earliest evidence known from Karnak is a polygonal column with a short vertical inscription giving the name of Wa'ankh Intef II and stating that this monument was made for Amen-Ra (Charloux and Mensan 2012, 188; Ullmann 2007, 4, fig. 2.2). Morenz has proposed a different reading of the beginning of the text on the column, accepting *imn* as an epithet, and not the god's name, and suggesting that originally the Karnak temple was for (Montu) Ra, the Hidden One, and it is slightly later under Mentuhotep II that Amen becomes the god (Morenz 2003, 115–117). There are two offering tables, a lintel, and two other stone fragments from Karnak with the name of Mentuhotep II (Habachi 1963, 31–36; Ullmann 2007, 4–5), so he must have added to or built a temple for Amen on the East Bank (Postel 2008, 335–339; Charloux and Mensan 2012, 219).

The red granite lintel of Mentuhotep II was reused in a wall in the northeast of the Karnak complex. It depicts the king seated on a throne with the symbol *sema-tawy* on the side. The god Horus and the goddess Wadjit, representing Upper Egypt, stand in front of him, while the god Seth and goddess Nehkbet, representing Lower Egypt, stand behind him. With those two pairs of deities, and the *sema-tawy*, the king emphasizes that he rules the entire country (Habachi 1963, 35–36, fig. 14; Gabolde 2018, 178, fig. 120). This block has been dated to the latter part of his reign (Ullmann 2007, 5), although it was recut after the Amarna Period (Gabolde 1998, 112).

Two granite offering tables of Mentuhotep II are also known from Karnak. One is inscribed with his name and "beloved of the lord of Abydos" (Habachi 1963, 32, fig. 12; Ullmann 2007, 4). The second, found in fragments, was larger and more complicated with four basins with inscriptions around and in between them, including small figures of Nile gods and nome personifications. The king's complete titulary is given, and he is called "beloved of all the gods of the Theban nome" (Habachi 1963, 34, fig. 13; Ullmann 2007, 4–5; Gabolde 2018, 176, fig. 118).

The Deir el-Bahari complex seems to have had three phases of development (Arnold 1974, 62), which were not progressive expansions of the monument but "major modifications of shape and religious meaning" (Arnold 2015b, 59). At first, there was a simple, large enclosure, with chapels and burials of six Hathor priestesses within the western half of the enclosure. Out in front of the enclosure on the east an underground passageway was cut, going west and ending in a chamber. Arnold's reconstruction suggests that, behind the chapels, to the north against the mountain was where the original Hathor shrine must have been (Arnold 2015b, 68, fig. 6). He gives two possible locations for this early Hathor shrine, both of which would have been covered over by later Eighteenth Dynasty construction: where Thutmose III built his Hathor sanctuary at the northwest corner of Mentuhotep II's temple or in the place where Hatshepsut built the uppermost part of her mortuary temple (Arnold 2015, 64–65).

The chapels of the priestesses were small, square, independent structures with a door on the east side. Inside was just room enough for a statue of the deceased, part of one of which was found (Naville 1910, pl. IXa). Painted carved relief on the outside of the chapels depicts offerings for the deceased, as well as the deceased sitting or standing with King Mentuhotep II, in a tall festive crown with two feathers. The style is very much that of the Theban area in the First Intermediate Period (Freed 1997, 151), and these scenes date to the earlier part of the king's reign, probably the years just after his regnal year fourteen. The inscriptions on the chapels give the king's second known Horus name, Netjery-hedjet, which he starts using sometime following regnal year 14 (Postel 2004, 178). These chapels were later included into the wall that was erected around the west side of the hypostyle hall of the temple's central platform. The shaft to each of their burials was located behind the chapel and thus behind the wall when it was constructed. The shaft went straight down and then turned east, so that the burial chamber was right under the chapel (Arnold 2008, 98–99, figs. 33–34).

The women have the titles "King's Wife Whom He Loves," "Sole Royal Ornament," and "Priestess of Hathor," titles that place them in a group with a special function and status, connected to the cult of Hathor, and that of the king, but not to the royal family and court (Sabbahy 1997, 164). Except for the title "King's Wife," the titles of these women do not fit those of a queen. Interestingly enough, their title as king's wife is only put on their shrines, where these women appear with the king; it never appears in their burial chambers or on their sarcophagi.

Mentuhotep II identifies himself with the fertility god Min in two large graffiti on the island of Konosso at the First Cataract. The king is shown as an ithyphallic figure, wearing two feathers on his head and holding the flail generally associated with Min (Habachi 1963, figs. 20–21). In each case, however, the name of Mentuhotep II appears in a cartouche. The epithet *Kamutef*, "Bull of His Mother" is represented by the depiction of Min, which is standing, mummy-like, ithyphallic, and with arms up and back, holding a flail. The epithet means "one who impregnates his own mother so that she gives birth to himself" and it emphasizes "the eternal and self-subsistent character of divine and pharaonic power" (Romanosky 2001, 415). Stated in another way, *Kamutef*, "being both father and son of itself, possesses a legitimacy that is not questionable" (Traunecker 2001, 221; Jacobsohn 1939, 28).

Another aspect of the cult of Min is the existence of a harem on earth for the god. The title of *hemet-Min*, "Min's wife," is known from the time of the Sixth Dynasty (Newberry 1912, 103, no. 4), and from the First Intermediate Period harems of local deities are known (Fischer 1956, 108n52). Mentuhotep II also depicts himself as Min but with a white crown, not feathers, in the upper, middle scene on the north wall of his chapel at Dendera (Habachi 1963, 26, fig. 8).

Since Mentuhotep II deifies and identifies himself with Min, it is tempting to explain the six wives with the shrines and tombs in his funerary complex as serving the king as a god on earth (Sabbahy 1982, 171). Such an interpretation would also explain the titles of these women, which are not the traditional ones of a king's wife.

The underground passageway and chamber to the east is known as the Bab el-Hosan. With the final building phase of this temple structure, the chamber of the Bab el-Hosan lay beneath the central platform. When the Bab el-Hosan was discovered in 1900, the chamber contained a large sandstone seated statue of Mentuhotep II in *heb sed* robe and double crown, lying on its side, wrapped in linen, and alongside it a "long wooden coffin" (Carter 1901, 202) (Figure 31). The king's skin is painted black, indicating he had become Osiris, and his beard is the curled one of a god. This chamber may have been originally planned for the king's burial but was then used for a symbolic Osiride burial, when a new burial chamber for the king was cut back in the mountain.

The platform of the temple was perhaps envisioned as a mound above the Bab el-Hosan chamber, while the garden of trees out in front, as evidenced by the tree holes and roots found (Arnold 1979, 21–24), symbolized the sacred cave and grove of Osiris (Junker 1913, 50–54). The trees in the garden also had

Figure 31 Seated statue of Mentuhotep II from the Bab el-Hosan, Deir el-Bahari (JE36195). Photo: Sally el-Sabbahy, Courtesy of the Egyptian Museum, Cairo

further symbolism, as they were sycamore and tamarisk, both of which had religious meaning. The *ba* or soul of Osiris was thought to rest in a tamarisk tree (Wilkinson 1998, 3), and the sycamore tree was associated with the goddess Hathor. Common epithets of Hathor, and known in the Memphite area in the Old Kingdom, were "Hathor, Mistress of the Sycamore tree" and "Hathor of the Southern Sycamore," which referred to a second cult of Hathor in the Memphite area (Galvin 1981, 253–256). One further religious association of the sycamore tree was that the sun was supposed to arise in the east "between sycamore-figs of turquoise" and in this way the garden tied into the rebirth of Mentuhotep II as the sun god (Wilkinson 1994, 3). There was also a shaft cut down, from the Bab el-Hosan chamber, perhaps added as part of an "Abydene burial" (Arnold 2007, 55), although containing only three wooden boats and rough red pottery (Carter 1901, 203).

The tomb of Queen Neferu (TT 319), one of the king's wives and seemingly the most important, belongs to the last stage of the temple's construction, as a relief fragment from the burial chamber carries the last form of the king's Horus name (Freed 1997, 151). Her tomb entrance is cut into the face of the stone just north of the large, open courtyard. The chapel of her tomb has fragmented remains of beautifully carved relief like that on the six chapels of the Hathor priestesses (Oppenheim et al. 2015, catalogue nos 34–37). Then a corridor leads down to her burial chamber, where the walls are covered with Coffin Texts (Winlock 1942, 102, fig. 8, pl. 13), some Pyramid Texts (Morales 2013, 579), a frieze d'objets and a band of inscription with the queen's titles. She is an *iry-pat*, or a noblewoman, "King's Wife," "King's Daughter," and "One Who Sees Horus and Seth," all titles used in the Old Kingdom (Sabbahy 1997, 165). In the Sixth Dynasty, wives of King Pepy II held the title *iry-pat*, but it was not used for royal women before that time. One title given to Neferu on the west wall of her burial chamber is "Mistress of Women," which becomes a popular title in the Twelfth Dynasty (Sabbahy 1997, 166n27). On the north wall of her burial chamber, Neferu is given two epithets that will be used again for women in the Late Period, who held the position of Divine Adoratrice: "pleasing in the columned hall by the smell of her fragrance" and "lovable possessor of charm." "Lovable possessor of charm" also appears again on the west side of her sarcophagus (Sabbahy 1997, 165). Both the titles of "King's Wife" and "King's Daughter" have added to them the phrase "Whom He Loves." Neferu also has one example of the title: "King's Oldest Daughter of His Body." As daughter of the king, Neferu was Mentuhotep II's sister. Her mother appears to have been a woman named I'h, as two mud shabti figures have the name "Nefru born of I'h" written on them in hieratic (Sabbahy 1982, 178n25; Hayes 1968, 327).

The courtyard by Neferu's tomb and the "outer northern colonnade of the temple" were used for the burials of more than thirty "religiously significant females" (Liszka 2018, 193). Two women, those found in Pits 23 and 26, had numerous tattoos on their bodies (Roehrig 2015, 527). One of the six priestesses and wives of Mentuhotep II buried in his temple complex, Amunet, also had these same kinds of tattoos (Roehrig 2015, 531). Morris has pointed out that these types of tattoos are found on *khener* (*ẖnr*) dancers, the women who dance in festivities for the goddess Hathor. There are also dolls from tombs in ancient Egypt known as paddle dolls, because of their shape. These dolls also have the same tattoo markings and were commonly offered to the goddess Hathor or put in tombs to associate the deceased with the dancers and the goddess (Morris 2011, 73). The majority of these dolls, 81 percent, come from Deir el-Bahari and are concentrated in the north court of the Mentuhotep II complex or on the south side of the causeway up to the temple (Morris 2011, 76, fig. 1). Clearly, Mentuhotep II planned the location of his funerary complex to stress his connection to his divine mother, Hathor, and therefore the legitimacy of his rule.

The carved relief at Schatt er-Rigal, a wadi just north of Gebel el-Silsila, depicts Mentuhotep II standing, wearing the double crown, and holding a staff and mace (Roth 2001, 568, fig. 90; Winlock 1947, pl. 12). Standing facing him on a smaller scale is his father, Intef III, wearing a nemes headcloth and uraeus and given the title "Beloved God's Father." Behind him, and on the same scale, is the treasurer Khety (called Akhtoy by earlier scholars). Standing behind the king on a smaller scale than all the other figures is his mother, "the King's Mother, Whom He Loves," I'h. She holds a staff with a lotus bud in her left hand and a bell-shaped lotus flower with curved stem in her right (Roth 2001, 190). This scene has been called an unmistakable proclamation of Mentuhotep II's divine birth (Darnell 2004, 26), based on Berlev's interpretation of the scene. The enormous figure of the king is positioned between his parents and, most importantly of all, his father carries the title *it-netjer* (*it- ntr*), "God's Father" (Habachi 1958, 189–190), which means that the son of his wife was produced by a sacred marriage with the sun god (Berlev 1981, 363) and Mentuhotep II is "Son of the Sun." Based on a stela in the British Museum (EA 1819) that depicts a woman named I'h with the titles "King's Daughter of His" and "Priestess of Hathor," standing behind an unnamed king, Troy suggests that this woman might be the mother of Mentuhotep II (Troy 1986, 73, fig. 47) and that she came from the ruling line of the early Eleventh Dynasty as well. A catalogue publication of this piece says the woman could be related to or mother of Mentuhotep II (Vandenbeusch, Semat, and Maitland 2016, 92–93).

Since a woman named I'h is mother of Mentuhotep II as well as his wife Neferu, they were undoubtedly full brother and sister. The last known evidence for a full brother–sister marriage was King Merenra and Queen Neith in the Sixth Dynasty. As the king's sister, Neferu must have been Mentuhotep II's highest ranking queen, although she was not the mother of his successor. Her importance is reflected not only in her tomb but in her titles and epithets, which are a mixture of Old Kingdom titles and new ones created for her.

The architecture of the temple complex of Mentuhotep II that was finally added into the enclosure with the chapels was influenced by the appearance of the earlier *saff* tombs at el-Tarif, which are characterized by pillared façades. Through a grove of sycamore and tamarisk trees (Arnold 1979, 21–24; Haase 2011, 188–190), a ramp, lined by heavy-looking, archaic-style standing statues of the king in his jubilee robe, led up onto a central square platform, with a pillared façade at its base and a second pillared façade up on the platform, beyond which a roofed colonnaded hall surrounded a smaller square "mound" in the center. Inscriptions on wood and alabaster tablets in the foundation deposits under this structure indicate that the platform was dedicated to Montu-Ra (Hayes 1968, fig. 92; Arnold 1974, 75), the Theban god of war and counterpart to Ra of Heliopolis (Werner 1985, 24–25). Gabolde has put forth the idea that a solar altar would have been on top of this platform (Gabolde 2015, 145–154). This possibility is based on the following facts: (1) there is now evidence of a solar altar at Karnak as early as the reign of Senusret I;

Figure 32 Damaged pillars still stand in the peristyle court, Mentuhotep II temple, Deir el-Bahari. Photo: Lisa Sabbahy

(2) the writing of the name of Mentuhotep's temple seems to have a pyramid or obelisk determinative; and (3) solar altars are always found in the later New Kingdom mortuary temples at Thebes, beginning with the nearby temple of Hatshepsut. Gabolde suggests a large offering stone with either a single squat obelisk or possibly two smaller ones were placed on the platform top and approached by a wooden ramp on the axis of the temple sanctuary at the back (Gabolde 2015, 151–152).

Behind the hall around the platform was an unroofed peristyle court, from which a corridor descended back into the mountain to the king's burial chamber (Figure 32). A corridor with vaulted sandstone ceiling led 150 meters into the rock to a granite-lined room, filled with an alabaster chapel "that had the shape of a god's shrine" to hold the king's wooden coffin (Arnold and Arnold 2015, 40).

Up on the level of the court, a hypostyle hall led back to a small rectangular sanctuary, with a statue niche at the back, cut into the mountain (Figure 33). The walls of this short hall had scenes of Mentuhotep II offering to deities, particularly Amen-Min and Hathor, and contained an altar, an offering table, and a large statue of the king set back in the niche (Edwards 1965, pl. 9, 2; Arnold 1997, 74–75, pls. 19, 25). The addition of a statue of the god Amen was probably made in the later years of Mentuhotep II (Arnold 1997, 74, 76, fig. 2) and was the first time that a deity had been placed in the cult chapel of a royal funerary temple. Associating the king's cult with a god's "was innovative and

Figure 33 Remains of the sanctuary at the back of the court, Mentuhotep II temple, Deir el-Bahari. Photo: Lisa Sabbahy

appeared to point to developments in the New Kingdom" leading to the royal mortuary temples, the "Houses of Millions of Years," that were in reality temples of Amen in which the dead king merged with a form of Amen (Arnold 2015b, 63). Mentuhotep II's mortuary temple becomes a place where the king is one among the gods; specifically, he is in a triad with his divine parents, his mother, Hathor, and his father Ra, in the form of Montu-Ra (Troy 1986, 55). Mentuhotep II's temple also serves as an Amen temple, as well as one honoring Osiris, whom the king joins in death. What is interesting here is that the same triad of Ra, Hathor, and the king as their child were the divinities found in the sun temples of the Fifth Dynasty.

One last queen's tomb, that of Tem, who was a king's mother, may have been added into the hypostyle hall of the sanctuary later, perhaps in the reign of Mentuhotep II's son, Sankhkara Mentuhotep III. Or, if her tomb was cut earlier, she must have died when her son was king, as her objects carry the title "King's Mother." An open passageway straight west was cut down between two columns in the southwest corner of the hypostyle hall, parallel to the passageway cut in the center of the hall, down to the king's tomb (Roth 2001, 569, fig. 91). It descended 18.5 meters to a square burial chamber (Arnold 1974, pl. 41). Tem's titles were found on her sarcophagus and on a fragment of a limestone offering table found in the rubble of the hypostyle hall (Arnold

1974, pl. 25b). Her titles are "King's Mother," "King's Wife Whom He Loves," "Great of Praise," and "Great of Affection," all titles that were typical of a king's mother in the Old Kingdom (Sabbahy 1997, 165). No earlier evidence is known for this woman, and it is possible that she only became important when her son, Mentuhotep II's oldest surviving son, became king. Tem does not use the title "King's Daughter" as Neferu does, and it is logical to assume Tem was not a member of the royal family.

Mentuhotep II also participated in the active construction of cult temples, particularly for Montu, and *ka*-chapels for himself. There is evidence that Mentuhotep II added to the Montu temples at Tod (Desroches-Noblecourt and Leblanc 1984, 83–86), Medamud, and Armant; built *ka*-chapels at Dendera and Gebelein, sites with temples for his divine mother, Hathor; built a cult chapel for Osiris at Abydos (Wegner 2015, 3–7) along with possible building at the early Osiris temple (Habachi 1963, 17); and added to the temple of Satit at Elephantine (Kaiser 1993, 147–152). There is no known structure of Mentuhotep II known north of Abydos, however. Morenz has described Mentuhotep II's building campaign as a sacro-political claim to legitimacy as king (Morenz 2010, 146–147), but it is particularly in his *ka*-chapels that Mentuhotep II legitimizes his reign and states his divinity.

Mentuhotep II's *ka*-chapel at Dendera was apparently still in situ northwest of the temple when it was discovered in 1916 and then moved to the Cairo Museum (JE 46068). In the vertical inscriptions on both sides of the entrance it states that this is the *ka*-chapel of Mentuhotep, beloved of Hathor and son of Ra, which he made as his monument (Habachi 1963, 20, fig. 5). On the back wall of the chapel, a large figure of the king is striding and smiting a papyrus plant, symbolizing his defeat of the Heracleopolitans in the north (O'Connor 1999, 216).

The scenes on the right and left sides of the chapel are smaller and divided into two registers with two scenes each. O'Connor has interpreted the scenes as presenting Mentuhotep II "in terms of the concordance between" his life and "cosmic order or *Maat*" (O'Connor 1999, 216). The left wall of the chapel is somewhat damaged, but the upper scene shows the king as a boy being suckled by Hathor. Behind Hathor is a depiction of Mentuhotep as the god Min. The king's divine birth is shown below, but only the disk and horns of Hathor, the king's crown, and one other headdress can be seen (O'Connor 1999, 219). On the opposite right wall, in the upper part on the right, the king, wearing a modius and two tall feathers like Amun, is brought to the goddess Hathor by Horackhty, "Lord of Dendera," while in the bottom scene, on the left, the king, or perhaps the *ka* statue of the king (O'Connor 1999, 218), is seated on a throne and provided with offerings, including milk. On the right, Hathor stands with the king and offers him eternal life (Habachi 1963, 24, fig. 7).

Along with the child god Ihy, Sema-tawy, Greek form Somtus, was also a son of Hathor. The association of this deity with Hathor is first known from a priest's title in the reign of Menkaura in the later Fourth Dynasty (Fischer 1968, 26). Sema-tawy appears next in the Eleventh Dynasty. A figure of Sema-tawy, Lord of Khadu, a cult place across the river from Dendera (Derchain-Urtel 1984, 1080), appears behind his father, Horackhty, in the scene of Mentuhotep II being presented to Hathor in the Dendera chapel. In two other scenes, in which there is a *sema-tawy*, a "tying together of the Two Lands" motif, it has been suggested that Mentuhotep II is being portrayed as Sema-tawy, son of Hathor and "may have been worshipped" in this form (Marochetti 2010, 26). Indeed, his relationship to Hathor as her son "is beyond dispute" (Gestermann 1984, 771). The first of these scenes is the main one on the rear wall of the Dendera chapel, where there is a *sema-tawy* motif filling the register below the king striding and smiting. The second scene is on the right wall of this chapel, down on the right side, where the king sits on a throne in a pavilion (O'Connor 1999, 218). On the side of his throne, as would be expected, is the *sema-tawy* motif that reflects the unity brought about by the king but also, in this case, the "staging" of him as Sema-tawy, Hathor's son (Morenz 2010, 163).

Gebelein, on the west bank of the Nile south of Thebes, is a site known from Predynastic times. It was an area that was hostile to the Theban rulers in the early part of the First Intermediate Period, which might have been why Mentuhotep built a chapel there to make a clear statement of his kingship. Marochetti has suggested that rather than a *ka*-chapel, such as the one at Dendera, or a local cult chapel for Hathor, the temple Mentuhotep II built at Gebelein was to celebrate his "royal power" and was a statement of his legitimacy (Marochetti 2010, 23). Based on his Horus name found at Gebelein, *Netjery-hedjet*, and the artistic style in the reliefs, Mentuhotep had the chapel built after regnal year 14 but before unification. Ten blocks from the chapel were found in 1893, reused in the much later Ptolemaic town, and numerous broken fragments were found scattered on the site of Gebelein in 1910 (Marochetti 2005, 146). One limestone block (Cairo 24/5/28/5) with two registers of decorated relief shows the king smiting foreigners in the lower register. The cartouche in front of him reads: "Son of Hathor of Dendera, Mentuhotep" (Marochetti 2010, 50–52). Six other fragments of relief come from a scene of Mentuhotep II wearing a white crown, followed by the god Sema-tawy, whose name is written above (Marochetti 2010, 80–83).

Petrie found five sandstone blocks in the enclosure of the god Osiris at Abydos that had been reused in foundations of the Eighteenth Dynasty and which he suggested had come from the earliest stone temple for Osiris (Petrie 1903, 14–15). The inscriptions on them have the full, final titulary of Mentuhotep II and are concerned with offerings and the making of a monument for Khentimentiu, the local god of Abydos, (Petrie 1903, pls. 24–25; Habachi 1963, 17–18).

In 2014, a *mahat* (*mḥt*) chapel of Mentuhotep II was found at Abydos at the northeast corner of the enclosure wall of the Seti I temple, the earliest Middle Kingdom religious structure known at Abydos (Wegner 2015). A *mahat* was a memorial built near the temple of Osiris at Abydos to protect a stela or statue of the owner (Haeny 1997, 115). A dedication text on the south wall of the chapel, oriented in the direction of the Early Dynastic royal tombs in the Umm el-Qa'ab says that this monument was built for "Osiris, Khentiamentiu, Wepwawet, and the gods who are in Abydos" and also mentions that he cut a canal for them, which must have been for the boat processions from the temple of Osiris (Wegner 2015, 5–6).

Before Mentuhotep II and the reunification of Egypt, the Eleventh Dynasty was a family of local rulers centered at Thebes, with a limited government structure, basically made up of a treasurer and a steward, the two officials that all elite private estates had (Grajetzki 2006, 21). Mentuhotep II brought about some changes, bringing back the office of vizier as well as "scribe of the king's document," both of which were well known in the Old Kingdom, while the old office of the "overseer of the double treasury" basically reappears as the "overseer of sealed things," or the treasurer (Grajetzki 2013, 213–221). The vizier, treasurer and steward, or "overseer of the house," were the three most important high officials. There is evidence for three viziers, one steward, and one treasurer from the reign of Mentuhotep II. They were of relatively equivalent rank and all three answered directly to the king (Allen 2003b). These officials are known from titles in their tomb inscriptions or from stelae. Since Mentuhotep II had his tomb at Deir el-Bahari, his high officials, for the most part, cut theirs in the cliff on the north side above the king's temple. Mentuhotep II remained centered at Thebes and does not seem to have been active north of the area of Abydos, and, as mentioned, there is no known religious structure of Mentuhotep II north of Abydos. The pre-unification art style found in Thebes disappears after Mentuhotep II's defeat of the Heracleopolitans, and it is suggested that he "took into his service artists of the Memphite tradition" and "seems to have deliberately ordered the northern style to be adopted in the south" (Robins 1990, 43). The sanctuary of the king's mortuary temple was one of the last parts of his complex to be completed, and its "decoration is clearly based on Memphite models" (Robins 1990, 43). Memphite or "northern" artistic traditions can also be seen in the Theban tombs of the high officials who served Mentuhotep II, particularly the tomb of Dagi (TT 103), who was his last vizier (Allen 1996, 22).

THE END OF THE ELEVENTH DYNASTY

Mentuhotep III, son of Mentuhotep II and Queen Tem, took the throne after his father, and, based on the Turin King List, he ruled for twelve years. His Horus name was "The One Who Has Sustained His Two Lands," and his prenomen, or crown name, was "The One Whom the *ka* of Ra Has Sustained" (Leprohon 2013, 55–56). Mentuhotep III is credited with building a small mud-brick temple, with three sanctuaries and what might be the earliest known brick pylon, up on "Thoth Hill," on the West Bank of Thebes. The king's titles were on the limestone jambs of the entrance, along with the statement that he made it as a monument for Horus (Vörös and Pudleiner 1997, 286). Mentuhotep III added to many of the same temples his father had; in particular, he added fine quality limestone relief decoration to the Montu temples of Tod and Armant (Oppenheim et al. 2015, catalogue no. 9).

There is no known tomb for Mentuhotep III. In the early 1920s, Winlock cleared an area in the wadi south of Deir el-Bahari revealing a causeway up to the platform with access to a closed but empty and unused burial chamber (Winlock 1921, 29–34). Based on graffiti in the area with the names of priests of Mentuhotep II and III, Winlock concluded that it was an unfinished tomb of Mentuhotep III (Winlock 1941, 155). This interpretation was accepted until 1991, when Dorothea Arnold published a new examination of the evidence and determined that it was instead an unfinished tomb for Amenemhat I, which had been closed up when he moved north to found a new royal residence at Itja-tawy and built his pyramid at Lisht (Arnold 1991). "The massive rock-cut tombs of the officials in the surrounding limestone cliffs were also left unfinished" (Arnold and Jánosi 2015, 55). Not all Egyptologists agree with Arnold's conclusions, but it still leaves no known completed tomb for Mentuhotep III.

There is also no evidence of a family connection between Mentuhotep III and Mentuhotep IV, who follows him on the throne. The only family member known for Mentuhotep IV is his mother, "King's Mother, Imi," named in an inscription in the Wadi Hammamat (Couyat and Montet 1913, pl. 36; Roth 2001, 570, fig. 93). There is no evidence to show this woman was married to Mentuhotep III, however, so a continuing ruling family cannot be assumed. The Turin King List does not include Mentuhotep IV at the end of the Eleventh Dynasty but records seven "missing" years after Mentuhotep III. It is not clear, however, if the name of Mentuhotep IV was in the list originally or if those years belonged to him (Willems 2014, 89).

Mentuhotep IV, whose throne name was Nebtawyra, "Lord of the Two Lands of Ra" (Leprohon 2013, 56), is known from a regnal year 1 rock inscription from Ain Sukhna on the west bank of the Gulf of Suez. The inscription announces the arrival of 3,000 men bringing turquoise and copper (Tallet 2012, 149, fig. 5), so they must have come from the Sinai. This king is also known from five inscriptions in the Wadi el-Hudi, dating to regnal year 1, and one dating to regnal year 2. The Wadi el-Hudi in the southern Eastern Desert is where the Egyptians, especially in the Middle Kingdom, went to get amethyst for jewelry and amulets (Sadek 1980, 4–15; Schenkel 1965, 260–263). All of the Wadi-el-Hudi inscriptions were written by or include the "expedition leader" Intef, but only in the fourth inscription (Sadek 1980, 10–11) does Intef have almost ten lines of self-praise similar to what is discussed next with the vizier Amenemhat.

There are other inscriptions from the reign of Mentuhotep IV in the Wadi Hammamat, where large numbers of men were sent to bring back a block of greywacke for the sarcophagus of the king. There are actually four rock inscriptions, all dated to different days of the same expedition into the wadi in regnal year 2. Two "miracles" were the subject of two of the inscriptions. One describes the finding of the perfect block of stone for the sarcophagus because a gazelle gave birth on it, and another that it rained and filled a cistern of water, so all the workmen were saved from thirst. The most relevant inscription for this discussion is the third, in which the vizier, Amenemhat reported on his role in this successful expedition. First, he gives himself a very long list of titles and epithets, beginning with status titles such as "Hereditary Prince" and *iry-pat*, and then his administrative titles such as "Judge," "Vizier," "Overseer of Works." He then has a long list of other titles and rather extraordinary epithets, all done in couplets, for example: "the one to whom the great ones come, bowing," "the entire land being on its belly"; "the one to whom is reported what exists and what does not exist," "the one who controls the affairs of the lord of the Two Lands."

After a number of couplets stressing his competence and extreme loyalty to the king, the vizier ends this introductory part stating that he is the "vizier of Horus, in his appearances, Amenemhat" (De Buck 1948, 75–76). The rest of the inscription describes how the king picked Amenemhat to lead this expedition out in front of his whole city and picked the choicest men in the land to accompany him, as well as how he managed to return with the sarcophagus as ordered, without losing any of the men or donkeys (De Buck 1948, 76).

Most Egyptologists accept that the vizier Amenemhat is the same man as King Amenemhat I, the first king of the Twelfth Dynasty. His exaggerated self - description in this expedition inscription helped paint a picture of an entitled high official who might have been picked by the king to follow him if he did not have a son; or perhaps, the vizier carried out a coup d'état and took over the kingship. Unfortunately, there is absolutely no evidence of how long Mentuhotep IV ruled, what happened to him, or how Amenemhat, if this vizier is the same person as the king, took the throne. It has also been shown that the aggrandizing self-description of Amenemhat is very close to that in another inscription done by the "Steward" Henu in the reign of Mentuhotep III, and so it should not be considered unique (Sweeney 2013; Leprohon 2001).

CHAPTER FIVE

THE BEGINNING OF THE TWELFTH DYNASTY

THE REIGN OF AMENEMHAT I (1985–1956)

A literary text, *The Prophecy of Neferti*, is used to shed light on the beginning of the reign of Amenemhat I (Berman 1985, 19). The text, written in the Eighteenth Dynasty of the New Kingdom but set in the Fourth Dynasty reign of King Sneferu, describes a future in which the situation in Egypt will be a time of civil strife, disorder, and foreign invasion. "Then a king will come from the South, Ameny, the justified, by name, son of a woman of Ta-seti, child of Upper Egypt" (Lichtheim 1973, 143). The name Ameny is short for Amenemhat (Posener 1956, 22–23). His mother is described as a Nubian, but the only other evidence we have for her is a limestone offering table in the collection of the Metropolitan Museum of Art (MMA 22.1.21), which was reused in a later settlement at Lisht (Mace 1922, fig. 11). The inscription, which is the same on each side, gives the offering formula for the *iry-pat*, "King's Mother," Nefert (Arnold 2015a, pl. 43). She is not called the daughter or wife of a king, so she was not part of the royal family. *The Prophecy of Neferti* says only that Ameny was the "son of a man" (Lichtheim 1973, 143), so that would seem to indicate also that Ameny was not of royal descent, although Posener believes the phrase "son of a man" designates someone of importance (Posener 1956, 50). It is possible that the "God's Father" Senusret, whose name is found at the end of a list of Eleventh Dynasty kings on a block from the chapel of Amenhotep I at Karnak, should be considered the father of Amenemhat I (Habachi 1958, 185–187).

138

The wife of Amenemhat I, who was the mother of his son and successor, Senusret I, is supposed to have had the name Nefri-ta-tjenen (?), which was inscribed on a carnelian statuette stolen from the Louvre during the Revolution of 1830 (Berman 1985, 12; Roth 2001, 220–224) and is only known through a description written by Champollion (Roth 2001, 22n1251). The daughter of Amenemhat I, and wife of her brother, or half-brother, Senusret I, was Neferu, some of whose titles are known from fragments of a broken black granite basin in the Metropolitan Museum of Art (MMA 34.1.10), which was found near her pyramid in her husband's complex at South Lisht. Only parts of two of her titles are preserved: "Mistress of All the Women" and "King's Wife" (Arnold 1992, 58n22, pl. 70). "Mistress of All the Women" is a common title in the Middle Kingdom and was first used in the Eleventh Dynasty by Neferu, queen and sister of Mentuhotep II. Neferu, wife of Senusret I, is also mentioned in an inscription along with her husband at Serabit el-Khadim in the Sinai where her titles are "His Sister," *iry-pat*, and "King's Wife" (Gardiner and Peet 1955, 86n71, pl. 21).

The highest regnal year known for Amenemhat I from a monument is thirty; the Turin Canon gives him a reign of twenty-nine years. Scholars are divided as to whether or not there was a co-regency of Amenemhat I and his eldest son Senusret I. If there was a co-regency, it started in Amenemhat I's year 20 and lasted for ten years. The main arguments against co-regencies, not only this one but co-regencies in general, have been put forward by Delia (1979, 1982) and Obsomer (1995, 45–136).

Amenemhat I's prenomen or crown name was "The One Who Has Satisfied the Heart of Ra," and his Horus name was "The One Who Has Satisfied the Heart of the Two Lands" (Leprohon 2013, 57), continuing the use of the name Ra in the crown name. At some point in his reign, Amenemhat I changed his Horus name to "The One Who Has Repeated Births," or *Wehem Mesut* (*wḥm-mswt*), and his Two Ladies and Golden Horus names change to that as well (Leprohon 2013, 58). A *Wehem Mesut* or "repeating of births" is usually translated into English as a "Renaissance."

Arnold suggested that the change in Horus name came at the same time in Amenemhat's reign as when he stopped the work on his tomb in Thebes and chose to move north. An inscription discovered at the harbor of Ain Sukhna shows that, in year 7, Amenemhat I was already using his *Wehem Mesut* Horus name (Abd el-Razik et al. 2002, 105). If his name change is tied to moving north, then that took place fairly early in his reign. *Amenemhat Itja-Tawy*, "Amenemhat is the seizer of the Two Lands," is almost always abbreviated *Itja-tawy*. The place where Amenemhat I based his new royal residence, and his royal necropolis, Lisht, nearby, is not known of until regnal year 20. Where then was Amenemhat for thirteen or more years, if he left Thebes when he changed his name by year 7?

Because there are so many blocks from the Memphite area reused in the building of the pyramid of Amenemhat I at Lisht, Arnold suggested that the king moved there first and perhaps started building a pyramid complex. At least a temple was completed, as there are papyrus fragments dating to year 14 that attest to cultic activities (Arnold 2015a, 62). Other evidence that supports the king's presence in the north are inscriptions in the tombs of two men, Ihy and Hetep, in the Teti pyramid cemetery at Saqqara (Silverman 2009, 47–78) (Figure 34). Both of these men were inspectors of the priests of King Teti's pyramid mortuary temple, and, in addition, Ihy had the same title connected with Amenemhat I. It is assumed that Hetep had this title as well, but a block of inscription in his tomb is broken away. The title in full is inspector of the mortuary priests of Amenemhat's pyramid, "Glorious and Favorite" (Ward 1982, 154, number 1327). Arnold, however, translates the pyramid name as "The-favorite-place-of-Amenemhat-is-transfigured" (Arnold 2015a, 3), which is probably closer to the ancient meaning. Does this pyramid title belong to Amenemhat I's second tomb but first pyramid in the Memphite area? Is this the pyramid that was taken apart to help build the king's second pyramid?

Ihy also has another cult title tied to Amenemhat, which has to do with a *ka*-chapel for the king, but the inscription only preserves the words: "Amenemhat *hwt-ka* ... beloved of his Lord, Ihy" (Silverman 2009, 57). One administrative title held by Ihy is very interesting: "Overseer of the Harem, Setepibra Itja-tawy" (Silverman 2009, 60). If Ihy worked at the royal palace in Itja-tawy, and also served at the mortuary temple of Teti at Saqqara, could Itja-tawy have been closer to the Memphite area than Lisht? Baines points out that the Itja-tawy is

Figure 34 Tomb of Ihy, Saqqara, across from the Teti pyramid. Photo: Lisa Sabbahy

often identified as being in the same place as the pyramids at Lisht, "but without good reason" (Baines 2013, 181). Based on the mention of Itja-tawy in the Twenty-Fifth Dynasty stela of King Piye, the town should have been located between Meydum and Memphis (Simpson 1963, 57).

It has been suggested that the "headless" or "capless" Lepsius Pyramid 29 could be the first one of the northern pyramids of Amenemhat I, although Arnold rejects this (Arnold 2003, 10). Some scholars believe Lepsius Pyramid 29 has many Old Kingdom characteristics and must have belonged to Menkauhor of the Fifth Dynasty (Hawass 2010, 159). Since it is just northeast of the Teti pyramid at Saqqara, and Ihy and Hetep were inspectors of the priests of the mortuary temples of both the Teti and Amenemhat pyramids, the location fits. It is possible Amenemhat I reused an Old Kingdom pyramid (Silverman 2009, 94).

In any case, by year 16, the temple that was completed and known to be functioning in year 14, location uncertain, was being taken apart, perhaps having been destroyed by an earthquake (Jánosi 2016, 1), and within two more years, a second pyramid complex was being built at North Lisht. Did the king choose to resettle slightly farther south, perhaps to be closer to northern Upper Egypt and closer to the nomarchs whose families were left in power after the reunification by Mentuhotep II? These nomarchs could either have been considered a power base for the king or, quite the opposite, have presented a growing threat to central power. Gundlach even suggests that, because northern Egypt was ignored by the Eleventh Dynasty, "vizier Amenemhat seized power" in order "to restore the kingship of the Old Kingdom" (Gundlach 2009, 52).

The pyramid complex of Amenemhat I at North Lisht was completed with a statue cult temple, rather than a funerary temple, by his son Senusret I, just after year 30 when Senusret became sole king. This sequence of architectural events, beginning with the building of the first temple, has been worked out by Dieter Arnold based on previous excavation records, going back to 1906, as well as the most recent excavations of the Metropolitan Museum at Lisht from 1991 to 1994 (Arnold 2015a, 18).

Some evidence has been found for a valley temple at North Lisht, and an open causeway, probably with brick walls, which led up to the pyramid. The statue cult temple on the east face of the pyramid was on two levels, as the bedrock goes up at that point. The limestone used to build the temple was quarried away in Ramesside times, but enough evidence was left to establish that it had a columned hall with an offering table in the middle, and then in the west against the face of the pyramid was a sanctuary with statue niches (Arnold 2015a, pl. 72). The substructure of the pyramid was unusual since the corridor into the pyramid on the north side goes in about 40 meters, where there is a small chamber with a shaft in the middle, which drops vertically down to the burial chamber. The burial chamber has not been explored in modern times, as it has always been below the water table.

In the substructure of the pyramid and cult temple foundations, many Old Kingdom blocks were found reused, which were discussed previously in Chapter 2. It does not appear that these blocks had been picked to associate Amenemhat I with older kings but because there may have been Old Kingdom structures in the Fayum or near Lisht that "probably fell into disuse during the First Intermediate Period and were later exploited as suitable sources for Amenemhat I's pyramid precinct" (Jánosi 2016, 13). There are also Middle Kingdom blocks reused, and they apparently come from three different sources: an earlier burial complex for Amenemhat I, "an unidentified building" in which both Amenemhat I and Senusret I are represented, and a building that had been prepared for Amenemhat I's *heb sed* (Jánosi 2016, 8). A lintel with an incomplete *heb sed* scene was found in the "foundation trench of the temple's north wall" (Jánosi 2016, 10n72, pls. 30–31), so it seems that Amenemhat was preparing for a *heb sed* but was assassinated before he celebrated it. A seated statue of the king found in Khataâna mentions the first *heb sed* but, again, does not prove it had already happened (Sourouzian 2005, 105).

Manetho, according to Africanus, states in his description of the Twelfth Dynasty: "Ammanemês, for 38 years: he was murdered by his own eunuchs" (Manetho trans. Waddell 1971, 67). The assassination is referred to in two Middle Kingdom texts, *The Story of Sinuhe* and *The Instructions of Amenemhat I for His son Senusret I*. In *Sinuhe*, Senusret I was in the Western Desert to fight the Libyans when a message came from the palace that the king had flown to heaven. In the *Instructions*, the king's death is described in more detail, as the king says he was falling asleep when "weapons for my protection were turned against me" and he was unable to protect himself. "No one is strong at night; no one can fight alone; . . . thus bloodshed occurred while I was without you" (Lichtheim 1973, 137). It is not stated outright, but clearly Amenemhat I is speaking to his son from the dead (Foster 1981, 46). Both texts were undoubtedly composed in the reign of Senusret I to justify and strengthen the legitimacy of his reign. In another line in the *Instructions*, Amenemhat states that he was killed "before the courtiers had heard I would hand over to you," and this is taken as proof that there was no co-regency between Amenemhat I and Senusret I. There is, of course, the problem of using a literary text as historical evidence, but in scholarly disputes against co-regencies "more weight is now given to statements in literary texts which are hard to explain on the assumption of a coregency" (Willems 2014, 91). This author accepts the co-regency of Amenemhat I and his son and questions the accuracy of relying on literature for specific historical facts. The *Instructions* have a "clear historical dimension, but we cannot make assumptions about the manner in which it is related to history, or to what extent it is historiographic" (Parkinson 2002, 9).

A co-regency between these two kings had been long accepted and was clearly backed up by Murnane's work on co-regencies, which literally opens with the sentence: "The Twelfth Dynasty begins with the first clearly attested instances of joint rule in Egyptian history" (Murnane 1977, 1). The evidence for a co-regency is a double-dated document that gives the regnal year of one king along with the regnal year of a second king. For example, the stela of Intef in the Cairo Museum (20516) gives the date year 30 of the reign of Amenemhat I, while also giving year 10 of the reign of Senusret I. This would mean that Senusret started a co-regency with his father in his father's twentieth year of reign and that they ruled together for ten years until his father's death. There is very clear evidence for their co-regency in a lintel found at Heliopolis with four horizontal lines, divided in half in the middle of the lintel with the birth and crown names of Amenemhat I on one half and those of Senusret I on the other. At the end of each line for each king is the statement "given life forever," which is an epithet applied to a living king (Awadalla 1990).

Jánosi states that "the archaeology and building history of Lisht-North leave little doubt that there was a joint rule of Amenemhat I and Senusret I" (Jánosi 2016, 1). Some type of temple, referred to as Temple A, had been built at the beginning of the co-regency and later taken down and its blocks used for the second building of Amenemhat I's pyramid. Relief scenes clearly show the two living kings, depicted as the same size and equal (Jánosi 2016, esp. 9).

It is virtually impossible to comment on the decorative scheme of Amenemhat I's pyramid complex, as literally every decorated block has been removed, except for those in the foundations and substructure of the pyramid, which originally came from the earlier burial complex, the "unidentified building," the *heb sed* building, or an Old Kingdom structure. Several blocks clearly belonging to Amenemhat I depict him with deities: a pillar shows the king embraced on different sides by Wadjit, Montu, and Sokar (Jánosi 2016, pls. 41–43); the king's Horus name is fed eternal life by Montu and Atum (Jánosi 2016, pl. 33); and the king is seated with Wadjit and Anubis in front of him and Behdety and Nekhbet behind him (Jánosi 2016, pl. 151).

Numerous other sites have pieces belonging to Amenemhat I, although, particularly in some of the Delta sites, they were taken there by later kings, who also had their names put on them. A colossal, granite, seated statue at Tanis probably came from Memphis, as part of the original inscription reads: "beloved of Ptah south of his wall" (Evers 1929, 17) (Figure 35). Cartouches with the name of King Merenptah of the Nineteenth Dynasty were cut on the chest and shoulders, but on the back and right side of the statue the name of Amenemhat I was left untouched (Berman 1985, 63) (Figure 36). A fragment of a door jamb was found reused in the temple of Nectanebo II at Bubastis. It preserves the titulary of Amenemhat I and says that he made it "as his monument for his mother Bastet, making a door in . . . " (Habachi 1957, 39, pl. 11a).

Figure 35 Colossal granite statue of Amenemhat usurped by Merenptah, found at Tanis (JE 37176). Photo: Sally el-Sabbahy, Courtesy of the Egyptian Museum, Cairo

Arnold remarked that Mentuhotep II "largely ignored Lower Egypt" and that it was only with Amenemhat I "that affairs in the Delta nomes ... received the attention of the king" (Arnold 1991, 20–21). An excavation at Ezbet Rushdi in the Eastern Delta in the early 1950s revealed a "nearly complete preserved ground plan" (Adam 1959, 209) of a temple built by Amenemhat I, with a court, hypostyle hall, and sanctuary with remains of an unidentified granite seated royal statue (Bietak and Dorner 1998). It has been suggested that the building was a *ka*-chapel, like that of Pepy I at Bubastis (Kees 1962, 2), but on a stela of year 5 of Senusret III found in the building it refers to the *hwt* of Amenemhat (Bietak and Dorner 1998, 18, fig. 6), which can mean a royal estate or administrative center. Nearby, at Kantir, the fallen blocks of a large granite door were found. An inscription on the lintel and door jambs states that Senusret III made this as his monument to renew what had been made by Amenemhat I (Habachi 1954, 451). Also found at the site was a seated statue of Amenemhat I, which is now in the Cairo Museum, as well as a limestone stela of an official, possibly, it is not clear, mentioning regnal year 2 and giving the name of Amenemhat I (Habachi 1954, 451–454).

As would be expected from a Theban king, Amenemhat I left traces of building at important religious sites in Upper Egypt. At Abydos, a red granite, rectangular offering table was found in the Osiris temple precinct carrying the name of Amenemhat I and saying that he made it as his monument for Osiris,

Figure 36 Side of the statue with original cartouche of Amenemhat I (JE37176). Photo: Sally el-Sabbahy, Courtesy of the Egyptian Museum, Cairo

Lord of Abydos (Mariette 1880, #1338). Blocks with relief decoration from a building of Amenemhat I were found at Coptos under the Ptolemaic temple remains (Berman 1985, 77). The temple of Armant has reused blocks of Amenemhat I in the Ptolemaic foundations and in the Roman floor. Berman points out that the name Amen has been chiseled away on all of them, so this structure must have still been standing in the reign of Akhenaten (Berman 1985, 78).

A granite offering table with the cartouches of Amenemhat I was found in the temple of the god Ptah at Karnak, although this could not have been its original place, as Amenemhat says "he made it as his monument for his father Amen-Ra, Lord of the Thrones of the Two Lands." The inscription continues, saying it was made "as a support for a granite naos" (Gabolde 2018, 214–215), which must have had a statue of Amen-Ra in it (Ullmann 2007, 5). There is also a dyad of the seated king Amenemhat I and a deity, unfortunately destroyed, that was found in the south of the Middle Kingdom court by Auguste Mariette in 1857 (Evers 1929, 22, fig. 4; Gabolde 2018, 218, 220, fig. 146). There is one other statue group that could date to either Amenemhat I or Senusret I, which consists of two figures of the king, two of Montu, and two of Hathor (Ullmann 2007, 5–6; Gabolde 2018, 206–209). The group statue came from the north side of the Middle Kingdom court, near where the solar altar was located.

Several cut-up blocks bearing the Horus and birth names of Amenemhat I were found at Luxor but must have originally been used in a structure at Karnak (Gabolde 2009, 2018, 221–222;). It would appear that the earliest Twelfth Dynasty Amen temple at Karnak was built by Amenemhat I on a sandstone platform (Carlotti et al. 2010, 158, figs. 2a–b) left in place when Senusret I enlarged the temple and created a north–south axis at the back (Gabolde 2018, figs. 148–149). The Amenemhat temple is reconstructed with a peristyle entrance court leading straight back to a sanctuary with three chapels.

Fischer makes the interesting statement that, between the time of the Sixth Dynasty and the rule of Thutmose III in the Eighteenth Dynasty, the names of Mentuhotep II and Amenemhat I "are by far the most frequently associated with Dendera" (Fischer 1968, n. 209), the main cult place of their divine mother Hathor. King Amenemhat I must have built, or added to, a structure at the temple complex of Hathor at Dendera. A granite lintel found in Graeco-Roman debris at Dendera and a granite column fragment "reused as a drainpipe" both carry the names of Amenemhat I and Hathor, Mistress of Dendera (Berman 1985, 76). There is also a faience foundation plaque from Dendera with a similar inscription stating that the king is beloved of Hathor (Weinstein 1973, 70). Two other objects bought in Upper Egypt, a cylinder seal (Berlin Museum 18488) and a bronze situla (Berlin Museum 18492), also have similar inscriptions (Fischer 1968, 52n209). A fragment of a slate bowl was found at the site of the North Lisht pyramid. On the outside are the birth and Horus names of Mentuhotep II, which had been earlier restored and read as the names of Mentuhotep IV, and on the inside, although written in a different style, was the Horus name, *Wehem Mesut*, of Amenemhat I. Alongside both of these royal sets of names was a further inscription "Beloved of Hathor, Mistress of Dendera" (Jánosi 2010, 8,2). An item such as this bowl from Dendera may have been purposely taken to the new capital at Itja-tawy to stress Amenemhat's legitimacy.

THE REIGN OF SENUSRET I (1956–1911)

When Senusret I took over sole rule of Egypt after the assassination of his father, he set about to cement the reunification of the Two Lands, which his father had set out to do once he moved north from Thebes. To justify and legitimize his kingship, particularly after the murder of his father, Senusret I followed the royal practices of the Old Kingdom, which had already been re-formed by Mentuhotep II as he reunified the land but with innovations that mark his reign as well as the later Twelfth Dynasty.

Senusret I is given a reign of 45 years by the Turin King List (Beckerath 1997, 132). He had a co-regency that started in year 20 of his father's reign, and then, after the death of his father in year 30 of his reign, Senusret I reigned as sole king for thirty-five years. His reign in the Turin King List is matched by a mention of year 45 in a graffito in Lower Nubia, south of Amada (Schneider 2006, 174) as well as year 44 on stela V, 4 in Leiden, which also gives year 2 for his son

Amenemhat II, providing proof of their co-regency (Simpson 1974b, pl. 30). Senusret I celebrated a *heb sed* in regnal year 31; it is attested in a number of inscriptions, for example on his obelisk at Heliopolis. His titulary is inscribed on each side of the obelisk, along with a statement that he set up the obelisk on the "first occasion of the heb sed" (Habachi 1977, 49).

When Amenemhat I changed his Horus name to *Wehem Mesut*, he also used this same name for his Two Ladies and Golden Horus names, therefore three of the five names of his titulary were identical. When Senusret I joined his father as co-regent, he also made his first three names the same: *Ankh Mesut* (*ʿnḫ-mswt*) , which has been variously translated as "The one who has lived the (re)birth" (Leprohon 2013, 58), "(Long) Live the (Re)birth" (Leprohon 1996, 167), and "Living by the Creation" or "Creation is alive" (Lorand 2015, 207). Senusret seemed to be making a statement that his father's reign was alive and well in his own reign; he was carrying on his father's legacy tradition. Senusret's throne name, *Kheperkara*, "The manifestation of the ka of Ra" (Leprohon 2013, 58) or "The ka of Ra comes to life" expressed that Senusret "is perceived as the royal living embodiment of the god Re accessing the throne of Egypt" (Lorand 2015, 208).

Some members of the family of Senusret I have been already discussed in the section "The Reign of Amenemhat I (1985–1956)." Senusret I's mother's name as read and written down by Champollion is "Nefri-ta-tjenen" (cited in Gauthier 1907, 263), which is an odd and possibly mistaken name or else one that might be transliterated differently by scholars nowadays. His wife was Neferu, who was his sister. She is known from the fragmentary basin and Sinai inscription with her father, Amenemhat I. She is also named in the beginning of *The Story of Sinuhe*, giving her the titles of a king's daughter and a king's wife, so the story was correct in those facts. It is possible that another sister was also wife of Senusret. One of the limestone blocks from the pyramid complex of Amenemhat I (MMA 09.180.121) has two short and broken vertical lines of inscription. The first still preserves "King's Daughter of His Body," and the second, part of a name: "///kayet" (Jánosi 2016, 81, pl. 79). At the complex of Senusret I, small subsidiary Pyramid 2 has two different inscriptions for a royal female named Itakayet. One, a fragment from the false door of the inner shrine, has the title "King's Daughter," followed by her name in one part of a vertical inscription and, in another, "His Daughter Whom He Loves," followed by her name (Arnold 1992, pl. 20d). Then, on a restored column from the mortuary chapel, is the vertical inscription: "*iry-pat*, great of affection and great of praise, *haty-a'a*, one who sees Horus and Seth, king's daughter whom he loves, Itakayet" (Arnold 1992, pl. 17c).

There could have been one woman named Itakayet, who was the daughter of King Amenemhat I and appeared on a block of relief decoration in his pyramid complex. She then could have married her brother, Senusret I, and been given Pyramid 2 as her tomb. The column from that tomb complex has three clear queen's titles: "One Who Sees Horus and Seth," "Great of Affection," and "Great of Praise," along with the other titles that are those of a princess. Such a situation might seem unusual, except that, in the Twelfth Dynasty, if a princess did not marry her brother and become a queen, she did not marry. Schmitz seems to have been the first to recognize this situation (Schmitz 1976, 202), and research by this author has reached a similar conclusion (Sabbahy 2004). The princesses that did not marry were buried near the pyramid of their fathers, and there are numerous burials of princesses at Twelfth Dynasty pyramids.

The earliest royal sibling marriage that there is some proof for is that of Netjerikhet and Hetephernebty in the Third Dynasty. In the Fourth Dynasty, there is clearer evidence of kings marrying their sisters. A brother–sister royal marriage with good evidence backing it is that of King Menkaura and his wife Queen Khamerernebty II. They were both the children of King Khafra and Queen Khamerernebty I, and their grandparents were related as well, although that evidence is not as clear. There is some evidence from the Fourth Dynasty for princes marrying their sisters, such as Ankhaf and Kawab, both brothers of Khufu, who married one of their sisters.

There is not clear evidence for sibling marriage again until the later part of the Sixth Dynasty, when Queen Neith first marries her brother, Merenra, and, upon his death, marries her half-brother, Pepy II. The next documented sibling marriage is Mentuhotep II and his sister Neferu in the later Eleventh Dynasty. Since Mentuhotep II set about to reunify Egypt in the traditions of the Old Kingdom, he must have been following Fourth Dynasty practice, which was based on the pattern of the sibling marriages of the gods and goddesses of the Heliopolitan creation. The Twelfth Dynasty clearly follows this marriage pattern as well, evidenced first in the reign of Senusret I. The Twelfth Dynasty did not allow a princess to marry unless she married her brother, which seems to be a way of protecting access to the throne, so that no one can claim legitimacy through marriage. Since the dynasty started out with an assassination, it would seem that protecting the royal line was of prime importance. Princess Khamaat, daughter of Userkaf of the Fifth Dynasty, was the first royal woman we know of who married outside the royal family. By the time of King Nyuserra, these marriages were common, but they certainly do not appear again in the Middle Kingdom.

Co-regency would also offer protection, because if anything happened to one king, there was still another ruling king in place. Since evidence points to the fact that Amenemhat I and Senusret I had a co-regency, did Amenemhat I begin this practice or did he follow an earlier practice started by Pepy I? Had there been earlier attempts on the life of Amenemhat I, like the conspiracies suggested in the reign of Pepy I? Senusret I followed the practice of his father and had a co-regency with his son, Amenemhat II, which lasted no more than four years (Murnane 1977, 5–6). As to what effect co-regency had on decision-making, palaces, status of royal family members, and other situations that might arise with dual kings and families, there is very little evidence. Assumptions are made that the elder king "retired" and the younger king was the active partner but that might just be based on the fact that in *The Story of Sinuhe* the royal father stayed at home while the royal son was on a military expedition.

There are more names of mothers preserved in the early Middle Kingdom than there are of wives. We know the mother of Mentuhotep II, Mentuhotep III, Mentuhotep IV, Amenemhat I, and Senusret I, but, while we know two queens of Mentuhotep II, not counting the women who were priestesses of Hathor, we do not have a queen's name for Mentuhotep IV; and for Amenemhat I and Senusret I, there seems to have been only one queen each, or perhaps two for Senusret. The king's mother was vastly more important for the king's legitimacy than his wife, and so the mother's name may well have appeared in many more instances and therefore has been preserved more often.

In Otto's study of the king's legitimacy in ancient Egypt, he points out three necessary aspects of kingship: effectiveness, birthright, and mythological backing (Otto 1969). The second aspect, that of birthright, is why the king's mother is so important; the transference of royal power passes through her to her son (Otto 1969, 400–402). The importance of the king's mother can be seen as early as the First Dynasty, as at least the names of three kings' mothers were included on the Palermo Stone, along with the name of their son, the king. In the Old Kingdom, beginning with the Fourth Dynasty, the king's mother was almost always shown wearing the vulture headdress, while other royal women had no special symbol or object that distinguished them and stated their position. A good example of a vulture headdress is that of Ankhenespepy II on the statuette of her and her son Pepy II.

The fact that the word for mother was *mwt* ties into the use of this headdress, as the ancient Egyptian name for vulture was also *mwt*. Goddesses could also wear a vulture headdress, and so the king's mother took on this divine attribute. By the end of the Middle Kingdom, in the Thirteenth Dynasty, princesses and queens all wear the vulture headdress, and it becomes the headdress of royal women and goddesses in general.

The literary texts that discuss the subject of Amenemhat I's assassination seem to describe it as a problem from within the palace, so it must have come from the harem. In *The Story of Sinuhe*, Sinuhe says that he ran away to the south rather than go back to the royal residence, saying: "I believed there would be turmoil and did not expect to survive it" (Lichtheim 1973, 224). In the Instructions of Amenemhat I, speaking from the dead, the king says: "He who ate my food raised opposition … Are rebels nurtured in the palace?" (Lichtheim 1973, 136–137). From the literary evidence, it sounds as if, after thirty years of rule, the conspiracy against the king came from within his own court. That seemed to have been the problem before in the Old Kingdom, with the possible assassination of King Teti and the foiled plot or plots against King Pepy I. With a minimum of seven queens, the harem of Pepy I must have had a number of young princes eager to take the throne, but with the early Middle Kingdom we have no evidence of large royal families or harems filled with queens.

Some scholars think that the vizier Amenemhat deposed Mentuhotep IV and seized power, and this has been a cause of contention. Gundlach suggests Amenemhat took over because the Eleventh Dynasty had "neglected the northern part of the country, the region of the former Tenth Dynasty" (Gundlach 2009, 52). Tidyman states that it is clear that "Nebtawyre was overthrown by his vizier, Amenemhet, and a civil war ensued in the vacuum that had been created" (Tidyman 1995, 108).

It is possible that there were still pockets of resistance, even after almost three decades of Amenemhat I's rule. There is some evidence of ongoing strife, particularly in the area of Thebes. In the 1920s, Winlock located a tomb in the cliffs north of Deir el-Bahari, Tomb 507, which contained the remains of about sixty male individuals, all of whom seem to have suffered trauma, such as blows to the head and being shot with arrows (Winlock 1945). Some of the individuals had obviously remained where they died for some time, as there was evidence of vultures having fed on them. The remains were originally dated to the reign of Mentuhotep II, and it was assumed they died during his attack on Heracleopolis, but, based on a paleographic study of the marks on the linen the remains were wrapped in, a re-dating to the reign of Senusret I has been put forth (Vogel 2003, 243n26).

The stela of Nesu-Montu (Louvre C 1), who has the title "Overseer of Troops" and was in charge of a Theban contingent, gives evidence for at least one battle on or by the river, probably in the Theban area, early in the reign of Senusret I. Although the date is damaged, the stela seems to date to year 24 of Amenemhat I (Obsomer 1993, 106), which, with a co-regency, would be year 4 of Senusret I. Nesu-Montu says that he led the battle and was victorious, overthrowing "the enemies of my lord" (Berman 1985, 119). There may have been resistance to the king, but it is probably unrealistic that anyone from outside the court could organize or carry out an attack on the king in his residence.

Based on foundation block marks, Senusret I had probably begun building his pyramid complex at South Lisht before year 10 of his co-regency with his father. His pyramid complex is a classic example of one from the Old Kingdom, monumental in size and with all the essential parts (Arnold 1988, 17). The causeway, however, with its Osiride figures of the king lining the interior walls (Arnold 1988, pl. 6), is more like the causeway of Mentuhotep II, which was

Figure 37 Osiride figure of Senusret I from Lisht (CG 398). Photo: Sally el-Sabbahy, Courtesy of the Egyptian Museum, Cairo

open and lined with *heb sed* figures of the king (Figure 37). The mortuary temple is badly destroyed, as the limestone was being removed from the pyramid complex by Ramesside times (Arnold 1988, 15), but it can be compared to those of the Old Kingdom: entry hall, peristyle court, transverse corridor, *antechambre carrée*, sanctuary, and storage magazines. The corridor to the burial chamber, which has never been explored since it is below the water level, goes down on the traditional north side of the pyramid. The descending corridor had been blocked by plugs that had been tunneled around in ancient times. Material from the king's burial, canopic jars and tops, alabaster food containers, and a piece of gold foil were found by Gaston Maspero's workmen

Figure 38 Seated statues of Senusret I found buried at Lisht (JE 31139). Photo: Sally el-Sabbahy, Courtesy of the Egyptian Museum, Cairo

(Arnold 1988, 70 n.233) and are in the collection of the Cairo Museum (Lorand 2011). There is an entrance chapel on the north side, above the descending corridor. Fragments of relief decoration from the chapel show offering bearers (Arnold and Jánosi 2015, 64, catalogue no. 13), and a block from the west wall depicts the king seated before an offering table (Arnold 1988, pl. 56).

Two sets of walls go around the pyramid. The outermost brick wall goes around the entire complex, and another inner limestone wall goes just around the king's pyramid. Every 5 meters on both the inner and the outer sides of this inner wall were vertical panels with the king's Horus name with a serekh-façade and at the bottom a scene of a Nile fertility figure (Arnold 1988, 59, pls. 30–36). In the space between the two walls is the king's "south tomb," a small pyramid on the southeast corner of his pyramid, just like that of Khufu at Giza, and then there are nine small subsidiary pyramids for family members. Only Pyramids 1 and 2 could be identified as belonging to specific family members, Queen Neferu and Princess (?) Itakayet.

Senusret I undertook a massive building program enlarging the temples at important religious sites, as well as producing large numbers of statues. There are fifty-one statues securely dated to Senusret I and others that are possibly his (Fay 2015, 81; Lorand 2011). Ten limestone seated statues of the king were found in a pit north of his mortuary temple in 1884 and are now in the Cairo Museum (Arnold 1988, 56) (Figure 38). The sides of the king's thrones have

Figure 39 Colossal standing statue of Senusret I from Memphis, usurped by Ramses II. Photo: Lisa Sabbahy

beautifully rendered *sema-tawy* reliefs with Horus and Seth or Nile fertility gods tying together the papyrus and the lotus. It is assumed that the statues were buried for safekeeping, but where they were placed originally in the complex, or meant to be placed, is unknown. Dohrmann has suggested that for a short period of time the statues were set in the columned court of the mortuary temple as part of the king's *heb sed*. The five statues with Horus and Seth on the sides of the thrones were set on the south side, and the ones with Nile gods were on the north.

Some of Senusret I's statues were of huge proportions, making him the first king since the Old Kingdom to commission colossal statues (Freed 2014, 891). As mentioned in Chapter 2 on the Fourth Dynasty, large monuments reflected power and that was undoubtedly the point. One of Senusret's standing colossal statues is on display in the Open-Air Museum at Mit Rahineh (Memphis). For years, it had been accepted as a statue of Ramses II, as he had his name carved on it, but Sourouzian has proved that it originally belonged to Senusret I (Sourouzian 1988, pl. 68) (Figure 39).

Figure 40 Space in the middle of Karnak that once held the Middle Kingdom temple of Senusret I. Photo: Lisa Sabbahy

Senusret I had an extensive building program, evidenced not only by archaeological remains but by lists of temples and statues from his reign, such as the inscription on the block found at the mosque of el-Azhar (Daressy 1903, 101–103). However, two sites in particular, Karnak and Heliopolis, will be discussed in some detail as they represent the two cult great centers of ancient Egypt and the sun god. Thebes was Senusret's family's nome and Karnak the cult place of the deity Amen-Ra adopted by the Thebans of the early Eleventh Dynasty. The vizier Mentuhotep, who was also overseer of all the king's works, was in charge of the building at Karnak, which began in regnal year 19. Mentuhotep also felt entitled enough to leave at least eleven statues of himself at the temple (Simpson 1991, 335) (Figure 40). Senusret left in place the sandstone flooring of his father's temple of Amen and redid the temple with a limestone platform, fifteen times larger (Gabolde 2018, 224–228; Lorand 2015, 212). The temple itself was also limestone. The façade of the temple "was preceded by a portico of twelve pillars, each one fronted by a colossus of the king in Osiride form" (Blyth 2006, 12) (Figure 41) that led to a large peristyle court with square pillars. The sides of the pillars each depict the king with one of the four most important gods: Atum of Heliopolis, Ptah of Memphis, Horus of Edfu, and Amen of Karnak.

Figure 41 Pillar with Osiride figure of Senusret I, Karnak (JE 48851). Photo: Sally el-Sabbahy, Courtesy of the Egyptian Museum, Cairo

On the north and south sides of the peristyle court were small chapels, suggested to have been for statues of kings of the Old Kingdom and First Intermediate Period that Senusret I wanted to honor and claim as "ancestral" to his own rule. Similar ancestor chapels were placed just slightly west of these by Amenhotep I in the New Kingdom and replaced later by Thutmose III (Blyth 2006, 37). Two statues that probably came from these Middle Kingdom chapels, Sahura (CG 42004) and Intef the Great (CG 42005), were found at Karnak, while a similar statue of Nyuserra in the British Museum (EA 870) was purchased but must have come from Karnak as well (Lorand 2013).

Beyond the peristyle court were further halls, led to by three large granite door sills that are still in situ today, but nothing else is left on the platform. After the last door sill, Gabolde suggests the axis of the room at the end, the sanctuary itself, was north–south rather than east–west like the rest of the temple, so that the pedestal with the naos for the god's statue was in the north. The large alabaster pedestal found in the court may well have come from the north sanctuary (Gabolde 2018, 330). The axis of this sanctuary may have been what influenced the axis of the later *Akh-menu*, which is also north–south.

A granodiorite naos of Senusret I found at Karnak, and now in the Cairo Museum (JE 47276), is not the one that was placed on the alabaster pedestal; it was probably set in a small limestone structure south of the temple and contained a *ka*-statue of the king (Gabolde 2018, 351–353) (Figure 42).

Because the Middle Kingdom temple was limestone it suffered terribly from later quarrying. The White Chapel erected for Senusret I's *heb sed* was also limestone, but since it was taken apart and used in the foundations of Amenhotep III's Third Pylon, it was saved and has been reconstructed. The chapel is square and up on a base approached from front and back by a ramp with stairs. In the center now is a barque-stand, but originally this place might have been for a statue base. Seidel proposes that a statue of King Senusret I and Amun-Ra-*Kamutef* (meaning *ka* of his mother) was there originally. A base was found with spaces for two standing statues, with the cartouches of Senusret I, at the later *Kamutef* temple south of Karnak (Seidel 1996, figs. 23–26). The chapel has four rows of four square pillars, carved in sunk relief on the sides of the pillars facing out, and raised relief on all the sides inside the chapel.

The base of the chapel is decorated on the outside with a list of the nomes of Lower Egypt on the north side and Upper Egypt on the south side. The measurements of the areas of the nomes are given, as are the measurements of the heights of the Nile floods. On the interior pillars, the king and the god Amen-Ra, or Amen-Ra *Kamutef*, are depicted, while on the exterior pillar sides Atum, Horus, Montu, and Ra-Harakhte appear with them. All of these gods have solar connections or ties to Heliopolis.

Figure 42 Naos of Senusret I from Karnak (JE 47276). Photo: Sally el-Sabbahy, Courtesy of the Egyptian Museum, Cairo

In fact, there may have been a cult chapel of Ra-Harakhte at Karnak, since the White Chapel mentions "Ra-Harakhte, Foremost of Karnak," which implies there was some type of sanctuary there (Gabolde 2018, 258n496). In the different scenes of embracing his father or being offered eternal life, Senusret is referred to as "Amen's Son," "His Son Whom He Loves," and the "Son of His Body Whom He Loves," all titles that parallel those of royal sons (Lacau and Chevrier 1969, pls. 20, 22). The scenes are repetitive and stress the crowning of the king. He is shown in the White Crown, the Red Crown, or the double crown when he is being presented to Amen or given eternal life, that is, the ankh symbol. When the king embraces his father Amun-Ra *Kamutef*, or kneels offering to him, he eithers wears a cap or a cap-crown with uraeus.

There was a solar altar at Karnak in the time of Senusret I. It was probably located on the north side of the Middle Kingdom court, since that would parallel the placement of the later solar altar of Thutmose III's Akh-menu. Fragments of the altar were discovered near the Seventh Pylon in 1905, and Senusret's cartouche is still readable on what would have been the north side; some other smaller pieces with broken inscription are known from the Pushkin Museum (Gabolde 2018, 246–247). The precedent for this altar may well have been a sun altar on the flat top of Mentuhotep's funerary complex at Deir el-Bahari (Gabolde 2015).

Along with Ra, one would expect depictions of the king with Hathor. One granodiorite group statue was found in the Middle Kingdom court in 1897, with the king standing next to a seated Hathor. It is particularly reminiscent of the triad from the valley temple of King Menkaura, with Hathor seated and a nome personification on one side and the king on the other (MFA 09.200) (Friedman 2008, 120, fig. 11a). The figure of the king in the Karnak dyad is broken away at the waist and Hathor's figure is broken away at the shoulders (Seidel 1996, 92, figs. 27a–d).

One last detail should be mentioned in terms of Senusret I's following of the religious program of the Eleventh Dynasty, which is that Senusret had a navigation scene, very similar to the one in the sanctuary of the Deir el-Bahari temple of Mentuhotep II. It was located on the south wall of the portico leading into the Amun Temple at Karnak and shows the king rowing the same type of boat in the presence of Amun *Kamutef* (Gabolde 1998, pl. 9). "This leads to the conclusion that the very same ritual journey is depicted in both cases" (Ullmann 2007, 8, 16, fig. 2.5).

The *Building Inscription of Senusret I*, also known as the Berlin Leather Roll (Berlin Museum 3029), is a hieratic text written on leather and dates to the reign of the Eighteenth Dynasty king Amenhotep II. It is accepted by many Egyptologists as a copy made from a Twelfth Dynasty stela or wall inscription at the temple of Atum of Heliopolis. The text itself gives a date of year 3, third month of inundation, day 8 of the reign of Senusret I. The text starts out by describing King Senusret I meeting with his courtiers. They were commanded to listen to the king and learn. At this point the king's speech becomes poetic, and some of the more interesting lines are quoted here: "He appointed me shepherd of this land, knowing who would herd it for him . . . I am a king by nature . . . I lorded in the egg. I ruled as a youth. He advanced me to the Lord of the Two Parts, a child yet wearing swaddling clothes . . . He fashioned me as palace–dweller, an offspring not yet issued from the thighs" (Lichtheim 1973, 116).

Senusret makes clear that he was destined to be king of Egypt, so his legitimacy is beyond question. Atum decided on his kingship before he was born, and the god's plans must be carried out. Senusret announces that: "I will construct a great house for my father Atum." His courtiers praise his plans. They point out that he possesses *Hu* (*ḥw*), which is the ability to speak with authority, as well as *Sia* (*siȝ*), the ability to recognize what needs to be done. These are two qualities that a legitimate king possesses. Then the king speaks to his royal seal bearer and overseer of the treasuries, who may have been the high official Mentuhotep, and tells him to take over and make the plans. In the next part, the king appears in front of the people and priests to carry out the "stretching of the cord," the ritual that started the building of a temple. At that point, the New Kingdom scribe stopped his copy.

Literary and royal texts from the time of the Twelfth Dynasty have often been called propaganda, particularly those from the reign of Senusret I. They were "intended to promote adherence to the pharaoh" (Franke 1995, 740) and above all to back his legitimacy as king. This need for legitimation is expressed in the *Building Inscription* through the use of predestination; the king was meant to be king before he was ever born; it is god's plan. Perhaps the idea of predestination is a way to state that assassination of the king is not possible, as a divine decision cannot be acted against. The theme of the king's predestination to rule appears again in *The Story of Sinuhe*, the official who ran away and ended up living in Syro-Palestine for much of his life. When describing the king to one of the foreign rulers, Sinuhe breaks into poetic style and begins: "He is a god without peer, No other comes before him; He is lord of knowledge, wise planner, skilled leader, One goes and comes by his will"; and then after bragging about the king's military skills, states: the "Victor while yet in the egg, Set to be ruler since his birth . . . He is unique, god-given" (Lichtheim 1973, 226).

Another important text that sheds light on the loyalty expected of elite officials in the reign of Senusret I is the so-called *Loyalist Instructions*. The emphasis on loyalty became a common theme in texts in the later Eleventh Dynasty, and it continued with the Middle Kingdom (Landgráfová 2019, 93). Being loyal to the king "was the most important aspect of ruling-class life"

(Grajetzki 2006, 160). This text is attributed to Mentuhotep, Senusret I's treasurer, who later in his reign became overseer of the king's works and vizier (Allen 2003b, 20–21, 25), although the first known copy is that on a stela from Abydos belonging to Sehetepibra, the royal seal-bearer and chief deputy treasurer of King Senwosret III (Leprohon 2009, 277). Sehetepibra copied parts of the autobiography of Mentuhotep from a stela at Abydos, and some scholars believe that the *Loyalist Instructions* were also copied from a text belonging to Mentuhotep (Simpson 1991, 337).

Assmann describes the *Loyalist Instructions* as an "educational text" written to ensure that members of the elite stay loyal to the kings of the new Twelfth Dynasty "by appealing to their innermost selves" (Assmann 1996, 136). The first few lines of the text demand: "Venerate the king in the inside of your bodies! Pledge allegiance to His Majesty in your hearts!" (Assmann 1996, 137; Posener 1976, 19). Assmann proposes that all the propagandistic literature, the *Building Inscription, The Story of Sinuhe*, and the *Loyalist Instructions*, were written for the same reason: "to impose pharaonic rule not just as a political system, but rather as a religion" (Assmann 1996, 142).

It has been suggested that Senusret I constructed the first large temple of the sun god at Heliopolis, changing a brick structure into stone and enlarging what earlier structure, or structures, had been there in the Old Kingdom. Quirke wonders if the Berlin Leather Roll is "indirect evidence" that Senusret's building at Heliopolis "made an impression on ancient posterity" (Quirke 2001, 87) and that is why a later scribe was interested in copying the text. It is not really known what was at Heliopolis in the Old Kingdom. Early excavators found blocks of a chapel of Netjerikhet at Heliopolis, but they could have been taken there sometime later. When Userkaf built the first of the sun temples of the Fifth Dynasty, it is assumed that its plan followed the plan of a sun temple at Heliopolis, but there is no actual proof. Although Menkaura's pyramid is off by a couple of meters, the southeast corners of the pyramids of Khufu and Khafra are on a line straight to Heliopolis. If they were purposely aligned this way, there must have been something tall or large enough at Heliopolis to be seen at a distance and make such an alignment possible. The first monument actually known to have been at Heliopolis is the quartzite obelisk of Teti I, which was not terribly tall, possibly 3 meters (Habachi 1977, 42). There was also a Heliopolis obelisk of Pepy I, later taken to Bubastis, but there are only fragments left.

The site of ancient Heliopolis is greatly damaged, suffering from a high water table and partially covered by modern buildings. Monuments preserved from the time of Senusret I are few. His obelisk is the biggest and most complete of what is left. It is pink granite and one of a pair; the other one fell down in 1158 CE (Habachi 1977, 48–49). A granite lintel with his titulary and that of his father, Amenemhat I, was found at Heliopolis in the late 1980s. Three quartzite blocks with the name of Senusret I were found reused in the Bab el-Tawfik in Cairo (Postel and Régen 2005). One is a block, with divisions marking four years of temple offerings, although none of the year entries are completely preserved. Across the top, it reads: "Senusret has done this as his monument for the *bau* (souls) of Heliopolis, the lords of the great temple of Heliopolis" (Postel and Régen 2005, 289, fig. 6). The donations include objects of metal and stone, as well as various food stuffs and animals for sacrifice. Different sanctuaries are named as recipients of these donations, including the temple of Hathor Nebet-hepet, "The Lady of Offerings," a cult perhaps founded by Senusret I (Postel and Régen 2005, 283). The second block is a door jamb with part of the king's name preserved. The third piece is the curved top of a stela. The names of the king are on each side, and in the middle is written "Atum, lord of Heliopolis," facing one way, and the "*bau* of Heliopolis, the lords of the great temple," written the other way (Postel and Régen 2005, 293, fig. 10).

In terms of administrative structure, the early Twelfth Dynasty is a combination of Old Kingdom practice along with the changes made under Mentuhotep II. The evidence is provided by private stelae and tomb inscriptions with titles, so not every part of Egypt will have equal evidence. Mentuhotep II's unification of Egypt "did not lead to a greater administrative homogeneity in the country" (Willems 2013, 384); quite the opposite. In Upper Egypt, the area that had been controlled by the Thebans, there was a governor, or nomarch. In Elephantine, Sarenput I, who was followed by his son, Sarenput II, and the other provincial centers had mayors, who were much below the status of a nomarch. In the area of northern Upper Egypt that had been controlled by the Heracleopolitans, there were also nomarchs, and in Asyut, Deir el-Bersheh and Beni Hasan, "no break in the line of nomarchs seems to occur after the Unification of Egypt" (Willems 2013, 385n134). At *Itja-tawy* was the king and the royal residence, with the high officials of the central administration, headed by the vizier, the steward, the overseer of the seal, and the overseer of the treasury. These high officials had mastabas at Lisht near the pyramid of the king. Most of these men were Theban "but a few were clearly from other parts of the country" (Allen 2003b, 14). In the early Middle Kingdom, there is some evidence that there could be more than one vizier (Grajetzki 2009, 22), and it seems, as in the later Old Kingdom, that an official could be a vizier in one of the provincial areas if needed. Like the Fifth and Sixth Dynasties of the Old Kingdom, and after, members of the royal family did not hold bureaucratic positions.

CONCLUSION

KINGSHIP AND ANCIENT EGYPTIAN CIVILIZATION ARE VIRTUALLY synonymous. Rule by a single king over the land of Egypt began in around 3300 BCE and was intrinsic to the country thereafter: pharaoh was Egypt. When central control came undone, as it did at the end of the Old Kingdom, the state was reunited and re-formed by a king claiming divine birth and authority, returning to the basic tenets of kingship developed early on in the first few dynasties and cemented in place by the beginning of the Old Kingdom. As seen in late Predynastic Hierakonpolis, the power of the king was symbolized quite physically not only in the strength of wild animals but in the ability to defeat them. The king's control of chaos, in the form of hunting animals and defeating foreigners, was depicted in art for the rest of pharaonic history.

The king rested his legitimacy on his identification with Horus, son of Osiris who inherited his father's kingship, as well as his descent from the sun god, Ra, the creator of all. Evidence of the king's relationship with the sun god can be seen beginning with the decorated ivory comb of King Djet and certainly clearly stated by the early Fourth Dynasty with King Sneferu's alignment of the pyramid complex from east to west, with the pyramid symbolizing the king's place of ascension. The king's father was the sun god and his mother was the goddess Hathor. As the sun god's wife, Hathor was also the king's wife, and so the queen of Egypt was Hathor. This divine position of the queen is not as well evidenced as the king's position as Ra, however. At times, the king's devotion to his mother, Hathor, such as in the reign of Mentuhotep II, becomes central to claiming legitimate kingship. Earlier relationships of the king and Hathor can be seen in the *meret* sanctuaries and sun temples, as well as in the statuary of the king with Hathor, such as the dyads and triads found in the valley temple of King Menkaura at Giza. Hathor is also closely associated with the goddesses Bastet and Sakhmet, and they can be interchangeable.

The kings of the early Old Kingdom built huge pyramid structures to make their power clear, and Sneferu even placed small pyramids throughout the provinces as local statements of the king's presence. In the late Fifth Dynasty, Pyramid Texts are inscribed in the pyramid chambers and clearly state the identification of the deceased king with that of the god Osiris. With the Twelfth Dynasty of the Middle Kingdom, King Senusret I stated his legitimacy in other ways as well. One was an extensive campaign of temple building in both Upper and Lower Egypt, and another took the form of literary works that extolled his rule as predestined by the gods and that loyalty to the king could not be questioned. With these types of literary texts appearing for the first time, one has to ask if this means that propaganda for his kingship was needed to be directed to the elite, as they were the ones who were literate; the physical statement of an enormous pyramid or colossal standing statue is clear to anyone.

Many facets of ancient Egyptian kingship, such as royal family relationships, cannot yet be understood. Except for the Fourth Dynasty, not much is known about the king's brothers. In the Fourth Dynasty, the princes are given the highest titles, such as vizier, and also carried out the responsibilities for the king's daily life in the palace. There is also some slight evidence of brother–sister marriage among royal siblings. Horus, the son of Osiris and Isis, was an only child; did that myth affect the status and position of the siblings of Horus the king? There does not seem to have ever been a title of "brother of the king," which might indicate that such a title simply could not exist.

Until the Middle Kingdom at Bubastis, Egyptologists have no archaeological remains of a harem and little knowledge of who lived in it and how it functioned. Only later, in the New Kingdom, from the reigns of King Amenhotep III, King Ramses II, and King Ramses III, is there both good archaeological and textual evidence for harems. In the Middle Kingdom, in particular, there is evidence that princesses either married their brother, the king, or did not marry. Unfortunately, the pyramid complexes of Amenemhat I and Senusret I are so badly damaged that there is scant evidence of their female family members.

The king marrying a sister or half-sister was documented earlier in the Fourth Dynasty and the Eleventh Dynasty; it also seems to have happened in the Seventeenth and early Eighteenth Dynasties of the New Kingdom. These were all times when there seems to have been a new family line claiming the kingship, and so this marriage pattern might have been a way to keep power concentrated within the family. It might also, since deities married siblings, have been a statement of divinity and therefore divine legitimacy to rule.

Even as divine the king needed help with control over the country, and early on the ancient Egyptians developed an efficient administrative structure to manage the resources of the country, all of which technically belonged the crown. A central administration headed by a vizier, and a provincial administration relying on nomarchs or mayors, began as early as the first two dynasties and was the backbone of government from then on. At first, all high offices were held by royal family members, but by the Fifth Dynasty that was no longer sustainable and men from elite families took over these jobs, often marrying a royal daughter as well. In the Old Kingdom, administrative power was centered in the Memphite area until into the Sixth Dynasty when the provincial nomarchs of Upper Egypt took on more control. With the breakdown of central government in the First Intermediate Period, nomarchs functioned as mini-kings and took care of their territory and people.

With King Mentuhotep II, the later Eleventh Dynasty reunites Egypt and begins what scholars call the Middle Kingdom, although Mentuhotep II remains in power and rules from Thebes. This king set about to present his legitimacy and power very much in the tradition of the Fourth Dynasty. He marries his sister, although she is not the mother of his successor. He proclaims that he is son of Hathor and builds numerous chapels connected to her. His funerary temple on the west side of Thebes was built on an area that was sacred to Hathor, and chapels for and burials of Hathor priestesses are incorporated into his temple. His temple sanctuary included a statue of the god Amen, of Karnak temple, and it has been suggested that the outer square of the temple had a solar altar on top of it. A solar altar is thought to have existed in Karnak temple at that time as well.

The early Twelfth Dynasty completes a re-formation of kingship in the tradition of the Old Kingdom by the king returning to the Memphite area to live and rule, as well as building pyramid complexes once again, at Lisht. Amenemhat I, the first king of this dynasty, is assassinated in the thirtieth year of his reign, resulting in a determined and extensive campaign of propaganda to uphold the rule of his son, Senusret I. Although the details of the king's death are unknown, two literary texts, *The Instructions of Amenemhat* and *The Story of Sinuhe*, indicate that it must have been the result of a harem conspiracy, just as in the earlier attempts on the king known from the Sixth Dynasty.

It would be very interesting to understand the makeup of a king's harem at this time. Did queens from earlier reigns continue to live in and be part of the harem? If so, it would be logical to assume that they would want their sons to take the throne. Although some scholars disagree, it would appear that throughout the Twelfth Dynasty there were co-regencies, so that the father king and his son and successor ruled together during the latter part of each reign, protecting their hold on the throne. How a co-regency with two kings would affect the structure of the harem and its inhabitants has never really been considered.

The early Twelfth Dynasty ruled the country with a handful of elite officials overseeing the administration. There was no intermarriage between princesses and high officials, however. This situation changes somewhat in the latter part of the dynasty, when the last existing nomarchs' sons are absorbed into the central administration, and from then on mayors in the nome capitals connect the provinces to the government.

This book began with an explanation of the background and origin of ancient Egyptian civilization in order to present the beginning of divine rule and the formation of the Egyptian state that led to the power and legitimacy of the ancient Egyptian king for the period of the Old Kingdom through the re-formation of a unified Egypt in the Twelfth Dynasty of the Middle Kingdom. In many ways, it is astonishing how much information Egyptologists have discovered about this period of ancient Egyptian civilization, although there is still so very much that is not yet understood. Hopefully the glimpses into the architectural monuments, family members, and government elite of the kings of this period will contribute to further understanding of the divine basis of ancient Egyptian kingship and how it was expressed and maintained.

BIBLIOGRAPHY

Abd el-Raziq, Mahmoud, Georges Castel, Pierre Tallet, and Victor Ghica. *Les inscriptions d'Ayn Soukhna*. Cairo: Institut Français d'Archéologie Orientale, 2002.

Adam, Chehata. "Report on the excavations of the Department of Antiquities at Ezbet Rushdi." *Annales du Service des Antiquties de l'Égypte* 56 (1959): 207–226.

Adams, Matthew, and David O'Connor. "The Royal Mortuary Enclosures of Abydos and Hierakonpolis." In *Treasures of the Pyramids*, edited by Zahi Hawass, 78–85. Vercelli: White Star, 2003.

AERAgram, "Pyramid Age Bakery Reconstructed." *AERAgram* 1 (1996): 6–7.

Afifi, Mahmoud. "King Userkare." In *Scribe of Justice, Egyptological Studies in Honour of Shafik Allam*, edited by Zahi Hawass, Khaled Daoud, and Ramadan Hussein, 55–58. Cairo: Ministry of State for Antiquities, 2011.

Ager, Sheila. "Familiarity Breeds: Incest and the Ptolemaic Dynasty." *The Journal of Hellenic Studies* 125 (2005): 1–34.

Ahram Online. "Fifth Dynasty Tomb and Name of a New Queen Discovered at Saqqara." English.ahram.org.eg. April 2, 2019.

Alexanian, Nicole. "Die Reliefdekoration des Chasechemui aus dem sogenannten *Fort* in Hierakonpolis." In *Les critères de datation stylistiques à l'ancien empire*, edited by Nicolas Grimal, 1–30. Cairo: Institut Français D'Archéologie Orientale, 1997.

Alexanian, Nicole. "The Relief Decoration of Khasekhemwy at the Fort." *Nekhen News* 11 (1999): 14–15.

Alexanian, Nicole, and Felix Arnold. "The Complex of the Bent Pyramid as a Landscape Design Project." In *10. Ägyptologische Tempeltagung: Ägyptische Tempel zwischen Normierung und Individualität*, edited by Martina Ullmann, 1–16. Wiesbaden: Harrassowitz, 2016.

Allam, Schafik. *Beiträge zum Hathorkult (bis zum Ende des Mittleren Reiches)*. Berlin: Bruno Hessling, 1963.

Allen, James. *The Ancient Egyptian Pyramid Texts*. Atlanta: Society for Biblical Literature, 2005.

Allen, James. "Why a Pyramid? Pyramid Religion." In *The Treasures of the Pyramids*, edited by Zahi Hawass, 22–27. Vercelli: White Star, 2003a.

Allen, James. "The High Officials of the Early Middle Kingdom." In *The Theban Necropolis: Past, Present and Future*, edited by Nigel Strudwick and John Taylor, 14–29. London: British Museum, 2003b.

Allen, James. "Some Theban Officials of the Early Middle Kingdom." In *Studies in Honor of William Kelly Simpson*, vol. 1, edited by Peter Der Manuelian, 1–26. Boston: Museum of Fine Arts, 1996.

Allen, James. "Re-wer's Accident." In *Studies in Pharaonic Religion and Society in Honour of J. Gwyn Griffiths*, edited by Alan Lloyd, 14–20. London: Egypt Exploration Society, 1992.

Altenmüller, Hartwig. "Der Himmelsaufstieg des Grabherrn: Zu den Szenen des *zšš w3d* in den Gräbern des Alten Reiches." *Studien zur Altägyptischen Kultur* 30 (2002): 1–42.

Altenmüller, Hartwig. "Old Kingdom: Fifth Dynasty, and Sixth Dynasty." In *Oxford Encyclopedia of Ancient Egypt*, edited by Donald Redford, 597–605. Oxford: Oxford University Press, 2001.

Altenmüller, Hartwig. "Das 'Fest des Weissen Nilpferds' und das 'Opfergefilde'." *Hommages à Jean Leclant*, vol. 1, 29–44. Cairo: Institut Français d'Archéologie Orientale, 1994.

Altenmüller, Hartwig. "Bemerkungen zur frühen und späten Bauphase des Djoserbezirkes in Saqqara." *Mitteilungen des Deutschen Archäologischen Instituts, Abteilung Kairo* 28 (1972): 1–12.

Angevin, Raphaël. "The Hidden Egyptian Workshop: The Lithic Grave Goods of King Khasekhemwy." *Antiquity* 89 (2015): 818–837.

Arnold, Dieter. *The Pyramid Complex of Amenemhat I at Lisht: The Architecture.* New York: Metropolitan Museum of Art, 2015a.

Arnold, Dieter. "Some Thoughts on the Building History of the temple of Mentuhotep Nebhepetre at Deir el-Bahri." *Bulletin of the Egyptological Seminar* 19 (2015b): 59–68.

Arnold, Dieter. *The Monuments of Egypt: An A–Z Companion to Ancient Egyptian Architecture.* Cairo: American University in Cairo Press, 2009.

Arnold, Dieter. "The Tombs of the Queens of Mentuhotep II." In *Queens of Egypt, From Hetepheres to Cleopatra*, edited by Christiane Ziegler, 94–101. Monaco and Paris: Grimaldi Forum and Somogy Art, 2008.

Arnold, Dieter. "Buried in Two Tombs? Remarks on 'Cenotaphs' in the Middle Kingdom." In *The Archaeology and Art of Ancient Egypt: Essays in Honor of David B. O'Connor*, edited by Zahi Hawass and Janet Richards, 55–62. Cairo: Conseil Suprême des Antiquities de l'Égypte, 2007a.

Arnold, Dieter. *Middle Kingdom Tomb Architecture at Lisht.* New York: Metropolitan Museum of Art, 2007b.

Arnold, Dieter. "Eine verlorene Pyramide?" In *Es werde niedergelegt als Schriftstück: Festschrift für Hartwig Altenmüller zum 65. Geburtstag*, edited by Nicole Kloth, Karl Martin, and Eva Pardey, 7–10. Hamburg: Helmet Buske, 2003.

Arnold, Dieter. "Royal Cult Complexes of the Old and Middle Kingdoms." In *Temples of Ancient Egypt*, edited by Byron Shafer, 31–85. Ithaca, NY: Cornell University Press, 1997.

Arnold, Dieter. *The Pyramid Complex of Senwosret I.* New York: Metropolitan Museum of Art, 1992.

Arnold, Dieter. *The Pyramid of Senwosret I.* New York: Metropolitan Museum of Art, 1988.

Arnold, Dieter. *The Temple of Mentuhotep at Deir el-Bahari.* New York: Metropolitan Museum of Art, 1979.

Arnold, Dieter. "Rituale und Pyramidentempel." *Mitteilungen des Deutschen Archäologischen Instituts, Kairo* 33 (1977): 1–14.

Arnold, Dieter. *Gräber des Alten und Mittleren Reiches in El-Tarif.* Mainz: Zabern, 1976.

Arnold, Dieter. *Der Tempel des Königs Mentuhotep von Deir el-Bahari*, vols. 1 and 2. Mainz: Philipp von Zabern, 1974.

Arnold, Dieter, and Dorothea Arnold. "A New Start from the South: Thebes during the Eleventh Dynasty." In *Ancient Egypt Transformed, The Middle Kingdom*, edited by Adele Oppenheim, Dorothea Arnold, and Kei Yamamoto, 38–41. New York: Metropolitan Museum of Art, 2015.

Arnold, Dieter, and Peter Jánosi. "The Move to the North: Establishing a New Capital." In *Ancient Egypt Transformed: The Middle Kingdom*, edited by A. Oppenheim, Dorothea Arnold, Dieter Arnold, and Kei Yamamoto,

58–67. New York: Metropolitan Museum of Art, 2015.

Arnold, Dorothea. "Royal reliefs." In *Egyptian Art in the Age of the Pyramids*, edited by Dorothea Arnold, Christiane Ziegler, and James P. Allen, 83–102. New York: Metropolitan Museum of Art, 1999a.

Arnold, Dorothea. "Scenes from a King's Thirty-Year Jubilee." In *Egyptian Art in the Age of the Pyramids*, edited by Dorothea Arnold, Christiane Ziegler, and James P. Allen, 196–198. New York: Metropolitan Museum of Art, 1999b.

Arnold, Dorothea. "Amenemhat I and the Early Twelfth Dynasty at Thebes." *Metropolitan Museum Journal* 26 (1991): 5–48.

Arnold, Felix. "The Necropolis of Dashur: Thirteenth Excavation Report of the work in spring 2016." Cairo: German Archaeological Institute, 2016.

Assmann, Jan. *The Mind of Egypt: History and Meaning in the Time of the Pharaohs*. New York: Metropolitan Books, 1996.

Awadalla, Atef. "Un document prouvant la corrégence d'Amenemhat et de Sesostris I." *GöttingerMiszellen* 115 (1990): 7–14.

Baines, John. *High Culture and Experience in Ancient Egypt*. Sheffield and Bristol: Equinox, 2013.

Baines, John. "Origins of Egyptian Kingship." In *Ancient Egyptian Kingship*, edited by David O'Connor and David Silverman, 95–156. Leiden: Brill, 1995.

Bárta, Miroslav. *Analyzing Collapse: The Rise and Fall of the Old Kingdom*. Cairo: American University in Cairo Press, 2019.

Bárta, Miroslav. "'Abusir Paradigm' and the Beginning of the Fifth Dynasty." In *The Pyramid: Between Life and Death: Proceedings of a Conference Held in Uppsala May 31–June 1*, edited by Irmgard Hein, Nils Billing, and Erika Meyer-Dietrich, 51–74. Uppsala: Uppsala University, 2016.

Bárta, Miroslav. "Long Term or Short Term? Climate Change and the Demise of the Old Kingdom." In *Climate Change and Ancient Societies*, edited by Susanne Kerner, Rachael Dann, and Pernille Bangsgaard, 177–195. Copenhagen: Museum Tusculanum Press, 2015.

Bárta, Miroslav. "Kings, Viziers and Courtiers: Executive Power in the Third Millennium B.C." *Ancient Egyptian Administration*, edited by Juan Carlos Moreno García, 153–176. Leiden and Boston: Brill, 2013a.

Bárta, Miroslav. "The Sun Kings of Abusir and Their Entourage: 'Speakers of Nekhen of the King.'" In *Diachronic Trends in Ancient Egyptian History*, edited by Miroslav Bárta and Hella Küllmer, 24–31. Prague: Charles University in Prague, Faculty of Arts, 2013b.

Bárta, Miroslav. "Architectural Innovations in the Development of the Non-Royal Tomb." In *Structure and Significance: Thoughts on Ancient Egyptian Architecture*, edited by Peter Jánosi, 105–130. Vienna: Verlag der Österreichischen Akademie der Wissenschaften, 2005.

Bárta, Miroslav. "The Title Inspektor of the Palace." *Archív Orientálni* 67 (1999): 1–20.

Bárta, Miroslav. "Archaeology and Iconography: *bd3* and *'prt* bread moulds and 'Speisetischszene' in the Old Kingdom." *Studien zur Altägyptischen Kultur* 22 (1995): 21–36.

Bárta, Miroslav, and Veronika Duliková. "Politics of Religious Symbols: Maat as a Concept of Rule, justice and Kingship." *EDAL* 6 (2017): 26–41.

Bárta, Miroslav, and Veronika Duliková. "Divine and Terrestial: The Rhetoric of Power in Ancient Egypt (The Case of Nyuserra)." In *Royal versus Divine Authority: Acquisition, Legitimization and Renewal of Power*, edited by Filip Coppens, Jiří Janák, and

Hana Vymaalová, 31–48. Wiesbaden: Harrassowitz, 2015.

Barta, Winfried. "Zur Lokalisierung und Bedeutung der mrt-Bauten." *Zeitschrift für ägyptische Sprache und Altertumskunde* 110 (1983): 98–104.

Batrawi, Ahmed. "Skeletal Remains from the Northern Pyramid of Sneferu." *Annales du Service des antiquities de l'Egypte* 51 (1951): 435–440.

Baud, Michel. "The Old Kingdom." In *A Companion to Ancient Egypt*, edited by Alan Lloyd, 63–80. Chichester: Wiley-Blackwell, 2014.

Baud, Michel. "Dynasties 6 and 8." In *Ancient Egyptian Chronology*, edited by Erik Hornung, Rolf Krauss, and David Warburton, 144–158. Leiden: Brill, 2006.

Baud, Michel. "Le palais en temple: Le culte funéraire des rois d'Abousir." In *Abusir and Saqqara in the Year 2000*, edited by Miroslav Bárta and Jaromír Krejčí, 347–360. Prague: Academy of Sciences of the Czech Republic, Oriental Institute, 2000.

Baud, Michel. "Études sur la statuaire de Rèdjedef: Rapport préliminaire sur la collection de l'Ifao." In *L'art de l'Ancien Empire égyptien: Actes du colloque organisé au Museé du Louvre par le Service culturel*, edited by Christiane Ziegler, 35–61. Paris: La documentation française, 1999a.

Baud, Michel. *Famille royale et pouvoir sous l'ancien empire égyptien*, vols. 1 and 2. Cairo: Institut Français d'Archéologie Orientale, 1999b.

Baud, Michel, and Vassil Dobrev. "De nouvelles annales de l'Ancien Empire égyptiens: Une "Pierre de Palerme" pour la VIe dynastie." *Bulletin de L'Institut Français d'Archéologie Orientale* 95 (1995): 23–92.

Baud, Michel, Dominique Farout, Yannis Gourdon, Nadine Moeller, and Auréliè Schenk. "Le cimetière d'Abou Rawach, nécropole royale de Rêdjedef (IVe dynastie)." *Bulletin de L'Institut Françíais d'Archéologie Orientale* 103 (2003): 17–71.

Baud, Michel, and Nadine Moeller. "A Fourth Dynasty royal necropolis at Abu Rawash." *Egyptian Archaeology* 28 (2006): 16–18.

Beckerath, Jürgen von. *Chronologie der Pharaonischen Ägypten*. Mainz: Philipp von Zabern, 1997.

Begelsbacher-Fischer, Barbara. *Untersuchungen zur Götterwelt des Alten Reiches*. Freiburg and Göttingen: Universitätsverlag and Vandenhoeck and Rupert, 1981

Behrmann, Almuth. *Das Nilpferd in der Vorstellungswelt der Alten Ägypter: Katalog*. Frankfurt am Main: Peter Lang, 1989.

Berger-El Naggar, Catherine, and Marie-Noëlle Fraisse. "Béhéou, 'aimée de Pépy', une nouvelle reine d'Égypte." *Bulletin de l'Institut Français d'Archéologie Orientale* 108 (2008): 1–27.

Berlev, Oleg. "Two Kings – two sons: On the worldview of the ancient Egyptians." In *Discovering Egypt from the Neva: The Egyptology Legacy of Oleg D. Berlev*, edited by Stephen Quirke, 19–35. Berlin: Achet-Verlag, 2003.

Berlev. Oleg. "The Eleventh Dynasty in the Dynastic History of Egypt." In *Studies Presented to Hans Jakob Polotsky*, edited by Dwight Young, 361–377. East Gloucester, MA: Pirtle and Polson, 1981.

Berman, Lawrence. "Amenemhat I." Ph.D. dissertation, Yale University, 1985.

Bestock, Laurel. *The Development of the Royal Cult at Abydos: Two Funerary Enclosures from the Reign of Aha*. Wiesbaden: Harrassowitz Verlag, 2009.

Bestock, Laurel. "The Early Dynastic Funerary Enclosures of Abydos." *Archaeo-Nil* 18 (2008a): 42–59.

Bestock, Laurel "The Evolution of Royal Ideology: New Discoveries from the Reign of Aha." In *L'Egypte pré-et proto-dynastique: Les origins de l'Etat. Predynastic* and Early Dynastic Egypt. Origin of the State. Toulouse (France) – 5–8 sept. 2005, edited by Béatrix Midant-Reynes and Yann Tristant with Joanne Rowland and Stan Hendrickx, 1091–1106. Leuven: Peeters, 2008b.

Bietak, Manfred, and Josef Dorner. "Der Tempel und die Siedlung des Mittleren Reichs bei 'Ezbet Ruschdi.'" *Ägypten und Levante* 8 (1998): 9–40.

Billing, Nils. *The Performative Structure: Ritualizing the Pyramid of Pepy I.* Leiden and Boston: Brill, 2018.

Billing, Nils. "Monumentalizing the Beyond: Reading the Pyramid before and after Pyramid Texts." *Studien zur Altägyptischen Kultur* 40 (2011): 53–66.

Bissing, F. W. von. *Das Re-Heiligtum der Königs Ne-Woser-Re (Rathures).* Berlin: Alexander Duncker, 1905.

Bissing, F. W. von, and Hermann Kees. *Das Re-Heiligtum des Königs Ne-Woser-Re (Rathures),* vol. 2: *Die kleine Festdarstellung.* Leipzig: J.C. Hinrichs'sche Buchhandlung, 1923.

Bleeker, C. J. *Hathor and Thoth: Two Key Figures of the Ancient Egyptian Religion.* Leiden: Brill, 1973.

Blyth, Elizabeth. *Karnak: Evolution of a Temple.* London: Routledge, 2006.

Borchardt, Ludwig. *Statuen und Statuetten von Königen und Privatleuten,* Catalogue Général I, Berlin, 1911.

Borchardt, Ludwig. *Das Grabdenkmal des Königs Sa-hu-re,* 3 vols. Leipzig: Hinrichs Verlag, 1910–1913.

Borchardt, Ludwig. *Das Grabdenkmal des Königs Ne-User-Re.* Leipzig: Hinrichs Verlag 1907.

Borchardt, Ludwig. *Das Re-Heiligtumdes Königs Ne-woser-re,* vol. 1. Berlin: Alexander Duncker, 1905.

Brovarski, Edward. "Overseers of Upper Egypt in the Old to Middle Kingdoms." *Zeitschrift für Ägyptische Spache und Altertumskunde* 140 (2013): 91–11.

Brovarski, Edward. "Abydos in the Old Kingdom and First Intermediate Period, Part II." In *For His Ka: Essays Offered in Memory of Klaus Baer,* edited by David Silverman, 15–44. Chicago: Oriental Institute of the University of Chicago, 1994.

Bryan, Betsy M. "Administration in the reign of Thutmose III". In *Thutmose III: A New Biography,* edited by Eric Cline and David O'Connor, 69–122. Ann Arbor: University of Michigan Press, 2006.

Buraselis, Kostas. "The problem of the Ptolemaic Sibling Marriage: A Case of Dynastic Acculturation?" In *Ptolemy II Philadelphus and His World,* edited by Paul McKechnie and Philippe Guillaum, 291–302. Leiden: Brill, 2008.

Bussmann, Richard. "Scaling the State: Egypt in the Third Millennium BC." *Archaeology International* 17 (2014): 79–93.

Bussmann, Richard. "Der Kult für die Königsmutter Anchenes-Merire I im Tempel Chontamenti. Zwei unpublizierte Türstürze der 6. Dynastie aus Abydos." *Studien zur Altägyptischen Kultur* 39 (2010): 101–119.

Callender, Vivienne. "Some Sixth Dynasty Queens: An historical perspective." In *Abusir and Saqqara in the Year 2015,* edited by Miroslav Bárta, Filip Coppens, and Jaromír Krejčí, 39–51. Prague: Faculty of Arts, Charles University, 2017.

Callender, Vivienne. "It's All in the Family: A 6th Dynasty Conundrum." In *Rich and Great: Studies in Honour of Anthony J. Spalinger on the Occasion of his 70th Feast of Thoth,* edited by Renata Landgráfová and Jana Mynárová, 19–28. Prague: Charles University, Faculty of Arts, 2016.

Callender, Vivienne. "Case Study of an Ancient Royal Woman: Queen Neith and the 6th Dynasty." In *Sex and the Golden Goddess II: World of the Love Songs,* edited by Hana Navratilova and Renata Langráfová, 1–13. Prague: Czech Institute of Egyptology, 2015.

Callender, Vivienne. "Queen Neit-ikrety /Nitokris." In *Abusir and Saqqara in the*

Year 2010, vol. 1, edited by Miroslav Bárta, Filip Coppens, and Jaromír Krejčí, 246–260. Prague, Czech Institute of Egyptology and Faculty of Arts, Charles University, 2011a.

Callender, Vivienne. In *Hathor's Image, Vol. 1: The Wives and Mothers of Egyptian Kings from Dynasties 1–VI*. Prague: Charles University, Faculty of Arts, 2011b.

Callender, Vivienne. "Observations on the Position of Royal Daughters in the Old Kingdom." In *Djedkare's Family Cemetery*, edited by Miroslav Verner and Vivienne Callender, 141–156. Prague: Czech Institute of Egyptology and Faculty of the Arts, Charles University, 2002.

Callender, Vivienne. "The Nature of the Egyptian Harim: Dynasties 1–20." *The Australian Centre for Egyptology* 5 (1994): 7–26.

Callender, Vivienne, and Peter Jánosi. "The Tomb of Queen Khamerernebty II at Giza." *Mittleilungen des Deutschen Archäologischen Instituts Abteilung Kairo* 53 (1997): 1–22.

Campagno, Marcelo. "Kinship and Family Relations." In *UCLA Encyclopedia of Egyptology*, edited by Elizabeth Frood and Willeke Wendrich, 2009. digital2.library.ucla.edu/viewItem.do?ark=21198/zz001nf68 f

Carlotti, Jean-François, Ernst Czerny, and Luc Gabolde. "Sondage autour de la plate-forme en grès de la 'Cour du Moyen Empire'." *Cahiers de Karnak* 13 (2010): 111–193.

Carter, Howard. "Report on the Tomb of Mentuhotep 1st at Deir el-Bahari Known as Bab El Hoçan." *Annales du Service des Antiquités de l'Égypte* 2 (1901): 201–205.

Caton-Thompson, Gertrude, and Elinor Gardner. *The Desert Fayum*. London: The Royal Anthropological Institute of Great Britain and Ireland, 1934.

Cerny, Jaroslav. "Consanguineous Marriages in Pharaonic Egypt." *Journal of Egyptian Archaeology* 40 (1954): 23–29.

Cervelló-Autuori, Josep. "The Sun-Religion in the Thinite Age: Evidence and Political Significance." In *Egypt at Its Origins 3: Proceedings of the Third International Conference 'Origin of the State: Predynastic and Early Dynastic Egypt', London 27th July-1st August 2008*, edited by Peter Fiske and Renée Friedman, 1125–1150. Leuven: Peeters, 2011.

Cervelló-Autuori, Josep. "The Origins of Pharaonic Titulary: A Cultural Approach." In *Das alte Ägypten und seine Nachbarn: Festschrift zum 65 Geburtstag von Helmut Satzinger*, edited by Monika Hasitzka, Johannes Diethart, and Günther Dembski, 43–57. Krems: Kremser Wissenschaftliche, 2003.

Cervelló-Autuori, Josep. "Back to the Mastaba tombs of the First Dynasty at Saqqara: Officials or Kings?" In *Egyptological Essays on State and Society*, edited by Rosanna Pirelli, 27–61. Naples: Università degli studi di Napoli L'Orientale, 2002.

Charloux, Guillaume. "The Middle Kingdom Temple of Amun at Karnak." *Egyptian Archaeology* 27 (2005): 20–24.

Charloux, Guillaume, and Romain Mensan. *Karnak avant la XVIIIᵉ dynastie: contributions à l'étude des vestiges en brique crue des premiers temples d'Amon-Rê* (Études d'égyptologie 11). Paris: Soleb, 2012.

Chlodnicki, Marek. "Trade and Exchange in the Predynastic and Early Dynastic Period in the Eastern Nile Delta". In *L'Egypte pré-et protodynastique: Les origines de l'Etat. Predynastic and Early Dynastic Egypt. Origin of the State. Toulouse (France) – 5–8 Sept. 2005*, edited by Béatrix Midant-Reynes and Yann Tristant with Joanne Rowland and

Stan Hendrickx, 489–500. Leuven: Peeters, 2008.

Clarke, Thérèse. "The Overseer of Upper Egypt in Egypt's Old Kingdom: A prosopographical study of the title-holders and a re-examination of the position within the Old Kingdom." BA thesis, Macquarie University, 2009.

Clère, J .J., and J. Vandier. *Textes de la Première Période Intermédiare et de la XIeme Dynastie*. Brussels: La Fondation Égyptologique Reine Élisabeth, 1948.

Cotelle-Michel, Laurence. "Présentation préliminaire des blocs de la chapelle de Sésostris l'er découverte dans le IXe pylône de Karnak." *Cahiers de Karnak* 11 (2003): 339–353.

Couyat, Jules, and Pierre Montet. *Les Inscriptions Hiéroglyphiques et Hiératiques du Ouâdi Hammamat*. Vols. 1 and 2. Cairo: Institut Français d'Archéologie Orientale, 1912–1913.

Ćwiek, Andrzej. "Relief Decoration in the Royal Funerary Complexes of the Old Kingdom: Studies in the Development, Scene Content and Iconography." Ph.D. dissertation, Warsaw University, 2003.

Ćwiek, Andrzej. "Date and Function of the So-called Minor Pyramids." *Göttinger Miszellen* 162 (1998): 39–52.

Daressy, Georges. "La nécropole des grands prêtres d'Héliopolis sous l'Ancien Empire." *Annales du Service des Antiquities d'Égypte* 16 (1916) 193–212.

Daressy, Georges. "Inscriptions hiéoglyphiques trouvées dans le Caire." *Annales du Service des Antiquitiés de l'Egypte* 4 (1903): 101–109.

Darnell, John . "The Eleventh Dynasty Inscription from Deir el-Ballas." *Revue d'Egyptologie* 59 (2008): 81–110.

Darnell, John. "The Route of Eleventh Dynasty Expansioninto Nubia: An Interpretation Based on the Rock Inscriptions of Tjehemau at Abisko." *Zeitschrift für ägyptische Sprache und Altertumskunde* 131 (2004): 23–37.

Dash, Glen. "Solar Alignments of Giza." *AERAgram* 12, 2 (2011): 3–8.

De Buck, Adrian. *Egyptian Readingbook*, vol. 1, Leiden: Nederlandisch Archaeologisch-Philologisch Instituut Voor Het Nabbije Oosten, 1948.

De Rouge, Emmanuel. *Inscriptions Hiéroglyphiques Copiées en Égypte*. Paris: F. Vieweg, 1877.

Debono, Fernand, and Bodil Mortensen. *El Omari: A Neolithic Settlement and Other Sites in the Vicinity of Wadi Hof, Helwan* (Archäologische Veröffentlichungen, Deutsches Archäologisches Institut, Abteilung Kairo 82). Mainz: Philipp von Zabern, 1990.

Delia, Robert. "A New Look at Some Old Dates: A Reexamination of Twelfth Dynasty Double Dated Inscriptions." *Bulletin of the Egyptological Seminar* 1 (1979):15–28.

Delia, Robert. "Doubts about Double Dates and Coregencies." *Bulletin of the Egyptological Seminar* 4 (1982): 55–69.

Derchain-Urtel, Maria-Theresia. "Somtus." In *Lexikon der Ägyptologie*, vol. 5, edited by Wolfgang Helck and Eberhard Otto, 1080–1081. Wiesbaden: Otto Harrassowitz, 1984.

Desroches-Noblecourt, Christiane, and Christian Leblanc. "Considérations sur l'existence desdivers temples de Monthou à traversles ages, dans le site de Tôd: État de la question en octobre 1983." *Bulletin de l'InstitutsFrançais d'Archéologie Orientale* 84 (1984): 81–109.

Das Götterdekret über das Abaton. Denkschriftender Kaiserlichen der Wissenschaften in Wien, Philosophisch-Historische Klasse 56. Vienna: A. Holder, 1913.

Dobrev, Vassil. "The South Saqqara Stone and the Sarcophagus of Queen Mother Ankhenespepy (JE 65908)." In *Abusir and Saqqara in the Year 2000*, edited by Miroslav Bárta and Jaromír Krejčí, 381–386. Prague: Academy of Sciences of the Czech Republic, Oriental Institute, 2000.

Dobrev, Vassil. "Considerations sur les titulatures des rois de la IVe dynastie égyptiennes." *Bulletin de l'Institut Français d'Archéologie Orientale* 93 (1993): 179–204.

Dobrev, Vassil, Audran Labrousse, and Bernard Mathieu. "La dixième pyramide à textes de Saqqâra: Ânkhesenpépy II, Rapport préliminaire de la campagne de fouilles 2000." *Bulletin de l'Institut Français d'Archéologie Orientale* 100 (2000): 275–296.

Dobrev, Vassil, and Jean Leclant. "Nedjeftet. Une nouvelle reine identifiée à Saqqara-Sud." *Bulletin de l'Institut Français d'Archéologie Orientale* 97 (1997): 149–156.

Dodson, Aidan, and Dyan Hilton. *The Complete Royal Families of Ancient Egypt.* Cairo: American University in Cairo Press, 2004.

Dorman, Peter. "The Biographical Inscription of Ptahshepses from Saqqara: A Newly Identified Fragment." *Journal of Egyptian Archaeology* 88 (2002): 95–102.

Dreyer, Günther. "Tomb U-j: A Royal Burial of Dynasty 0 at Abydos." In *Before the Pyramids: The Origins of Egyptian Civilization*, edited by Emily Teeter, 131–138. Chicago: Oriental Institute of the University of Chicago, 2011.

Dreyer, Günther. "Tombs of the First and Second Dynasties." In *Treasures of the Pyramids*, edited by Zahi Hawass, 74–77. Vercelli: White Star, 2003.

Dreyer, Günther. "Der erste König der 3. Dynastie." In *Stationen, Beiträge zur Kulturgeschichte Ägyptens*, edited by Heike Guksch and Daniel Polz, 31–34. Mainz: Philipp von Zabern, 1998.

Dreyer, Günther. "Recent Discoveries in the U-Cemetery at Abydos." In *The Nile Delta in Transition: 4th–3rd Millennium B. C*, edited by Edwin van den Brink, 293–300. Tel Aviv: Pinkhas, 1992.

Dreyer, Günther. "Umm el-Qaab: Nachuntersuchungen im frühzeitlichen Königsfriedhof, 3./4. Vorbericht." *Mitteilungen des Deutschen Archäologischen Instituts, Abteilung Kairo* 46 (1990): 53–90.

Dreyer, Günther. "Ein Siegel der frühzeitlichen Königsnekropole von Abydos." *Mitteilungen des Deutschen Archäologischen Instituts Abteilung Kairo* 43 (1987): 33–43.

Dreyer, Günther, Eva-Maria Engel, Ulrich Hartung, Thomas Hikade, E. Christiana Köhler, and Frauke Pumpenmeier. "Nachuntersuchungen im fühzeitlichen Königsfriedhof, 7/8 Vorbericht." *Mitteilungen des Deutschen Archäologischen Instituts Abteiling Kairo* 52 (1996): 11–81.

Dreyer, Günther, Rita Hartmann, Ulrich Hartung et al. "Umm el-Qaab – Nachuntersuchungen im früzeitlichen Könihgsfriedhof, 13/14/15. Vorbericht." *Mitteilungen des Deutschen Archäologischen Instituts Abteiling Kairo* 59 (2003): 67–138.

Dreyer, Güther, and Werner Kaiser. "Zu den kleinen Stufenpyramiden Ober- und Mittelägyptens." *Mitteilungen des Deutschen Archäologischen Instituts Abteiling Kairo* 36 (1980): 43–59.

Drioton, Étienne. "Une Corégence de Pépi Ier et de Mérenrê (?)." *Annales du Service des Antiquities de l'Égypte* 45 (1947): 55–56.

Dulíková, Veronika. "The Reign of King Nyuserre and Its Impact on the Development of the Egyptian State: A Multiplier Effect Period during the Old Kingdom." Ph.D. dissertation, Charles University, 2016.

Dulíková, Veronika. "Some Notes on the Title of 'Vizier' during the Old Kingdom, Especially on the Hieroglyphic Phallus-Sign in the Vizier's Titles." In *Abusir and Saqqara in the Year 2010/1*, edited by Miroslav Bárta, Filip Coppens, and Jaromír Krejčí, 327–336. Prague: Czech Institute of Egyptology, 2011.

Dulíková, Veronika, and Radek Marík. "Complex Network Analysis in Old Kingdom Society: A Nepotism Case." In *Abusir and Saqqara in the Year 2015*, edited by Miroslav Bárta, Filip Coppens, and Jaromír Krejčí, 63–83. Prague: Faculty of Arts, Charles University, 2017.

Dunham, Dows. "The Biographical Inscriptions of Nekhebu in Boston and Cairo." *Journal of Egyptian Archaeology* 24, (1938): 1–8.

Dunham, Dows, and William Kelly Simpson. *The Mastaba of Queen Mersyankh III*. Boston: Museum of Fine Arts, 1974.

Edel, Elmar, and Steffen Wenig. *Die Jahreszeitenreliefs aus den Sonnenheiligtum des Königs Ne-user-Re*. Berlin: Akademie Verlag, 1974.

Edwards, I. E. S. "The Pyramid of Seila and Its Place in the Succession of Snofru's Pyramids." In *Chief of Seers: Egyptian Studies in Memory of Cyril Aldred*, edited by Elizabeth Goring, Nicolas Reeves, and John Ruffle, 88–96. London: Kegan Paul International, 1997.

Edwards, I. E. S. *The Pyramids of Egypt*. Penguin Books, Harmondsworth, 1975.

Edwards, I. E. S. "Lord Dufferin's Excavations at Deir El-Bahri and the Clandeboye Collection." *Journal of Egyptian Archaeology* 51 (1965): 16–28.

Eiwanger, Josef. *Merimde-Benisalame 3: Die Funde der jüngeren Merimdekultur*. Mainz: Von Zabern, 1992.

Eiwanger, Josef. *Merimde-Benisalame 1: Die Funde der Urschicht*. Mainz: Von Zabern, 1984.

El-Awady, Tarek. *Sahure – The Pyramid Causeway: History and Decoration Program in the Old Kingdom. Abusir XVI*. Prague: Charles University in Prague, 2009.

El-Awady, Tarek. "The Royal Family of Sahura: New Evidence." In *Abusir and Saqqara in the Year 2005*, edited by Miroslav Bárta, Filip Coppens, and Jaromír Krejči, 191–218. Prague: Czech Institute of Egyptology and Faculty of Arts, Charles University, 2006

Emery, Walter. *Archaic Egypt*. Baltimore, MD: Penguin Books, 1961.

Emery, Walter. *Great Tombs of the First Dynasty, Vol. 3*. London: Egypt Exploration Society, 1958.

Emery, Walter *Great Tombs of the First Dynasty, Vol. 2*. Oxford: Oxford University Press, 1954.

Emery, Walter. *Great Tombs of the First Dynasty, Vol. 1: Excavations at Saqqara*. Cairo: Government Press, 1949.

Engel, Eva-Maria. "The Organisation of a Nascent State: Egypt until the Beginning of the 4th Dynasty." In *Ancient Egyptian Administration*, edited by Juan Carlos Moreno García, 19–40. Leiden and Boston: Brill, 2013.

Engel, Eva-Maria. "The Royal Tombs at Umm el-Qa'ab," *Archeo-Nil* 18 (2008): 30–41.

Engel, Eva-Maria. "Die Enwicklung des Systems der ägyptischen Nomoi in der Frühzeit." *Mitteilungen des Deutschen Archäologischen Instituts Abteilung Kairo*, 62 (2006): 151–160.

Engel, Eva-Maria. "The Domain of Semerkhet." In *Egypt at its Origins: Studies in Memory of Barbara Adams*, edited by S. Hendrickx, R. Friedman, Krzysztof Cialowicz, and Marek Chlodnicki, 705–710. Leuven: Peeters, 2004.

Ernst, Herbert. "Der Kult in den Opferhöfen der Totentempel des Alten und Mittleren Reiches." *Studien zur Altägyptischen Kultur* 29 (2001): 41–53.

Espinel, A. D. "The Boundary Stelae of Djoser's Funerary Complex at Saqqara: An Interpretation through Artistic and Textual Evidence." In *Egyptology at the Dawn of the Twenty-first Century, Proceedings of the Eighth International Congress of Egyptologists Cairo, 2000*, edited by Zahi Hawass, 215–220. Cairo: American University in Cairo Press, 2003.

Evers, Hans. *Staat aus dem Stein. Denkmäler: Geschichte und bedeutung der Ägyptischen Plastikwährend des Mittleren Reichs.* Munich: Verlag F. Bruckmann, 1929.

Fakhry, Ahmed. *The Monuments of Sneferu at Dahshur, Vol. 2: The Valley Temple, Part I: The Temple Reliefs.* Cairo: Government Press, 1961a.

Fakhry, Ahmed. *The Monuments of Sneferu at Dahshur, Vol. 2: The Valley Temple, Part II: The Finds.* Cairo, Government Press, 1961b.

Faltings, Dina A. "The Chronological Frame and Social Structure of Buto in the Fourth Millennium BCE." In *Egypt and the Levant: Interrelations from the 4th through the early 3rd millennium BCE*, edited by Edwin van den Brink and Thomas Levy, 165–170. London and New York: Leicester University Press, 2002.

Faulkner, R. O. *The Ancient Egyptian Pyramid Texts.* Oxford: Clarendon Press, 1969.

Faulkner, R. O. "The King and the Star-Religion in the Pyramid Texts." *Journal of Near Eastern Studies* 25 (1966): 153–161.

Fay, Biri. "Thoughts on the Sculpture of Sesostris I and Amenemhat II Inspired by the Meket-re Study Day." In *The World of Middle Kingdom Egypt (2000–1550 BC)*, edited by Gianluca Miniaci and Wolfram Grajetzki, 81–83. London: Golden House Publications, 2015.

Fay, Biri. "Royal Women as Represented in Sculpture During the Old Kingdom. Part II: Uninscribed Sculptures." In *L'art de l'Ancien Empire égyptien, Actes du colloque organisé du Louvre par le Service culturel les 3 et 4 avril 1999*, 99–147. Paris: La documentation Française, 1998.

Fay, Biri. "Royal Women as Represented in Sculpture during the Old Kingdom." In *Les critères de datation stylistiques à l'ancien empire*, edited by Nicolas Grimal, 159–186. Cairo: Institut Français D'Archéologie Orientale, 1997.

El-Fikey, Said Amer. *The Tomb of the Vizier Re'-Wer at Saqqara.* Warminister: Aris & Phillips, 1980.

Firth, Cecil, and James Quibell. *The Step Pyramid: Excavations at Saqqara.* Cairo: Imprimerie de l'Institut Français d'Archéologie Orientale, 1935. 2 vols.

Fischer, Henry. *Egyptian Women of the Old Kingdom and of the Heracleopolitan Period.* New York: Metropolitan Museum of Art, 2000.

Fischer, Henry. "Marginalia." *Göttinger Miszellen* 122 (1991): 21–30.

Fischer, Henry. *The Orientation of Hieroglyphs. Part 1: Reversals.* New York: Metropolitan Museum of Art, 1977.

Fischer, Henry. "Some Emblematic Uses of Hieroglyphs with Particular Reference to an Archaic Ritual Vessel." *Metropolitan Museum Journal* 5 (1972): 5–23.

Fischer, Henry. *Dendera in the Third Millennium B.C.* Locust Valley, NY: J. J. Augustin, 1968.

Fischer, Henry. *Inscriptions from the Coptite Nome Dynasties VI–XI.* Rome: Pontificum Institutum Biblicum, 1964.

Fischer, Henry. "A Daughter of the Overlords of Upper Egypt in the First Intermediate Period." *Journal of the American Oriental Society* 76 (1956): 99–110.

Flentye, Laurel. "Royal and Non-royal Statuary of the Fourth Dynasty from the Giza Necropolis." In *Abusir and Saqqara in the Year 2015*, edited by Miroslav Bárta, Filip Coppens, and Jaromír Krejčí, 123–144. Prague: Faculty of Arts, Charles University, 2017.

Flentye, Laurel. "Royal Statuary of the Fourth Dynasty from the Giza Necropolis in the Egyptian Museum, Cairo." *Bulletin of the Egyptological Seminar* 19 (2015): 277–292.

Flentye, Laurel. "The Decorative Programmes of the Pyramid

Complexes of Khufu and Khafre at Giza." In *Old Kingdom, New Perspectives: Egyptian Art and Archaeology, 2750–2150 BC*, edited by N. Strudwick and H. Strudwick, 77–92. Oxford, Oxbow Books, 2011a.

Flentye, Laurel. "The Development of the Giza Necropolis in the Early Fourth Dynasty." In *Abusir and Saqqara in the Year 2010/1*, edited by M. Bárta, F. Coppens, and J. Krejčí, 337–361. Prague: Charles University in Prague, 2011b.

Flentye, Laurel. "The Development of the Eastern and the GIS Cemeteries at Giza during the Fourth Dynasty: The Relationship between Architecture and Tomb Decoration." In *The Old Kingdom Art and Archaeology: Proceedings of the Conference, Prague, May 31–June 4, 2004*, edited by Miroslav Bárta, 133–144. Prague: Publishing House of the Academy of Sciences of the Czech Republic, 2006.

Foster, John. "The Conclusion to the Testament of Ammenemes, King of Egypt." *Journal of Egyptian Archaeology* 67 (1981): 36–47.

Frandsen, Paul. *Incestuous and Close-Kin Marriage in Ancient Egypt and Persia: An Examination of the Evidence*. Copenhagen: Tusculanum Press, 2009.

Franke, Detlef. "The Middle Kingdom in Egypt." In *Civilizations of the Ancient Near East*, edited by J. Sasson, 735–748. New York: Simon and Schuster Macmillan, 1995.

Franke, Detlef. "The career of Khnumhotep III of Beni Hasan and the so-called 'decline of the nomarchs'." In *Middle Kingdom Studies*, edited by Stephen Quirke, 51–68. Surrey: Sia Publishing, 1991.

Franke, Detlef. *Altägyptische Verwandtschaft sbezeichungen im Mittleren Reich*. Hamburg: Borg GMBH, 1983.

Freed, Rita. "Sculpture of the Middle Kingdom." In *A Companion to Ancient Egypt*, edited by Alan Lloyd, 882–912. Chichester: Wiley-Blackwell, 2014.

Freed, Rita. "Observations on the Dating and Decoration of the Tombs of Ihy and Hetep at Saqqara." In *Abusir and Saqqara in the Year 2000*, edited by Miroslav Bárta and Jaromír Krejčí, 207–214. Prague: Academy of Sciences of the Czech Republic, Oriental Institute, 2000.

Freed, Rita. "Relief Styles of the Nebhepetre Montuhotep Funerary Temple Complex." In *Chief of Seers: Egyptian Studies in Memory of Cyril Aldred*, edited by Elizabeth Goring, Nicholas Reeves, and John Ruffle, 148–163. London: Kegan Paul International, 1997.

Friedman, Florence Dunn. "The Names of Menkaure." In *The Perfection that Endues … Studies in Old Kingdom Art and Archaeology*, edited by Kamil Kuraszkiewicz, Edyta Kopp, and Danial Takcs, 124–132. Warsaw: Zaklad Egiptologii, 2018.

Friedman, Florence Dunn. "The Cultic Relationship of the Menkaure Triads to the Small Step Pyramids." In *Royal versus Divine Authority, 7. Symposium zur ägyptischen Königideologie*, edited by Filip Coppens, Jirí Janák, and Hana Vymazalová, 95–108. Wiesbaden: Harrassowitz, 2015a.

Friedman, Florence Dunn. "Economic Implications of the Menkaure Triads." In *Towards a New History for the Egyptian Old Kingdom*, edited by Peter Der Manuelian and Thomas Schneider, 18–59. Leiden: Brill, 2015b.

Friedman, Florence Dunn. "Reading the Menkaure Triads, Part I." In *Palace and Temple: Architecture – Decoration – Ritual. Cambridge, July 16–17, 2007*, edited by Rolf Gundlach and Kate Spence, 1–34. Wiesbaden: Harrassowitz, 2011a.

Friedman, Florence Dunn. "Reading the Menkaure Triads: Part II (Multi-directionality)." In *Old Kingdom, New Perspectives: Egyptian Art and*

Archaeology, 2750–2150 BC, edited by Nigel Strudwick and Helen Strudwick, 93–114. Oxford, Oxbow Books, 2011b.

Friedman, Florence Dunn. "The Menkaure Dyad(s)." In *Egypt and Beyond: Essays Presented to Leonard H. Lesko upon his Retirement from the Wilbour Chair of Egyptology at Brown University June 2005*, edited by Stephen Thompson and Peter Der Manuelian, 109–144. Brown University: Department of Egyptology and Ancient Western Asian Studies, 2008.

Friedman, Florence Dunn. "Notions of Cosmos in the Step Pyramid Complex." In *Studies in Honor of William Kelly Simpson*, vol. 1, edited by Peter Der Manuelian, 337–351. Boston: Museum of Fine Arts, 1996.

Friedman, Florence Dunn. "The Underground Relief Panels of King Djoser at the Step Pyramid Complex." *Journal of the American Research Center in Egypt* 32 (1995): 1–42.

Friedman, Renée "Hierakonpolis." In *Before the Pyramids. The Origins of Egyptian Civilization*, edited by Emily Teeter, 33–44. Chicago: Oriental Institute Publications 33, 2011.

Friedman, Renée "Hierakonpolis Locality HK29A: The Predynastic Ceremonial Center Revisited." *Journal of the American Research Center in Egypt* 45 (2009): 79–103.

Friedman, Renée, "Excavating Egypt's Early Kings: Recent Discoveries in the Elite Cemetery at Hierakonpolis." In *L'Egypte pré-et protodynastique: Les origines de l'Etat. Predynastic and Early Dynastic Egypt. Origin of the State. Toulouse (France) – 5–8 sept. 2005*, edited by Béatrix Midant-Reynes and Yann Tristant with Joanne Rowland and Stan Hendrickx, 1157–1194. Leuven: Peeters, 2008a.

Friedman, Renée. "The Cemeteries of Hierakonpolis." *Archeo-Nil* 18 (2008b): 8–29.

Friedman, Renée. "New Observations on the Fort at Hierakonpolis." In *The Archaeology and Art of Ancient Egypt: Essays in Honor of David B. O'Connor*, vol. 1, edited by Zahi Hawass and Janet Richards, 309–336. Cairo: Supreme Council of Antiquities, 2007.

Friedman, Renée, "Excavating Egypt's Early Kings." *Nekhen News* 17 (2005): 4–6.

Friedman, Renée. "Investigations in the Fort of Khasekhemwy." *Nekhen News* 11 (1999): 8–12.

Friedman, Renée, Wim Van Neer, and Veerle Linseele. "The Elite Predynastic Cemetery at Hierakonpolis: 2009–2010 Update." In *Egypt at Its Origins 3: Proceedings of the Third International Conference 'Origin of the State: Predynastic and Early Dynastic Egypt', London 27th July–1st August 2008*, edited by Peter Fiske and Renée Friedman, 157–191. Leuven: Peeters, 2011.

Gabolde, Luc. *Karnak, Amon-Rê: La Genèse d'un Temple, La Naissance d'un Dieu*. Cairo: Institut Français d'Archéologie Orientale, 2018.

Gabolde, Luc. "The 'Kernbau' of the Temple of Mentuhotep II at Deir el-Bahari: A Monumental Sun Altar?" In *Joyful in Thebes: Egyptological Studies in Honor of Betsy M. Bryan*, edited by Richard Jasnow and Kathlyn Cooney, 145–154. Atlanta: Lockwood Press, 2015.

Gabolde, Luc. "Un assemblage au nom d'Amenemhat Ier dans les magasins du temple de Louxor." In *Causing His Name to Live: Studies in Egyptian Epigraphy and History in Memory of William Murnane*, edited by Peter Brand and Louise Cooper, 103–107. Leiden: Brill, 2009.

Gabolde, Luc. *Le "grand château d'Amon" de Sesostris Ier à Karnak: La decoration du temple d'Amon-Rê au moyen empire* (Mémoires de l'Académie des Inscriptions et des Belles-Lettres,

Nouvelle Série, 17). Paris: Institut de France, 1998.

Galvin, Marianne. "The Priestesses of Hathor in the Old Kingdom and the 1st Intermediate Period." Ph.D. dissertation, Brandeis University, 1981.

Gardiner, Alan. *Egyptian Grammar*, 3rd ed. Oxford: Griffith Institute, 2001.

Gardiner, Alan. *The Royal Canon of Turin*. Oxford: Griffith Institute, 1959.

Gardiner, Alan. "The Mansion of Life and the Master of the King's Largess." *Journal of Egyptian Archaeology* 24 (1938): 83–91.

Gardiner, Alan, and Eric Peet. *The Inscriptions of Sinai*, 2 vols. London: Egypt Exploration Society, 1952 and 1955.

Garstang, John. *Mahasna and Bet Khallaf*. London: Egyptian Research Account, 1901.

Gauthier, Henri. *Le Livre des Rois d'Égypte* vol. 1. Cairo: Institut Français d'Archéologie Orientale, 1907.

Gestermann, Louise. "Hathor, Harsomtus und *Mntw-htp.w* II." In *Studies zu Sprache und Religion Ägyptens: Zu Ehren von Wolfhart Westendorf*, vol. 2, 763–776. Göttingen: Hubert & Co., 1984.

Goedicke, Hans. "Abusir – Saqqara – Giza." In *Abusir and Saqqara in the Year 2000*, edited by Miroslav Bárta and Jaromír Krejčí, 397–412. Prague: Academy of Sciences of the Czech Republic, Oriental Institute, 2000.

Goedicke, Hans. "The Death of Pepy II – Neferkare." *Studien zur Altägyptischen Kultur* 15 (1988): 111–122.

Goedicke, Hans. "The Unification of Egypt under Monthuhotep Neb-hepet-Re (2200 B.C.)." *The Society for the Study of Egyptian Antiquities* 12 (1982): 157–164.

Goedicke, Hans. *Reused Blocks from Lisht*. New York: Metropolitan Museum of Art, 1971.

Goedicke, Hans. *Königliche Dokumente aus dem Alten Reich*. Wiesbaden: Otto Harrassowitz, 1967.

Goedicke, Hans. "Bemerkung zum Alter der Sonnenheiligtümer." *Bulletin de L'Institut Française D'Archéologie Orientale* 56 (1956): 151–153.

Goelet, Ogden, Jr. "The term śtp-s3 in the Old Kingdom and Its Later Development." *Journal of the American Research Center in Egypt* 23 (1986): 85–98.

Gourdon, Yannis. "The Royal Necropolis of Djedefra at Abu Rawash (Seasons 2001–2005)." In *Abusir and Saqqara in the Year 2005*, edited by Miroslav Bárta, Filip Coppens, and Jaromír Krejčí, 247–256. Prague: Charles University in Prague, 2006.

Goyon, Georges. "La chaussée monumentale et le temple de la vallée de la pyramide de Khéops." *Bulletin de l'Institut Français d'Archéologie Orientale* 67 (1967): 49–69.

Gozzoli, Roberto. *The Writing of History in Ancient Egypt during the First Millennium BC (ca. 1070–180 BC): Trends and Perspectives*. London: Golden House Publications, 2006.

Graefe, Erhart. "Die Gute Reputation des Königs 'Snofru'." In *Studies in Egyptology: Presented to Miriam Lichtheim*, vol. 1, edited by Sarah Israelit-Groll, 257–263. Jerusalem: The Magnes Press, 1990.

Grajetzki, Wolfram. "Setting a State Anew: The Central Administration from the End of the Old Kingdom to the End of the Middle Kingdom." In *Ancient Egyptian Administration*, edited by Juan Carlos Moreno García, 215–258. Leiden and Boston: Brill, 2013.

Grajetzki, Wolfram. *Court Officials of the Egyptian Middle Kingdom*. London: Duckworth, 2009.

Grajetzki, Wolfram. *The Middle Kingdom of Ancient Egypt*. London: Duckworth, 2006.

Grajetzki, Wolfram. *Ancient Egyptian Queens: A Hieroglyphic Dictionary*. London: Golden House Publications, 2005.

Griffiths, J. Gwyn. *The Origins of Osiris and His Cult*. Leiden: Brill, 1980.

Grimal, Nicolas. *A History of Ancient Egypt*. Oxford: Blackwell, 1988.

Gundacker, Roman. "The Original Programme of Texts in the Sarcophagus Chamber of King Pepy I." In *The Pyramids, Between Death and Life. Proceedings of the Workshop Held at Uppsala University, Uppsala, May 31–June 1 2012*, edited by Irmgard Hein, Nils Billing, and Erika Meyer-Dietrich, 207–248. Uppsala: Uppsala University, 2016.

Gundacker, Roman. "The Chronology of the Third and Fourth Dynasties According to Manetho's *Aegyptiaca*." In *Towards a New History for the Egyptian Old Kingdom*, edited by Peter Der Manuelian and Thomas Schneider, 76–199. Leiden and Boston: Brill, 2015.

Gundlach, Rolf. "Die Chapelle Blanche und das Tempelbauprogramm Sesostris I. in Theban." In *8. Ägyptologische Tempeltagung: Interconnections between temples, Warschau, 22.–25. September 2008*, edited by Monika Dolińska and Horst Beinlich, 81–109. Wiesbaden: Harrassowitz, 2010.

Gundlach, Rolf. "'Horus in the Palace': The Centre of State and Culture in Pharaonic Egypt." In *Egyptian Royal Residences: 4th Symposium on Egyptian Royal Ideology*, edited by Rolf Gundlach and John Taylor, 45–68. Wiesbaden, Harrassowitz, 2009.

Gundlach, Rolf. *Die Königsideologie Sesostris' I. anhand seiner Titulatur*. Wiesbaden: Harrassowitz, 2008.

Gundlach, Rolf. *Der Pharao und Sein Staat*. Darmstadt: Wissenschaftliche Buchgesellschaft, 1998.

Gundlach, Rolf. "Mentuhotep IV. Und Min – Analyse der Inscriften M 110, M 191 und M192a aus dem Wâdi Hammâmât." *Studien zur Altägyptischen Kultur* 8 (1980): 89–114.

Guyot, Frédéric 2008. "The Origins of the 'Naqadan Expansion' and the Interregional Exchange Mechanisms between Lower Nubia, Upper and Lower Egypt, the South Levant and North Syria during the First Half of the 4th Millennium B.C." In *L'Egypte pré-et protodynastique: Les origins de l'Etat. Predynastic and Early Dynastic Egypt. Origin of the State. Toulouse (France) – 5–8 sept. 2005*, edited by Béatrix Midant-Reynes and Yann Tristant with Joanne Rowland and Stan Hendrickx, 707–740. Leuven: Peeters, 2008.

Haase, Michael. "Tempel und Gärten." In *Ägyptische Gärten*, edited by Christian Tietze, 177–200. Weimar: Christian Tietze Press, 2011.

Habachi, Labib. *The Obelisks of Egypt: Skyscrapers of the Past*. New York: Charles Scribner's, 1977.

Habachi, Labib. *Features of the Deification of Ramesses II*. Glückstadt: J. J. Augustin, 1969.

Habachi, Labib. "King Nebhepetre Menthuhotep: His Monuments, Place in History, Deification and Unusual Representations in the Form of Gods." *Mitteilungen des Deutschen Archäologischen Instituts, Abteilung Kairo*, 19 (1963): 16–52.

Habachi, Labib. "God's fathers and the Role They Played in the History of the First Intermediate Period." *Annales du Service des Antiquitiés de l'Égypte* 55 (1958): 167–190.

Habachi, Labib. *Tell Basta*. Cairo: Institut Français d'Archéologie Orientale, 1957.

Habachi, Labib. "Khatâ'na-Qantir: Importance." *Annales du Service des Antiquités del'Égypte* 52 (1954): 443–562.

Haeny, Gerhard. "New Kingdom "Mortuary Temples" and "Mansions of Millions of Years." In *Temples of Ancient Egypt*, edited by Byron Shafer, 86–226. Ithaca, NY: Cornell University Press, 1997.

Hamdan, Mohamed, Fekri Hassan, Roger Flower, Suzanne Leroy, Nahla Shallaly, and A. Flynn. "Source of Nile Sediments in the Floodplain at Saqqara Inferred from

Mineralogical, Geochemical, and Pollen Data, and their Palaeoclimatic and Geoarchaeological Significance." *Quaternary International* 501B (2019): 272–288.

Hamilton, Caleb. "Conflict in the Iconography of the Protodynastic and Early Dynastic Periods." In *Rich and Great: Studies in Honour of Anthony J. Spalinger on the Occasion of his 70th Feast of Thoth*, edited by Ranata Landgráfová and Jana Mynárová, 99–114. Prague: Charles University in Prague, 2016.

Haring, Ben. "Administration and Law: Pharaonic." In *A Companion to Ancient Egypt*, vol. 1, edited by Alan Lloyd, 218–236. Chichester and Malden, MA: Wiley-Blackwell. 2014.

Harpur, Yvonne. *Decoration in Egyptian Tombs of the Old Kingdom*. London: KPI, 1987.

Harrington, Nicola. 2004. "Human Representation in the Predynastic Period: The Locality HK6 Statue in Context." In *Egypt at its Origins: Studies in Memory of Barbara Adams. Proceedings of the International Conference 'Origin of the State, Predynastic and Early Dynastic Egypt, Krakow, 28th August – 1st September 2002*, vol. 1, edited by Stan Hendrickx, Marek Chlodnicki, Barbara Adams, and Renée Friedman, 25–43. Leuven: Peeters, 2004.

Hassan, Fekri, Alejandro Jiménez Serrano, and Geoffrey Tassie. "The Sequence and Chronology of the Protodynastic and Dynasty I Rulers." In *Archaeology of Early Northeastern Africa: Studies in Memory of Lech Krzyżaniak*, edited by Marek Chlodnicki, Karla Kroeper, and Michal Kobusiewicz, 687–722. Poznan: Archaeological Museum, 2006.

Hassan, Selim. *Excavations at Giza, 1938–39, Vol. 10: The Great Pyramid of Khufu and Its Mortuary Chapel*. Cairo: Government Press, 1960.

Hassan, Selim. *The Great Sphinx and Its Secrets*. Cairo: Government Press, 1953.

Hassan, Selim. *Excavations at Giza, 1932–1933, Vol. 4*. Cairo: Government Press, 1943.

Hawass, Zahi. "The Discovery of the Pyramid of Queen Sesheshet (?)at Saqqara." In *Times, Signs and Pyramids: Studies in Honour of Miroslav Verner on the Occasion of His Seventieth Birthday*, edited by Vivienne Callender, Ladislav Bareš, Miroslav Bárta, Jiri Janák, and Jaromír Krejčí, 173–189. Prague: Faculty of Arts, Charles University, 2011.

Hawass, Zahi. "The Excavations of the Headless Pyramid, Lepsius XXIX." In *Perspectives on Ancient Egypt, Studies in Honor of Edward Brovarski*, edited by Zahi Hawass, Peter Der Manuelian and Ramadan Hussein, 153–170. Cairo: Conseil Suprême Antiquités de l'Égypte, 2010.

Hawass, Zahi. "Recent Discoveries in the Pyramid Complex of Teti at Saqqara." In *Abusir and Saqqara in the Year 2000*, edited by Miroslav Bárta and Jaromír Krejčí, 413–444. Prague: Academy of Sciences of the Czech Republic, 2000.

Hawass, Zahi. "The Funerary Establishments of Khufu, Khafra and Menkaura During the Old Kingdom." Ph.D. Dissertation, University of Pennsylvania, 1987.

Hawass, Zahi. "The Khufu Statuette: Is it an Old Kingdom Sculpture?" In *Mélanges Gamal Eddin Mokhtar*, vol. 1, 379–394. Cairo: Institut Français d'Archéologie Orientale du Caire, 1985.

Hayes, Harold. "The Entextualization of the Pyramid Texts and the Religious History of the Old Kingdom." In *Towards a New History for the Egyptian Old Kingdom*, edited by Peter Der Manuelian and Thomas Schneider, 315–336. Leiden and Boston: Brill, 2015.

Hayes, Harold. *Organization of the Pyramid Texts: Typology and Disposition*. Leiden: Brill, 2012, 2 vols.

Hayes, William. *The Scepter of Egypt: Part 1*. New York: Metropolitan Museum of Art, 1968.

Helck, Wolfgang. "Zum Stauensockel des Djoser." In *Gegengabe: Festschrift für Emma Brunner-Traut*, edited by Ingrid Gamer-Wallert and Wolfgang Helck, 143–150. Tübingen: Attempto Verlag, 1992.

Helck, Wolfgang. *Untersuchungen zur Thinitenzeit (ÄA 45)*. Wiesbaden: Harrassowitz, 1987.

Helck, Wolfgang. "Heliopolis und die Sonnenheiligtümer." In *Sundries in Honour of Torgny Säve-Söderbergh*, 67–72. Uppsala: BOREAS, Uppsala Studies in Ancient Mediterranean and Near Eastern Civilizations 13, 1984.

Helck, Wolfgang. "Die 'Weihinschrift' aus dem Taltempel des Sonnenheiligtum des Königs Neuserre bei Abu Gurob." *Studien zur Altägyptische Kultur* 5 (1977): 47–77.

Helck, Wolfgang. *Untersuchungen zu den Beamtentiteln des Ägyptischen Alten Reichs*. Glückstadt: J. J. Augustin, 1954.

Hendrickx, Stan. "Les grands mastabas de la lre dynastie à Saqqara." *Archeo-Nil* 18 (2008): 60–88.

Henige, David. "How Long did Pepy II Reign?" *Göttinger Miszellen* 221 (2009): 41–48.

Hirsch, Eileen. "Residences in the Texts of Senwosret I." In *Egyptian Royal Residences. 4th Symposium on Egyptian Royal Ideology*, edited by Rolf Gundlach and John Taylor, 69–82. Wiesbaden, Harrassowitz, 2009.

Hölscher, Uvo. *The Temples of the Eighteenth Dynasty, The Excavations of Medinet Habu*, vol. 2. Chicago: University of Chicago Press, 1939.

Hölscher, Uvo. *Das Grabdenkmal des Königs Chephren*. Leipzig: J.C. Hinrichs, 1912.

Hopkins, Keith. "Brother-sister Marriage in Roman Egypt." *Comparative Studies in Society and History* 22 (1980): 303–355.

Hornung, Erik. *History of Ancient Egypt: An Introduction*. Ithaca, NY: Cornell University Press, 1999.

Hornung, Erik, Rolf Krauss, and David Warburton (eds.). *Ancient Egyptian Chronology*. Leiden and Boston: Brill, 2006.

Huebner, Sabine. "Brother-Sister Marriage in Roman Egypt: A Curiosity of Mankind or a Widespread Family Strategy?" *The Journal of Roman Studies* 97 (2007): 21–49.

Jacobsohn, Helmuth. *Die dogmatische Stellung des Königs in der Theologie der alten Ägypter*. Hamburg: Augustin, 1939.

Jacquet-Gordon, H. K. *Les noms des domains funéraires sous l'ancient empire égyptien* (Bibliotéque d'étude 34). Cairo: French Institute, 1962.

Jaeschke, Helena. "The HK6 Statue Fragments." In *Egypt at Its Origins: Studies in Memory of Barbara Adams. Proceedings of the International Conference 'Origin of the State, Predynastic and Early Dynastic Egypt, Krakow, 28th August – 1st September 2002*, vol. 1, edited by Stan Hendrickx, Marek Chlodnicki, Barbara Adams, and Renée Friedman, 25–43. Leuven: Peeters, 2004.

James, T.G.H. *Corpus of Hieroglyphic Inscriptions in the Brooklyn Museum*, vol. 1. Brooklyn: The Brooklyn Museum, 1974.

Janák, Jiří, Hana Vymazalová, and Filip Coppens. "The Fifth Dynasty 'Sun Temples' in a Broader Context." In *Abusir and Saqqara in the Year2010/1*, edited by Miroslav Bárta, Filip Coppens, and Jaromír Krejčí, 430–442. Prague: Czech Institute of Egyptology, Faculty of Arts, Charles University, 2011.

Jánosi, Peter. *The Pyramid Complex of Amenemhat I at Lisht: The Reliefs*. New York: Metropolitan Museum of Art, 2016.

Jánosi, Peter. "What did the Court in the Pyramid Temple of Khafre at Giza look like?" In *The Pyramid: Between Life and Death*, edited by Irmgard Hein, Nils Billing, and Erika Meyer-Dietrich, 27–50. Uppsala: Uppsala University BOREAS 36, 2016.

Jánosi, Peter. "Montuhotep-Nebtawyre and Amenemhat I: Observations on the Early Twelfth Dynasty in Egypt." *Metropolitan Museum Journal* 45 (2010): 7–20.

Jánosi, Peter. *Die Pyramidenanlagen der Königinnen*. Vienna: Österreichischen Akademie der Wissenschaften, 1996.

Jánosi, Peter. "The Queens of the Old Kingdom and Their Tombs." *Bulletin of the Australian Centre for Egyptology* 3 (1992): 51–57.

Jánosi, Peter. "Die Pyramidenanlage der 'anonymen Königin' des Djedkare-Isesi." *Mitteilungen des Deutschen Archäologischen Instituts Abteilung Kairo* 45 (1989): 187–202.

Jaroš-Deckert, Brigitte. *Das Grab des Jnj-iti. f. Grabung im Asasif*, vol. 5. Mainz am Rhein: Philipp von Zabern, 1984.

Jéquier, Gustave. *Les Pyramides des Reines Neit et Apouit*. Cairo: Institut Français d'Archéologie Orientale, 1933.

Jéquier, Gustave. *Le Mastabat Faraoun*, Cairo: Imprimerie de l'Institut Français d'Archéologie Orientale, 1928a.

Jéquier, Gustave. *La Pyramide D'Oudjebten*. Cairo: Institut Français d'Archéologie Orientale, 1928b.

Jones, Dillwyn. *An Index of Ancient Egyptian Titles, Epithets and Phrases of the Old Kingdom*, vol. 2. Oxford: Archaeopress, 2000.

Junker, Hermann. *Giza VII*. Vienna and Leipzig: Hölder – Pichler –Tempsky, 1944.

Junker, Hermann. Vorläufiger Bericht über die Grabung der Akademie der Wissenschaften in Wien auf der neolithischen Siedelung von Merimde-Benisalâme (Westdelta) vom 1. bis 30.

März 1929, Vienna: *Akademie der Wissenschaften in Wien, Philosophisch-Historische Klasse* (1929–1940).

Kahl, Jochem. "Dynasties 0–2". In *Ancient Egyptian Chronology*, edited by Erik Hornung, Rolf Krauss, and David Warburton, 94–115. Leiden: Brill, 2006.

Kahl, Jochem. *'Ra is my Lord', Searching for the Rise of the Sun God at the Dawn of Egyptian History*. Wiesbaden, Harrassowitz: 2007.

Kahl, Jochem. "Das Alter der Sonnenheiligtümer." *Göttinger Miszellen*, 143 (1994): 81–84.

Kahl, Jochem, Tine Bagh, Eva-Maria Engel, and Susanne Petschel. "Die Funde und dem 'Menesgrab' in Nagada: ein Zwischenbericht." *Mitteilungen des Deutschen Archäologischen Instituts Abteilung Kairo* 57 (2001): 171–186.

Kahl, Jochem, Nicole Kloth, and Ursula Zimmermann. *Die Inschriften der 3. Dynastie: Eine Bestandsaufnahme*, Wiesbaden, Harrassowitz: 1995.

Kahlbächer, Andrea. "Bon appetit! Bread and reed in the funerary repast imagery of the Old and Middle Kingdoms." *The Bulletin of the Australian Centre of Egyptology* 24 (2013): 7–20.

Kaiser, Werner. "Zur unterirdischen Anlage der Djoserpyramide und ihrer entwicklungs geschichtlichen Einordnung." *Gegengabe: Festschrift für Emma Brunner-Traut*, edited by Ingrid Gamer-Wallert and Wolfgang Helck, 167–190. Tübingen: Attempto Verlag, 1992.

Kaiser, Werner. "Zur inneren Chronologie der Naqadakultur." *Archaeologia Geographica* 6 (1957): 69–77.

Kaiser, Werner, and Martin Bommas. "Stadt und Tempel von Elephantine, 19. /20. Grabungsbericht." *Mitteilungen des Deutschen Archäologischen Instituts, Abteilung Kairo* 49 (1993): 133–187.

Kanawati, Naguib. "The Memphite Control of Upper Egypt during the

Old Kingdom: The Cases of Edfu, Abydos, and Akhmim." In *Ancient Memphis, "Enduring Is the Perfection"*, edited by Linda Evans, 238–252. Leuven and Paris: Peeters, 2012.

Kanawati, Naguib. "The Vizier Nebet and the Royal Women of the Sixth Dynasty." In *Thebes and Beyond: Studies in Honour of Kent R. Weeks*, edited by Zahi Hawass and Salima Ikram, 115–126. Cairo: Conseil suprême des antiquités, 2010.

Kanawati, Naguib. "Weni the Elder and his Royal Background." In *En Quête de la Lumiére, In Quest of Light: Mélanges in Honorem Ashraf A. Sadek*, edited by Alicia Maravelia, 33–49. Oxford: Archeopress, 2009.

Kanawati, Naguib. *Mereruka and King Teti: The Power behind the Throne*. Cairo: Supreme Council of Antiquities Press, 2007.

Kanawati, Naguib. *Conspiracies in the Egyptian Palace: Unis to Pepy I*. London and New York: Routledge, 2003.

Kanawati, Naguib. "A New *ḥȝ t/rnpt-zp* for Teti and its Implication for Old Kingdom Chronology." *Göttinger Miszellen* 177 (2000): 25–32.

Kanawati, Naguib. "Deux conspirations contre Pépy Ier." *Chronique d'Égypte* 56 (1981a): 203–217.

Kanawati, Naguib. "The living and the dead in Old Kingdom tomb scenes." *Studien zur Altägyptischen Kultur* 9 (1981b): 213–226.

Kanawati, Naguib. *Governmental Reforms in Old Kingdom Egypt*. Warminster: Aris and Phillips, 1980.

Kanawati, Naguib. "Was Jbj of Deir el-Gebrawi a Polygamist?" *Studien zur Altägyptischen Kultur* 5 (1977): 123–129.

Kanawati, Naguib. "The Mention of More Than One Eldest Child in Old Kingdom Inscriptions." *Chronique D' Égypte* 51 (1976): 235–251.

Kanawati, Naguib. "Polygamy in the Old Kingdom of Egypt." *Studien zur Altägyptischen Kultur* 4 (1974): 149–160.

Kanawati, Naguib, and Joyce Swinton. *Egypt in the Sixth Dynasty, Challenges and Responses*. Wallasy: Abercromby Press, 2018.

Kaplony, Peter. *Steingefässe mit Inscriften der Frühzeit und des Alten Reich*. Brussels: Fondation Égyptologique Reine Élisabeth, 1968.

Kaplony, Peter. *Die Inschriften der Ägyptischen Frühzeit*, Vols. 1–3. Wiesbaden: Harrassowitz, 1963.

Kaufman, Herbert. "The Collapse of Ancient States and Civilizations as an Organizational Problem." In *The Collapse of Ancient States and Civilizations*, edited by Norman Yoffee and George Cowgill, 219–235. Tucson, University of Arizona Press, 1988.

Kees, Hermann. *Der Götterglaube im Alten Ägypten*. Berlin: Akademie Verlag, 1980.

Kees, Hermann."Ein Handelsplatz des MR im Nordostdelta." *Mitteilungen des Deutschen Archäologischen Instituts, Abteiling Kairo* 18 (1962): 1–13.

Kees, Hermann. *Das Re-Heiligtim des Königs Ne-Woser-Re*, vol. 3, *Die grosse Festdarstellung*. Leipzig: J.C. Hinrichs'sche Buchhandlung, 1928.

Kemp, Barry. "The 'pyramid' at Zawiyet Sultan (Zawiyet al-Meitin)." *Mitteilungen des Deutschen Archäologischen Instituts Abteilung Kairo* 70–71 (2014–2015): 239–246.

Kemp, Barry. *Ancient Egypt: Anatomy of a Civilization*, 2nd ed. London: Routledge, 2006.

Kemp, Barry. "The Osiris Temple at Abydos." *Mitteilungen des Deutschen Archäologischen Instituts Abteilung Kairo* 23 (1968): 138–155.

Kemp, Barry. "The Egyptian 1st Dynasty Royal Cemetery." *Antiquity* 41 (1967): 22–32.

Khaled, Mohamed Ismail. "The Old Kingdom Royal Funerary Domains: New Evidence from the Causeway of the Pyramid Complex of Sahura."

Ph.D. thesis, Charles University, 2008a.

Khaled, Mohamed Ismail. "Old Kingdom funerary domains: a question of dating!" In *Chronology and Archaeology in Ancient Egypt (The Third Millennium B.C.)*, edited by Hana Vymazalová and Miroslav Bárta, 194–213. Prague: Czech Institute of Egyptology, Charles University, 2008b.

El-Khouli, Ahmed, and Naguib Kanawati. *The Old Kingdom Tombs of El-Hammamiya*. Sydney: Australian Centre for Egyptology, 1990.

Klemm, Dietrich, and Rosemary Klemm. *The Stones of the Pyramids: Provenance of the Building Stones of the Old Kingdom Pyramids*. Berlin and New York: DeGruyter, 2010.

Köhler, E. Christiana. "Early Dynastic Society at Memphis." In *Zeichen aus dem Sand: Streiflichter aus Ägyptens Geschichte zu Ehren von Günter Dreyer*, edited by Eva-Maria Engel, Vera Müller, and Ulrich Hartung, 381–399. Wiesbaden: Harrassowitz, 2008a.

Köhler, E. Christiana. "The Interaction between and the Roles of Upper and Lower Egypt in the Formation of the Egyptian State: Another Review." In *L'Egypte pré-et protodynastique. Les origins de l'Etat. Predynastic and Early Dynastic Egypt. Origin of the State. Toulouse (France) – 5–8 sept. 2005*, edited by Béatrix Midant-Reynes and Yann Tristant with Joanne Rowland and Stan Hendrickx, 514–543. Leuven: Peeters, 2008b.

Köhler, E. Cristiana, and Jana Jones. *Helwan II: The Early Dynastic and Old Kingdom Funerary Relief Slabs*. Rahden: Marie Leidorf, 2009.

Kraemer, Bryan. "A Shrine of Pepy I in South Abydos." *Journal of Egyptian Archaeology* 103, (2017): 13–34.

Krauss, Rolf. "Stellar and Solar Components in Ancient Egyptian Mythology and Royal Ideology." In *Astronomy and Power: How Worlds are Structured. Proceedings of the SEAC 2010 Conference*, edited by Michael Rappenglück, Nicholas Campion, and Fabio Silva, 137–141 (BAR International Series 2794). Bar Publishing, 2016.

Krejčí, Jaromír. *The Royal Necropolis in Abusir. Abusir XVIII*. Prague: Charles University, Faculty of Arts, 2010.

Krejčí, Jaromír. "Several Remarks on the Abusir Pyramid Necropolis: Its Minor Tombs and Their Place in the Chronology of the Royal Cemetery." In *Chronology and Archaeology in Ancient Egypt (The Third Millennium B.C.)*, edited by Hana Vymazalová and Miroslav Bárta, 124–136. Prague: Charles University, Faculty of Arts, 2008.

Krejčí, Jaromír, Vivienne Callender, and Miroslav Verner. *Abusir XII, Minor Tombs in the Royal Necropolis I*. Prague: Czech Institute of Egyptology, 2008.

Krejčí, Jaromír, Katarine Kytnarová, Hana Vymazalová, Adéla Pokorná, and Jaromír Beneš. *Mastaba of Werkare, Vol. 1: Abusir XXIV*. Prague: Charles University, Faculty of Arts, 2014.

Kuhlmann, Klaus. "Der 'Wasserburg des Djedefre' (Chufu 0I/I), Ein Lagerplazmit Expeditionsinschriften der 4. Dynastie im Raum der Oase Dachla." *Mitteilungen des Deutschen Archäologischen Instituts Abteilungen Kairo* 61 (2005): 243–290.

Kuper, Rudolph and Frank Förster. "Khufu's 'mefat' expeditions into the Libyan Desert." *Egyptian Archaeology* (2003): 25–28.

Kuraszkiewicz, Kamil. "An afterworld for Netjerykhet." In *Old Kingdom, New Perspectives, Egyptian Art and Archaeology 2750–2150 BC*, edited by Nigel Strudwick and Helen Strudwick, 139–142. Oxford: Oxbow Books, 2011.

Kuraszkiewicz, Kamil. "Netjerikhet's Traces in the West." In *Abusir and Saqqara in the Year 2005*, edited by Miroslav Bárta, Filip Coppens, and

Jaromír Krejčí, 274–281. Prague: Czech Institute of Egyptology, Charles University, 2006.

Labbé-Toutée, Sophie, and Christine Ziegler. "100. Head of King Userkaf." In *Egyptian Art in the Age of the Pyramids*, edited by The Metropolitan Museum of Art, 314–315. New York: Harry N. Abrams, 1999.

Labrousse, Audran. *Le Temple Funéraire du Roi Pépy Ier*. Cairo: Institut Français d'Archéologie Orientale, 2019.

Labrousse, Audran. "Les reines de la sale aux offrandes de Pepy Ier." In *Cinquante ans d'éternité: Jubilé de la Mission archéologique française de Saqqâra*, edited by Remi Legros, 167–179. Cairo: Institut Français d'Archéologie Orientale, 2015.

Labrousse, Audran. "Recent Discoveries at the Necropolis of King Pepy I." In *Ancient Memphis, 'Enduring Is the Perfection'* edited by Linda Evans, 299–308. Leuven and Paris: Peeters, 2012.

Labrousse, Audran. "Huit épouses du roi Pépy Ier." In *Egyptian Culture and Society, Studies in Honour of Naguib Kanawati*, edited by Alexandra Woods, Ann McFarlane, and Susanne Binder, 297–314. Cairo: Conseil suprême des antiquités de l'Égypte, 2010.

Labrousse, Audran. "L'architecture des pyramides de reines à la fin de la VIᵉ dynastie." In *Des Néferkarê aux Montouhotep*, edited by Laure Pantalacci and Catharine Berger El-Naggar, 203–214. Lyon: Maison de l'Orient et de la Méditerranée, 2005.

Labrousse, Audran. "The Pyramids of the Sixth Dynasty." In *The Treasures of the Pyramids*, edited by Zaki Hawass, 265–281. Vercelli: White Star, 2003.

Labrousse, Audran. "Une épouse du roi Mérenrê Ier: la reine Ânkhesenpépy II." In *Abusir and Saqqara in the Year 2000*, edited by Miroslav Bárta and Jaromír Krejčí, 485–490. Prague: Acedemy of Sciences of the Czech Republic, Oriental Institute, 2000.

Labrousse, Audran. "Discovery of the Pyramid of Queen Ankhesenpepy II." *Egyptian Archaeology* 13 (1998): 9–10.

Labrousse, Audran. "Un bloc décoré du temple funéraire de la mère royale Néferhétephés." In *Études sur l'Ancien Empire et la nécropole de Saqqâra dédiées à Jean-Philippe Lauer*, edited by Catharine Berger and Bernard Mathieu, 263–270. Université Paul Valéry-Montpellier III, 1997.

Labrousse, Audran. "The Pyramids of Pepy I and His Queens at Saqqara." *Egyptian Archaeology* 8 (1996): 3–6.

Labrousse, Audran. "Les reines de Téti, Khouit et Ipout Ire, recherches architecturales." In *Hommages à Jean Leclant*, vol. 1, 231–244. Cairo: Institut Français d'Archéologie Orientale, 1994.

Labrousse, Audran, and Jean-Philippe Lauer. *Les Complexes Funeraires d'Ouserkaf et de Neferhetepes*, vols. 1–2. Cairo: Institut Français d'Archéologie Orientale, 2000.

Labrousse, Audran, and Jean Leclant. "Nouveaux documents sur le reine Ankhenespépy II, mère de Pépy II." In *Stationen: Beiträge zur Kultturgeschichte Ägyptens*, edited by Heike Guksch and Daniel Polz, 95–100. Mainz: Philipp von Zabern, 1998.

Lacau, Pierre, and Henri Chevrier. *Une Chappelle de Sésostris Ier a Karnak*. Cairo: Institut Français d'Archéologie Orientale, 1969.

Lacau, Pierre., and Jean-Philippe Lauer. *La pyramide á degrès*, vol. 4. Cairo: French Institute, 1959.

Lacheer, Claudia. "Das Grab des Hetepsechemui/Raneb in Saqqara ideen zur Baugeschichtlichen Entwicklung." In *Zeichen um dem Sand, Streiflichter aus Ägyptens Geschichte zu Ehren von Günter Dreyer*, edited by Eva-Maria Engel, Vera Müller, and Ulrich Hartung, 427–451. Wiesbaden: Harrassowitz, 2008.

Lacovara, Peter. *The New Kingdom Royal City*. London and New York: Kegan Paul International, 1997.

La Loggia, Angela. "Egyptian Engineering in the Early Dynastic Period: The Sites of Saqqara and Helwan." *British Museum Studies in Ancient Egypt and Sudan* 13 (2009): 175–196.

Langráfová, Renata. "Self-Presentation in the 11th Dynasty." In *Living Forever, Self-Presentation in Ancient Egypt*, edited by Hussein Bassir, 89–104. Cairo, American University in Cairo Press, 2019.

Landgráfová, Renata. *Faience Inlays from the Funerary Temple of King Raneferef, Abusir XIV*. Prague: Czech Institute of Egyptology, Charles University in Prague, 2006a.

Landgráfová, Renata. "The Function of the Faience Inlays in the Funerary Temple of Raneferef at Abusir." In *The Old Kingdom, Art and Archaeology. Proceedings of the Conference Prague, May 31–June 4, 2004*, edited by Miroslav Bárta., 203-208. Prague: Publishing House of the Academy of Sciences of the Czech Republic, 2006b.

Lange, Eva. "Die Ka-Anlage Pepys I. in Bubastis im Kontext königlicher Ka-Anlagen des Alten Reiches." *Zeitschrift für Ägyptischen Sprache und Altertumskunde* 133 (2006): 121–140.

Lange-Athinodorou, Eva, and Ashraf es-Senussi. "A Royal *ka*-temple and the Rise of Old Kingdom Bubastis." *Egyptian Archaeology* 53 (2018): 20–24.

Lansing, Ambrose. "The Egyptian Expedition 1934–1935. The Museum's Excavations at Hierakonpolis." *Bulletin of the Metropolitan Museum of Arts* 30 (1935): 37–45.

Lauer, Jean-Philippe. "Le développement des complexes funéraires royaux en Égypte depuis les temps prédynastiques jusqu'à la fin de l'Ancien Empire." *Bulletin de l'institut Française d'Archéologie Oriental* 79 (1979): 355–394.

Lauer, Jean-Philippe. "Note complément aire sur le temple funéraire de Khéops." *Annales du Service des Antiquities de l'Égypte* 49 (1949): 111–123.

Lauer, Jean-Philippe. *Étude complément aires sur les monuments du Roi Zoser À Saqqarah*. Cairo: French Institute, 1948.

Leclant, Jean. "Noubounet: Une nouvelle reine d' Égypte." In *Gegengabe: Festschrift für Emma Brunner-Traut*, edited by Ingrid Gamer-Wallert and Wolfgang Helck, 211–220. Tübingen: Attempto Verlag, 1992.

Leclant, Jean, and Gisèle Clerc. "Fouilles et travaux en Égypte et au Soudan, 1996–1997." *Orientalia* 67, no. 3 (1998): 315–444.

Leclant, Jean, and Giséle Clerc. "Fouilles et travaux en Égypte et au Soudan, 1995–1996." *Orientalia* 66, no. 3 (1997): 222–363.

Leclant, Jean, and Anne Minault-Gout. "Fouilles et travaux en Égypte et au Soudan, 1998–1999." *Orientalia* 69 (2000): 209–329.

Lehner, Mark. "The monument and the formerly so-called Valley Temple of Khentkawes I: Four observations." In *Royal versus Divine Authority, 7th Symposium on Egyptian Royal Authority*, 215–274. Wiesbaden: Harrassowitz Verlag, 2015.

Lehner, Mark. "On the Waterfront: Canals and Harbors in the Time of Giza Pyramid-Building." *AERAgram* 15, nos. 1–2 (2014): 14–23.

Lehner, Mark. "The Lost Port City of the Pyramids." *AERAgram* 14, no. 1 (2013): 2–7.

Lehner, Mark. "The Horizon at Giza." *AERAgram* 12, no. 2 (2011): 9.

Lehner, Mark. "The Sphinx." In *The Treasures of the Pyramids*, edited by Zahi Hawass, 173–189. Vercelli: White Star, 2003.

Lehner, Mark. *The Complete Pyramids*. London: Thames and Hudson, 1997.

Lehner, Mark, and Zahi Hawass. *Giza and the Pyramids.* Cairo: American University in Cairo Press, 2017.

Leprohon, Ronald. "Self-Presentation in the Twelfth Dynasty." In *Living Forever, Self-Presentation in Ancient Egypt,* edited by Hussein Bassir, 105–124. Cairo; American University in Cairo Press, 2019.

Leprohon, Ronald. *The Great Name: Ancient Egyptian Royal Titulary.* Atlanta: Society of Biblical Literature, 2013.

Leprohon, Ronald. "The Stela of Sehetepibre (CG 20538): Borrowings and Innovation." In *Archaism and Innovation: Studies in the Culture of Middle Kingdom Egypt,* edited by David Silverman, William Kelly Simpson, and Josef Wegner, 277–293. New Haven, CT and Philadelphia: Yale University and University of Pennsylvania Museum, 2009.

Leprohon, Ronald. "Remarks on Private Epithets Found in the Middle Kingdom Wadi Hammamat Graffiti." *The Journal of the Society for the Study of Egyptian Antiquities* 28 (2001): 124-146

Leprohon, Ronald. "The Programmatic Use of the Royal Titulary in Twelfth Dynasty." *Journal of the American Research Center in Egypt* 33 (1996): 165–171.

Lesko, Barbara. "Queen Khamerernebty II and her Sculpture." In *Ancient Egyptian and Mediterranean Studies in Memory of William A. Ward,* edited by Leonard Lesko, 149–162. Providence: Department of Egyptology, Brown University, 1998.

Lichtheim, Miriam. *Ancient Egyptian Literature, Vol. 1: The Old and Middle Kingdoms.* Berkeley: University of California Press, 1973.

Lieven, Alexandra von. "The Soul of the Sun Permeates the Whole World." *Pandanus* 4/2 (2010): 29–60.

Linseele, Veerle, Wim Van Neer, and Renée Friedman. "Special Animals from a Special Place? The Fauna from HK29A at Predynastic Hierakonpolis." *Journal of the American Research Center in Cairo* 45 (2009): 105–136.

Liszka, Kate. "Discerning Ancient Identity: The Case of Aashyet's Sarcophagus (JE 47267)." *Journal of Egyptian History* 11 (2018): 185–207.

Lloyd, Alan. *Ancient Egypt: State and Society.* Oxford: Oxford University Press, 2014.

Logan, Thomas. "The Origins of the *Jmy-wt* Fetish." *Journal of the American Research Center in Egypt* 27 (1990): 61–70.

Lorand, David. "The Archetype of Kingship: Who Senwosret claimed to be, How and Why?" In *The World of Middle Kingdom Egypt (2000–1550 BC) I,* edited by Gianlucca Miniaci and Wolfram Grajetzki, 205–220. London: Golden House Publications, 2015.

Lorand, David. "Une 'Chapelle des Ancêtres' à Karnak sous Sésostris Ier?" *Cahiers de Karnak* 14 (2013): 447–466.

Lorand, David. *Arts et politique sous Sésostris Ier: Littérature, sculpture et architecture dans leur context historique.* Brussels: Turnhout, 2011.

Lorton, David. "Book review of *Der Königliche Harim im alten Ägypten und seine Verwaltung* by Elfriede Reise." *Journal of the American Research Center in Egypt* 11 (1974): 98–101.

Mace, Arthur. "Excavations at Lisht." *Metropolitan Museum of Art Bulletin* 17, (1922): 4–18.

Malek, Jaromir. "Old-Kingdom Rulers as 'Local Saints' in the Memphite Area during the Middle Kingdom." In *Abusir and Saqqara in the Year 2000,* edited by Miroslav Bárta and Jaromír Krejčí, 241–258. Prague: Academy of Sciences of the Czech Republic, Oriental Institute, 2000.

Malek, Jaromir. "A Chronological Scheme and Terminology for the Early Part of

Egyptian History: A Contribution to a Discussion." *Discussions in Egyptology* 15 (1989): 37–50.

Malek, Jaromir. *In the Shadow of the Pyramids*. Cairo: American University in Cairo Press, 1986.

Malek, Jaromir. "The Original Version of the Royal Canon of Turin." *Journal of Egyptian Archaeology* 68 (1982): 93–106.

Malek, Jaromir. "Princess Inti, the Companion of Horus." *The Society for the Study of Egyptian Antiquities Journal* 10, 3 (1980): 229–242.

Der Manuelian, Peter. "The Lost Throne of Queen Hetepheres from Giza: An Archaeological Experiment in Visualization and Fabrication." *Journal of the American Research Center in Egypt* 53 (2017): 1–46.

Mariette, Auguste. *Les mastabas de L'ancien empire*. Hildesheim and New York: Georg Olms, 1976.

Mariette, Auguste. *Catalologue général des monuments d'Abydos découverts pendant les fouilles de cette ville*. Paris: Imprimerie Nationale, 1880.

Marochetti, Elisa. *The Reliefs of the Chapel of Nebhepetre Mentuhotep at Gebelein*. Leiden: Brill, 2010.

Marochetti, Elisa. "The temple of Nebhepetre Mentuhotep at Gebelein: Preliminary report." In *Das Néferkarê aux Montouhotep: travaux archéologiques en cours sur la finde la Vie dynastie et la première intermédiare; actes du colloque CNRS-Université Lumière-Lyon 2, tenu le 5-7 juillet 2001*, edited by Laure Pantalacci and Catherine Berger-El-Naggar, 145–163. Lyon and Paris: Maison de l'Orient et de la Méditerranée and de Boccard, 2005.

Martin-Pardey, Eva. *Untersuchungen zur ägyptischen Provinzialverwaltungen bis zum Ende des Alten Reiches*. Hildesheim: Gebrüder Gerstenberg, 1976.

Maspero, Gaston. *Les mastabas de l'ancien empire*. Hildesheim: Georg Olms, 1976 (reprint of Paris: F. Vieweg, 1889).

Mathieu, Bernard. "Mais qui est donc Osiris? Ou la politique sous le linceul de la religion." *ENiM* 3 (2010): 77–107.

Mathieson, Ian. "The National Museum of Scotland Saqqara Survey Project 1990–2000." In *Abusir and Saqqara in the Year 2000*, edited by Miroslav Bárta and Jaromír Krejčí, 33–42. Prague: Academy of Sciences of the Czech Republic, 2000.

McCorquodale, Kim. *Representations of the Family in the Egyptian Old Kingdom (BAR International Series 2513)*. Oxford: Archaeopress, 2013.

MacNamara, Liam. "The Revetted Mound at Hierakonpolis and Early Kingship: A Re-Interpretation. " In *Egypt at Its Origins 2*, edited by Béatrix Midant-Reynes and Yann Tristant, 901–936. Leuven: Peeters, 2008.

Megahed, Mohamed. "The *Antichambre Carrée* in the Old Kingdom: Decoration and Function." In *Rich and Great: Studies in Honour of Anthony J. Spalinger on the Occasion of his 70th Feast of Thoth*, edited by Renata Landgráfová and Jana Mynárová, 239–258. Prague: Charles University, Faculty of Arts, 2016.

Megahed, Mohamed, and Peter Jánosi. "The Pyramid Complex of Djedkare at Saqqara South: Recent Results and Future Prospects." In *Abusir and Saqqara in the Year 2015*, edited by Miroslav Bárta, Filip Coppens, and Jaromír Krejčí, 237–256. Prague: Faculty of Arts, Charles University, 2017.

Midant-Reynes, Béatrix. *The Prehistory of Egypt: From the First Egyptians to the First Pharaohs*. Oxford: Blackwell, 1992.

Moeller, Nadine. "The First Intermediate Period: A Time of Famine and Climate Change." *Ägypten und Levante* 15 (2005): 153–167.

Morales, Antonio. "Iteration, Innovation and Dekorum in Opferlisten des Alten Reichs." *Zeitschrift für Ägyptische Sprache und Altertumskunde* 142 (2015a): 55–69.

Morales, Antonio. "Text-building and Transmission of Pyramid Texts in the Third Millennium BCE: Iteration, Objectification, and Change." *Journal of Ancient Near Eastern Religions* 15 (2015b): 169–201.

Morales, Antonio. "Los dos Cuerpos del Rey: Cosmos y Política de la Monarquía Egipcia." *ARYS* 12 (2014): 47–86.

Morales, Antonio. "The Transmission of the Pyramid Texts in the Middle Kingdom: Philological Aspects of a Continuous Tradition in Egyptian Mortuary Literature." Ph.D. dissertation, University of Pennsylvania, 2013.

Morales, Antonio. "Traces of Official and Popular Veneration to Nyuserra Iny at Abusir. Late Fifth Dynasty to Middle Kingdom." In *Abusir and Saqqara in the Year 2005*, edited by Miroslav Bárta, Filip Coppens, and Jaromír Krejčí, 311–341. Prague: Czech Institute of Egyptology, Charles University, 2006.

Moreno García, Juan Carlos. "Building the Pharaonic State: Territory, Elite and Power in Ancient Egypt in the 3rd Millennium BCE." In *Experiencing Power, Generating Authority: Cosmos, Politics and the Ideology of Kingship in Ancient Egypt and Mesopotamia*, edited by Jane Hill, Philip Jones, and Antonio Morales, 185–217. Phila-delphia: University of Pennsylvania Museum, 2013a.

Moreno García, Juan Carlos. "The Study of Ancient Egyptian Administration." In *Ancient Egyptian Administration*, edited by Juan Carlos Moreno García, 1–18. Leiden and Boston: Brill, 2013b.

Moreno García, Juan Carlos, "The Territorial Administration of the Kingdom in the 3rd Millennium." In *Ancient Egyptian Administration*, edited by Juan Carlos Moreno García, 85–151. Leiden and Boston: Brill, 2013c.

Moreno García, Juan Carlos. "The State and the Organization of the Rural Landscape in 3rd Millennium BC Pharaonic Egypt." In *Aridity, Change and Conflict in Africa*, edited by Michael Bollig, Olaf Bubenzer, Ralf Vogelsang, and Hans-Peter Wotzka, 313–330. Cologne: Heinrich-Barth-Institut, 2007.

Moreno García, Juan Carlos. "Deux familles de potentats provinciaux et les assises de leur pouvoir: Elkab et el-Hawawish sous la Vie dynastie." *Revue d'Égyptologie* 56 (2005): 95–128.

Moreno García, Juan Carlos. *Hwt et le milieu rural égyptien du IIIe millénaire*. Paris: Librairie Honoré Champion, 1999.

Morenz, Ludwig D. "Texts before Writing: Reading (Proto-) Egyptian Poetics of Power." In *Experiencing Power, Generating Authority: Cosmos, Politics and the Ideology of Kingship in Ancient Egypt and Mesopotamia*, edited by Jane Hill, Philip Jones, and Antonio Morales, 121–149. Philadelphia: University of Pennsylvania Museum of Archaeology and Anthropology, 2013.

Morenz, Ludwig. *Die Zeit der Regionen im Spiegel der Gebelein-Region*. Leiden and Boston: Brill, 2010.

Morenz, Ludwig. "Die Thebanischen Potentaten und ihr Gott. Zur Konzeption des GottesAmunund der (Vor) Geschichte des Sakralzentrums Karnak in der XI. Dynastie." *Zeitschrift für Ägyptische Sprache und Altertumskunde* 130 (2003): 110–119.

Morenz, Ludwig. "Die Götter und ihr Redetext: Die ältestbelegte Sakral-Monumentalisierung von Textlichkeit auf Fragmenten der Zeit des Djoser aus Heliopolis." In *5. Ägyptologische Tempeltagung, Würzburg, 23.–26. September 1999*, edited by Horst Beinlich, Jochen Hallof, Holger Hussy, and Christiane von Pfeil, 137–158. Wiesbaden: Harrassowitz, 2002.

Morenz, Ludwig. "Zur urspünglich heliopolitanischen Herkunft zweier

Fragmente Pepy I. aus Bubastis." *Discussions in Egyptology* 45 (1999): 61–64.

Morenz, Ludwig. 1994. "Zur Dekoration der früzeitlichen Tempel am Beispiel zweier Fragmente des archaischen Tempels von Gebelein." In *Ägyptische Tempel – Struktur, Funktion und Programm*, edited by Rolf Gundlach and Matthias Rochholz, 217–238. Hildesheim: Gerstenberg Verlag. 1994.

Morgan, Jacques de. *Recherches sur les origines de l'Égypte, vol. II: Ethnographie prehistorique et tombeau royal de Negadah.* Paris: Ernest Leroux, 1897.

Morris, Ellen. "The Pharaoh and Pharaonic Office." In *A Companion to Ancient Egypt*, edited by Alan Lloyd, 201–217. Chichester: Wiley-Blackwell, 2014.

Morris, Ellen. "Paddle Dolls and Performance." *Journal of the American Research Center in Egypt* 47 (2011): 71–104.

Morris, Ellen. "Sacrifice for the State: First Dynasty Royal Funerals and the Rites at Macramallah's Rectangle." In *Performing Death: Social Analysis of Funerary Traditions in the Ancient Near East and Mediterranean*, edited by Nicola Laneri, 15–37. Chicago: University of Chicago, 2008.

Morris, Ellen. "On the Ownership of the Saqqara Mastabas and the Allotment of Political and Ideological Power at the Dawn of the State." In *The Archaeology and Art of Ancient Egypt: Essays in Honor of David B. O'Connor*, vol. 2, edited by Zahi Hawass and Janet Richards, 171–190. Cairo: Supreme Council of Antiquities, 2007.

Morris, Ellen. "Lo, Nobles Lament, the Poor Rejoice": State Formation in the Wake of Social Flux." In *After Collapse: The Regeneration of Complex Societies*, edited by Glen Schwartz and John Nichols, 58–71. Tucson: University of Arizona Press, 2006.

Mortensen, Bodil. "Change in the Settlement Pattern and Population in the Beginning of the Historical Period." *Ägypten und Levante* II (1991): 11–38.

Moursi, Mohamed. *Die Hohenpriester des Sonnengottes von der Frühzeit Ägyptens bis zum Ende des Neuen Reiches.* Munich: Deutscher Kunstverlag, 1972.

Muhlestein, Kerry. "Transitions in Pyramid Orientation: New Evidence from the Seila Pyramid." *Studien zur Altägyptischen Kultur* 44 (2015): 249–258.

Müller, Vera. "Do Seal Impressions Prove a Change in the Administration During the Reign of King Den." In *Seals and Sealing Practices in the Near East: Developments in Administration and Magic from Prehistory to the Islamic Period*, edited by Ilone Regulski, Kim Duistermaat, and Peter Verkinderen, 17–32. Leuven: Peeters, 2012.

Müller-Wollermann, Renate. "End of the Old Kingdom." *UCLA Encyclopedia of Egyptology*, 1–9, 2014. http://digital2 .library.ucla.edu/viewItem.do?ar k=21198/zz002hzfs1

Munro, Peter. *Der Unas-Friedhof Nord-West, Das Doppelgrab der Königinnen Nebet und Khenut.* Mainz am Rhein: Philipp von Zabern, 1993.

Murnane, William. *Ancient Egyptian Coregencies, SAOC 40.* Chicago: The Oriental Institute of the University of Chicago, 1977.

Myśliwiec, Karol. "The 'Dry Moat' West of the Netjerykhet Enclosure." In *The Old Kingdom Art and Archaeology, Proceedings of the Conference, Prague 2004*, edited by Miroslav Bárta, 233–237. Prague: Publishing House of the Academy of Sciences of the Czech Republic, 2006.

Naville, Edouard. *Bubastis.* London: Kegan Paul, Trench, Trübner & Co., 1891.

Navrátilova, Hana. *The Visitors' Graffiti of Dynasties XVIII and XIX in Abusir and Northern Saqqara.* Prague: Czech Institute of Egyptology, 2007.

Newberry, Percy. "The Inscribed Tombs of Ekhmim." *Annals of*

Archaeology and Anthropology, 4 (1912): 101–120.

Nolan, John. "Fifth Dynasty Renaissance at Giza." *Aregram* 13, no. 2 (2012): 2–5.

Nolan, John. "Mud Sealings and Fourth Dynasty Administration at Giza." Ph.D. dissertation, University of Chicago, 2010.

Nováková, Vera. "The Household of an Egyptian Dignitary: The Case of Ptahshepses." *Prague Egyptological Studies* 19 (2017): 95–109.

Nuzzolo, Massimiliano. *The Fifth Dynasty Sun Temples. Kingship, Architecture and Religion in Third Millennium BC Egypt.* Prague: Charles University, Faculty of Arts, 2018.

Nuzzolo, Massimiliano. "Human and Divine: The King's Two Bodies and the Royal Paradigm in Fifth Dynasty Egypt." In *Constructing Authority, 8th Symposium on Egyptian Royal Ideology*, edited by Támas Bács and Horst Beinlich, 185–214. Wiesbaden: Harrassowitz, 2017.

Nuzzolo, Massimiliano. "The Fifth Dynasty Sun Temples and Their Relationship with the Contemporary Pyramids." In *Pyramids; Between Life and Death*, edited by Irmgard Hein, Nils Billing, and Erika Meyer-Dietrich, 163–186. Uppsala: Uppsala University BOREAS 36, 2016.

Nuzzolo, Massimiliano. "The Bent Pyramid of Sneferu at Dahshur: A Project Failure or an Intentional Architectural Framework?" *Studien zur Altägyptischen Kultur* 44 (2015a): 259–282.

Nuzzolo, Massimiliano. "The Sed-Festival of Niuserra and the Fifth Dynasty Sun Temples." In *Towards a New History for the Egyptian Old Kingdom*, edited by Peter Der Manuelian and Thomas Schneider, 366–392. Leiden and Boston: Brill, 2015b.

Nuzzolo, Massimiliano. "Royal Authority, Divine Legitimation. Topography as an Element of Acquisition, Confirmation and Renewal of Power in the Fifth Dynasty." In *Royal versus Divine Authority: Acquisition, Legitimization and Renewal of Power*, edited by Filip Coppens, Jiří Janák, and Hana Vymazalová, 289–304. Wiesbaden: Harrassowitz, 2015c.

Nuzzolo, Massimiliano. "The V Dynasty Sun Temples Personnel." *Studien zur Altägyptischen Kultur* 39 (2010): 289–308.

Nuzzolo, Massimiliano. "Sun Temples and Kingship in the Ancient Egyptian Kingdom." In *Proceedings of the Ninth International Congress of Egyptologists*, edited by Jean-Claude Goyon and Christine Cardin, 1401–1410. Leuven: Peeters, 2007.

Nuzzolo, Massimiliano, and Jaromír Krejčí. "Heliopolis and the Solar Cult in the Third Millennium BC." *Ägypten und Levante* 27 (2017): 357–380.

Nuzzolo, Massimiliano, and Rosanna Pirelli. "New Archaeological Investigation in the Sun Temple of Niuserra in Abu Ghurab". In *Abusir and Saqqara in the Year 2010*, vol. 2, edited by Miroslav Bárta, Filip Coppens, and Jaromír Krejčí, 664–679. Prague: Czech Institute of Egyptology, Charles University in Prague, 2011.

Obsomer, Claude. *Sésostris Ier: Étude chronologique et historique du règne.* Brussels: Connnaissance de l'Egypte Ancienne, 1995.

Obsomer, Claude. "La Date de Nésou-Montou (Louvre C1)." *Revue d'Égyptologie* 44 (1993): 103–140.

O'Connor, David. *Abydos: Egypt's First Pharaohs and the Cult of Osiris.* Cairo: American University in Cairo Press, 2009.

O'Connor, David. "The Ownership of Elite Tombs at Saqqara in the First Dynasty." In *Studies in Honor of Ali Radwan*, edited by Khaled Daoud, Shafia Bedier, and Sawsan Abd el-Fatah, 223–231. Cairo: Supreme Council of Antiquities, 2005.

O'Connor, David. "The Dendereh chapel of Nebhepetre Mentuhotep: A new perspective." In *Studies on Ancient Egypt in Honour of H.S. Smith*, edited by Anthony Leahy and John Tait, 21220. London: Egypt Exploration Society, 1999.

O'Connor, David. "New Funerary Enclosures (Talbezirke) of the Early Dynastic Period at Abydos." *Journal of the American Research Center in Egypt* 26 (1989): 51–86.

Oppenheim, Adela. "A New Boundary Stela of the Pharaoh Netjerikhet (Djoser) Found in the Pyramid Complex of Senwosret III, Dahshur." *Bulletin of the Egyptological Seminar* 17 (2007): 153–182.

Oppenheim, Adela. "Decorative Programs and Architecture in the Pyramid Complexes of the Third and Fourth Dynasties." In *Structure and Significance: Thoughts on Ancient Egyptian Architecture*, edited by Peter Jánosi, 455–476. Vienna: Österreichischen Akademie der Wissenschaften, 2005.

Oppenheim, Adela. "103. Cast of a Block with Running Troops and an Inscription with the Name and Titles of King Userkaf" and "104. Running Troops." In *Egyptian Art in the Age of the Pyramids*, 318–321. New York: Metropolitan Museum of Art, 1999.

Oppenheim, Adela, Dorothea Arnold, Dieter Arnold, and Kei Yamamoto. *Ancient Egypt Transformed: The Middle Kingdom*. New York: Metropolitan Museum of Art, 2015.

Ormeling, Marinus. "Planning the Construction of First Dynasty Mastabas at Saqqara. Modelling the Development of the Pre-Stairway Mastabas." In *Egypt at Its Origins 5*, edited by Béatrix Midant-Reynes and Yann Tristant, 401–432. Leuven: Peeters, 2017.

Otto, Eberhard. "Legitimation des Herrschens im pharaonischen Ägypten." *Saeculum* 20 (1969): 385–407.

Papazian, Hratch. "The State of Egypt in the Eighth Dynasty." In *Towards a New History for the Egyptian Old Kingdom: Perspectives on the Pyramid Age*, edited by Peter Der Manuelian and Thomas Schneider, 393–428. Leiden and Boston: Brill, 2015.

Papazian, Hratch. *Domain of Pharaoh*. Hildesheim: Hildesheimer Ägyptologische Beiträge, 2012.

Papazian, Hratch. "The Temple of Ptah and Economic Contacts Between Memphite Cult Centers in the Fifth Dynasty." In *8. Ägyptologische Tempeltagung: Interconnections between temples, Warschau, 22.–25. September 2008*, edited by Monika Dolińska and Horst Beinlich, 137–153. Wiesbaden: Harrassowitz, 2010.

Papazian, Hratch. "Perspectives of the Cult of Pharaoh during the Third Millennium B.C.: A Chronological Overview." In *Chronology and Archaeology in Ancient Egypt (The Third Millennium B.C.)*, edited by H. Vymazalová and M. Bárta, 61–80. Prague: Czech Institute of Egyptology, Charles University, 2008.

Papazian, Hratch. "Domain of Pharaoh: The Structure and Components of the Economy of Ancient Egypt." Ph.D. dissertation, University of Chicago, 2005.

Parkinson, R. B. *Poetry and Culture in Middle Kingdom Egypt*. London and New York: Continuum, 2002.

Payraudeau, Frédéric. "Considérations sur quelques titres des reines de l'Ancien Empire à l'epoque ptolémaïque." *Cinquante ans d'éternité: jubilé de la mission archéologique française de Saqqâra*, edited by R. Legros, 209–248. Cairo: Institut Française d'Archéologie Orientale, 2015.

Perry, Patricia. "Sources of Power in Predynastic Hierakonpolis: Legacies for Egyptian Kingship." In *Egypt at its Origins 3: Proceedings of the Third International Conference 'Origin of the State: Predynastic and Early Dynastic*

Egypt', London 27th July–1st August 2008, edited by Peter Fiske and Renée Friedman, 1271–1292. Leuven: Peeters, 2011.

Petrie, W. M. F. *Abydos, Part II*. London: Egypt Exploration Fund, 1903.

Petrie, W. M. F. *Diospolis Parva*. London: Egypt Exploration Fund, 1901.

Petrie, W. M. F. *The Royal Tombs of the First Dynasty*. London: Egypt Exploration Fund, 1900.

Picton, Jan. "Living and Working in a New Kingdom 'Harem Town'." In *Women in Antiquity*, edited by Stephanie Budin and Jean Turfa, 229–242. London and New York: Routledge, 2016.

Pinch, Geraldine. *Votive Offerings to Hathor*. Oxford: Griffith Institute, 1993.

Porter, Bertha, and Rosalind Moss. *Topographical Bibliography of Ancient Egyptian Texts, Reliefs and Paintings: Vol. 3, Part 2: Saqqara to Dahshur*. Oxford: Griffith Institute, 1981.

Posener, Georges. L'enseignement loyaliste: Sagesse éyptienne du Moyen Empire. Geneva: Librairie Droz, 1976.

Posener, Georges. *Littérature et politique dans L'Égypte de la XIIe Dynastie*. Paris: Librairie Ancienne Honoré Champion, 1956.

Posener-Krieger, Paule. *Les archives du temple funéraire de Néferirkarê-Kakai*, 2 vols. Cairo: Institut Français d'Archéologie Orientale du Caire, 1976.

Posner-Krieger, Paule, Miroslav Verner, and Hana Vymazalová. *The Pyramid Complex of Raneferef: The Papyrus Archive, Abusir X*. Prague: Czech Institute of Egyptology, Faculty of Arts, Charles University, 2006.

Postel, Lilian. "Une nouvelle mention des campagnes nubiennes de Montouhotep II à Karnak." In *Hommages à Jean-Claude Goyon*, edited by Luc Gabolde, 329–340. Cairo: Institut Français d'Archéologie Orientale, 2008.

Postel, Lilian. *Protocole des souverains égyptiens et dogme monarchique au début du Moyen Empire*. Turnhout: Brepols, 2004.

Postel, Lilian. "'Rame' or 'course'? Enquête lexicographique sur le terme [hepet]." Bulletin *de l'Institut Français d'Archéologie Orientale* 103 (2003): 377–420.

Postel, Lilian, and Isabelle Régen. "Annales héliopolitaines et fragments de Sésostris Ier dans la porte Bâb al-Tawfiq au Caire." *Bulletin de l'Institut Français d'Archéologie Orientale* 105 (2005): 229–293.

Quibell, James. *Hierakonpolis: Part I*. London: Bernard Quaritch, 1900.

Quibell, James. *Hierakonpolis: Part II*. London: Egypt Research Account, 1902.

Quirke, Stephen. *The Cult of Ra: Sun-Worship in Ancient Egypt*. London: Thames and Hudson, 2001.

Quirke, Stephen. *Ancient Egyptian Religion*. London: British Museum Press, 1992.

Radwan, Ali. "Step Pyramids." In *The Treasures of the Pyramids*, edited by Zahi Hawass, 86–111. Vercelli: White Star, 2003.

Raue, Dietrich. "Pottery from the Hierakonpolis Fort." *Nekhen News* 11 (1999): 13.

Reader, Colin. "The Netjerikhet Stela and the Early Dynastic Cult of Ra." *Journal of Egyptian Archaeology* 100 (2014): 421–436.

Redford, Donald. "History and Egyptology." In *Egyptology Today*, edited by Richard Wilkinson, 23–35. Cambridge: Cambridge University Press, 2008.

Regulski, Ilona. "Reinvestigating the Second Dynasty at Saqqara." In *Abusir and Saqqara in the Year 2010*, edited by Miroslav Bárta, Filip Coppens, and Jaromír Krejčí, 694–708. Prague: Charles University in Prague, 2010.

Regulski, Ilone. "Investigating a New Dynasty 2 Necropolis at South Saqqara." *British Museum Studies in*

Ancient Egypt and the Sudan 13 (2009): 221–237.

Regulski, Ilone. "The Origin of Writing in Relations to the Emergence of the Egyptian State." In *L'Egypte pré-et proto-dynastique: Les origins de l'Etat. Predynastic and Early Dynastic Egypt. Origin of the State. Toulouse (France) – 5–8 Sept. 2005*, edited by Béatrix Midant-Reynes and Yann Tristant with Joanne Rowland and Stan Hendrickx, 983–1008. Leuven: Peeters, 2008.

Regulski, Ilone. "Second Dynasty Ink Inscriptions from Saqqara Paralleled in the Abydos Material from the Royal Museums of Art and History in Brussels" In *Egypt at Its Origins: Studies in Memory of Barbara Adams: Proceedings of the International Conference 'Origin of the State, Predynastic and Early Dynastic Egypt, Krakow, 28th August – 1st September 2002*, vol. 1, edited by Stan Hendrickx, Marek Chlodnicki, Barbara Adams, and Renée Friedman, 949–970. Leuven: Peeters, 2004.

Reiser, Elfriede. *Der königlicke Harim im alten Ägypten und seine Verwaltung.* Vienna: Verlag Notring, 1972.

Reisner, George. "The Servants of the Ka." *Bulletin of the Museum of Fine Arts* 32 (1934): 1–12.

Reisner, George. "The Bed Canopy of the Mother of Cheops." *Bulletin of the Museum of Fine Arts* 30 (1932): 55–60.

Reisner, George. *Mycerinus: The Temples of the Third Pyramid at Giza.* Cambridge, MA: Harvard University Press, 1931.

Reisner, George, and William Smith. *A History of the Giza Necropolis*, vol. 2. Cambridge, MA: Harvard University Press, 1955.

Richards, Janet. "Kingship and Legitimation." In *Egyptian Archaeology*, edited by Willeke Wendrich, 55–84. Chichester: Wiley-Blackwell, 2010.

Ricke, Herbert. *Der Harmachistempel des Chefren in Giseh. Beiträge zur Ägyptischen Bauforschung und Altertumskunde* 10. Wiesbaden: Franz Steiner, 1970.

Ricke, Herbert. *Das Sonnenheiligtum des Königs Userkaf.* Cairo: Institut für Ägyptische Bauforschung und Altertumskunde, 1965.

Ricke, Herbert. *Bemerkingen zur Ägyptischen Baukunst des Alten Reichs II.* Cairo: Institut für Ägyptische Bauforschung und Altertumskunde, 1950.

Rizkana, Ibrahim, and Jürgen Seeher. *Maadi, III: The Non-lithic Small Finds and the Structural Remains of the Predynastic Settlement* (Archäologische Veröffentlichungen, Deutsches Archäologisches Institut, Abteilung Kairo 80). Mainz: Zabern, 1989.

Rizkana, Ibrahim, and Jürgen Seeher. *Maadi, II: The Lithic Industries of the Predynastic Settlement* (Archäologische Veröffentlichungen, Deutsches Archäologisches Institut, Abteilung Kairo 65). Mainz: Zabern, 1988.

Rizkana, Ibrahim, and Jürgen Seeher. *Maadi, I: The Pottery of the Predynastic Settlement* (Archäologische Veröffentlichungen, Deutsches Archäologisches Institut, Abteilung Kairo 64). Mainz: Zabern, 1987.

Robins, Gay. "The Reign of Nebhepetre Mentuhotep II and the Pre-unification Theban Style of Relief." In *Beyond the Pyramids, Egyptian Regional Art from the Museo Egizio, Turin*, edited by Gay Robins, 39–45. Atlanta: Emory University Museum of Art and Archaeology, 1990.

Roehrig, Catharine. "Two Tattooed Women from Thebes." *Bulletin of the Egyptological Seminar* 19 (2015): 537–536.

Roehrig, Catharine. "Fragments of a Royal Head" In *Egyptian Art in the Age of the Pyramids*, edited by Dorothea Arnold, Christiane Ziegler, and James Allen, 254. New York: Metropolitan Museum of Art, 1999.

Roehrig, Catherine, and Anna Serotta. "The Stela of King Raneb." In *Dawn of*

Egyptian Art, edited by Diana Craig Patch, Marianne Eaton-Krauss, and Susan Allen, 210. New York: Metropolitan Museum of Art, 2011.

Romanosky, Eugene. "Min." In *The Oxford Encyclopedia of Ancient Egypt*, edited by Donald Redford, 413–415. Oxford: Oxford University Press, 2001.

Römer, Malte. "Zum Problem von Titulatur und Herkunft bei den Ägyptischen "Königssöhnen" des Alten Reiches." Ph.D. Dissertation, Freie Universität Berlin, 1977.

Roth, Ann Macy. "Upper Egyptian Heliopolis: Thebes, Archaism, and the Political Ideology of Hatshepsut and Thutmose III." *Bulletin of the Egyptological Seminar* 19 (2015): 537–552.

Roth, Ann Macy. *A Cemetery of Palace Attendants*, Boston: Museum of Fine Arts, 1995.

Roth, Ann Macy. "Social Change in the Fourth Dynasty: The Spatial Organization of Pyramids, Tombs, and Cemeteries." *Journal of the American Research Center in Egypt* 30 (1993): 33–56.

Roth, Silke. "*Harem*," UCLA *Encyclopedia of Egyptology*, 2012. https://escholarship.org/uc/item/k3663r3

Roth, Silke. *Die Königsmütter des Alten Ägypten von der Frühzeit bis zum Ende der 12. Dynastie*, Wiesbaden: Harrassowitz, 2001.

Rydström, Kjell. "HRY SŠT3, 'In Charge of Secrets', The 3000 Year Evolution of a Title." *Discussions in Egyptology* 28 (1994): 53–85.

Ryholt, Kim. "The Late Old Kingdom in the Turin King-list and the Identity of Nitocris." *Zeitschrift für Ägyptische Sprache und Altertumskunde* 127 (2000): 87–100.

Rzepka, Slawomir. "Old Kingdom graffiti in Deir el-Bahari." In *Es werde niedergelegt als Schriftstück. Festschrift für Hartwig Altenmüller zum 65. Geburtstag*, edited by Nicole Kloth, Karl Martin, and Eva Pardey, 379–385. Hamburg: Helmut Buske, 2003.

Sabbahy, Lisa. "Ancient Egyptian Queens' Names." *The Journal of the Society for the Study of Egyptian Antiquities* 34 (2007): 149–157.

Sabbahy, Lisa. "The Female Family of Amenemhat II: A Review of the Evidence." In *Hommages à Fayza Haikal*, 239–244. Cairo: Institut Français d'Archéologie Orientale, 2004.

Sabbahy, Lisa. "The King's Mother in the Old Kingdom with Special Reference to the Title s3 t-ntr." *Studien zur Altägyptischen Kultur*, 25 (1998): 305–310.

Sabbahy, Lisa. "The Titulary of the Harem of Nebhepetre Mentuhotep, Once Again." *Journal of the American Research Center in Egypt* 34 (1997): 163–166.

Sabbahy, Lisa. "Evidence for the Titulary of the Queen from Dynasty One." *Göttinger Miszellen* 135 (1993): 81–87.

Sabbahy, Lisa. "The Development of the Titulary and Iconography of the Ancient Egyptian Queen from Dynasty One to Early Dynasty Eighteen." Ph.D. dissertation, University of Toronto, 1982.

Sabbahy, Lisa. "The Titulary of Queens Nbt and Hnwt." *Göttinger Miszellen* 52 (1981): 37–42.

Sadek, Ashraf. *Wadi el-Hudi: The Amethyst Mining Inscriptions*, 2 vols. Warminster: Aris and Phillips, 1980.

Saied, Ahmed. "Der Sonnenkult und der Sonnengott in der Vor-und Frühgeschichte Ägyptens." In *Studies in Honor of Ali Radwan*, edited by Khaled Daoud, Shafia Bedier, and Sawsan Abd el-Fatah, 287–294. Cairo: Supreme Council of Antiquities, 2005.

Saleh, Mohamed. *Three Old Kingdom Tombs at Thebes*. Mainz am Rhein: Philipp van Zabern, 1977.

el Sawi, Ahmad. *Excavations at Tell Basta*. Prague: Charles University, 1979.

Schäfer, Heinrich. *Ein Bruckstück altagyptischer Annalen*. Berlin: Verlag der Akademie der Wissenschaften, 1902.

Schenkel, Wolfgang. *Memphis – Herakleopolis – Theben: Die Epigrapischen Zeugnisse der 7.-11. Dynastie Ägyptens*. Wiesbaden: Harrassowitz, 1965.

Schmitz, Bettina. *Untersuchungen zum Titel S3-Njśwt "Königssohn."* Bonn: Rudolf Habelt Verlag, 1976.

Schneider, Thomas. "Periodizing Egyptian History: Manetho, Convention, and Beyond." In *Historiographie in der Antike*, edited by Klaus-Peter Adam, 183–197. Berlin: Walter de Gruyter, 2008.

Schneider, Thomas. "The Relative Chronology of the Middle Kingdom and the Hyksos Period (Dyns. 12–17)." In *Ancient Egyptian Chronology*, edited by Erik Hornung, Rolf Krauss, and David Warburton, 168–196. Leiden and Boston: Brill, 2006.

Schott, Siegfried. "Ein Kult der Götten Neith." In *Das Sonnenheligtum des Königs Userkaf, Vol. 2: Die Funde by Emar Edel*, 123–138. Wiesbaden: Schweizerisches Institut für ägyptische Bauforschung and Altertumskunde, 1950.

Seidel, Matthias. *Die königlichen Statuengruppen*, vol. 1. Hildesheim: Gerstenberg Verlag, 1996.

Seidlmayer, Stephan. "The Relative Chronology of the First Intermediate Period." In *Ancient Egyptian Chronology*, edited by Erik Hornung, Rolf Krauss, and David Warburton, 159–167. Leiden: Brill, 2006.

Seidlmayer, Stephan. "The First Intermediate Period (c. 2160–2055 BC)." In *The Oxford History of Ancient Egypt*, edited by Ian Shaw, 108–136. Oxford: Oxford University Press, 2000.

Seidlmayer, Stephan. "Town and State in the Early Old Kingdom: A View from Elephantine." In *Aspects of Early Egypt*, edited by Jeffry Spencer, 108–127. London: British Museum Press, 1996.

Seipel, Wilfried. "Untersuchungen zu den Ägyptischen Königinnen der Frühzeit und des alten Reiches." Ph.D. Dissertation, University of Hamburg, 1980.

Serrano, Alejandro Jiménez. *Royal Festivals in the Late Predynastic Period and the First Dynasty*, BAR International Series 1076. Oxford: Archeopress, 2002.

Sethe, Kurt. *Urkunden des Alten Reichs*, vol. 1. Leipzig: J.C. Hinrich'sche Buchhandlung, 1933

Sethe, Kurt. *Die Altägyptischen Pyramidentexte nach den Papierabdrücken und Photographien des Berliner Museums*, vol. 4. Leipzig: J.C. Hinrichs, 1922.

Shalomi-Hen, Racheli. "The Dawn of Osiris and the Dusk of the Sun-Temples: Religious History at the End of the Fifth Dynasty." In *Towards a New History for the Egyptian Old Kingdom*, edited by Peter Der Manuelian and Thomas Schneider, 456–469. Leiden and Boston: Brill, 2015.

Shaw, Garry. *The Pharaoh: Life at Court and on Campaign*. New York: Thames and Hudson, 2012.

Shaw, Garry. "The Meaning of the Phrase *m Hm n Stp-s3*." *Journal of Egyptian Archaeology* 96 (2010): 175–190.

Shaw, Ian. "Seeking the Ramesside Royal Harem: New Fieldwork at Medinet el-Gurob." In *Ramesside Studies in Honour of K.A. Kitchen*, edited by Mark Collier and Stephen Snape, 453–464. Bolton: Rutherford Press, 2011.

Shaw, Ian. *Ancient Egypt: A Very Short Introduction*. Oxford: Oxford University Press, 2004.

Shaw, Ian (ed.). *The Oxford History of Ancient Egypt*. Oxford: Oxford University Press, 2000.

Silverman, David. "Non-Royal Burials in the Teti Pyramid Cemetery and the Early Twelfth Dynasty." In *Archaism and Innovation: Studies in the Culture of Middle Kingdom Egypt*, edited by David

Silverman, William Kelly Simpson, and Josef Wegner, 47–101. New Haven, CT and Philadelphia: Yale University and University of Pennsylvania, 2009.

Simpson, William Kelly. "Studies in the Twelfth Egyptian Dynasty: Year 25 in the Era of the Oryx Nome and the Famine Years in Early Dynasty 12." *Journal of the American Research Center in Egypt* 38 (2001): 7–8.

Simpson, William Kelly. "Mentuhotep, Vizier of Sesostris I, Patron of Art and Architecture." *Mitteilungen des Deutschen Archäologischen Instituts Abteilungen Kairo* 47 (1991): 331–340.

Simpson, William Kelly. "Polygamy in Egypt in the Middle Kingdom." *Journal of Egyptian Archaeology* 60 (1974a): 100–105.

Simpson, William Kelley. *The Terrace of the Great God at Abydos: The Offering Chapels of Dynasties 12 and 13.* New Haven, CT and Philadelphia: Peabody Museum of Yale University and University Museum of University of Pennsylvania, 1974b.

Simpson, William Kelly. "Studies in the Twelfth Egyptian Dynasty: I–II." *Journal of the American Research Center in Egypt* 2 (1963): 53–63.

Smith, Mark. *Following Osiris: Perspectives on the Osirian Afterlife from Four Millennia.* Oxford: Oxford University Press, 2017.

Smith, Mark. "Osiris and the Deceased in Ancient Egypt: Perspectives from Four Millennia." *Annuaire de l'École pratique des hautes études, Section des sciences religieuses* [Online], 121 | 2014.

Smith, William Stevenson. *The Art and Architecture of Ancient Egypt.* New Haven, CT and London: Yale University Press, 1998.

Smith, William Stevenson. "The Old Kingdom in Egypt." In *The Cambridge Ancient History*, 3–72. Cambridge: Cambridge University Press, 1965.

Smith, William Stevenson. *A History of Egyptian Sculpture and Painting in the Old Kingdom.* Oxford: Oxford University Press, 1946.

Solà-Sagalés, Irene Cordón. "Four Daughters of the King from the Second Dynasty: Epigraphic and Iconographic Analysis of the Stele of Hepetkhenmet, Satba, Shepsetipet (?) and Sehefner." In *Proceedings of the Tenth International Congress of Egyptologists, University of the Aegean, Rhodes 22–29 May 2008*, vol. 2, edited by Panagiotis Kousoulis and Nicholas Lazaridis, 1547–1558. Leuven: Peeters, 2015.

Sourouzian, Hourig. "La reine et le papyrus." In *Times, Signs and Pyramids: Studies in Honour of Miroslav Verner on the Occasion of His Seventieth Birthday*, edited by Vivienne Callender, Ladislav Bareš, Miroslav Bárta, Jirí Janák, and Jaromír Krejčí, 341–350. Prague: Faculty of Arts, Charles University, 2011.

Sourouzian, Hourig. "Features of Early Twelfth Dynasty Royal Sculpture." *Bulletin of the Egyptian Museum* 2 (2005): 103–124.

Sourouzian, Hourig. "Standing royal colossi of the Middle Kingdom reused by Ramses II." *Mitteilungen des Deutschen Archäologischen Instituts Abteilungen Kairo* 44 (1988): 229–254.

Spalinger, Anthony. "Dated texts of the Old Kingdom." *Studien zur Altägyptischen Kultur* 21 (1994): 275–320.

Spencer, Patricia, "Petrie and the Discovery of Earliest Egypt." In *Before the Pyramids: The Origins of Egyptian Civilization*, edited by Emily Teeter, 17–24. Chicago: The University of Chicago, 2011.

Stadelmann, Ranier. "The heb-sed Temple of Senefru at Dahshur." In *Abusir and Saqqara in the Year 2010*, vol. 2, edited by Miroslav Bárta, Filip Coppens and Jaromír Krejčí, 736–746. Prague: Faculty of Arts, Charles University, 2011a.

Stadelmann, Ranier. "Where were the Queens of the Early Dynastic Period and the Queens of Djoser Time Buried." In *Times, Signs and Pyramids: Studies in Honour of Miroslav Verner on the Occasion of His Seventieth Birthday*, edited by Vivienne Callender, Ladislav Bares, Miroslav Bárta, Jiri Janak, and Jaromír Krejčí, 375–390. Prague: Faculty of Arts, Charles University, 2011b.

Stadelmann, Rainer. "The Prince Kawab, Oldest Son of Khufu." In *Offerings to the Discerning Eye: An Egyptological Medley in Honor of Jack A. Josephson*, edited by Sue D'Auria, 295–299. Leiden and Boston: Brill, 2010a.

Stadelmann, Rainer. "Snofru-Builder and Unique Creator of the Pyramid of Seila and Maidum." In *Echoes of Eternity: Studies presented to Gaballa Aly Gaballa*, edited by Ola El-Aguizy and Mohamed Sherif Ali, 31–38. Wiesbaden: Harrassowitz, 2010b.

Stadelmann, Rainer. "Inscriptional evidence for the reign of Seneferu at Dahshur." In *Chronology and Archaeology in Ancient Egypt (The Third Millennium B.C.)*, edited by Hana Vymazolová and Miroslav Bárta, 104–110. Prague: Faculty of Arts, Charles University, 2008.

Stadelmann, Rainer. "King Huni: His Monuments and His Place in the History of the Old Kingdom." In *The Archaeology and Art of Ancient Egypt: Essays in Honor of David B. O'Connor*, vol. 2, edited by Zahi Hawass and Janet Richards, 425–432. Cairo: Supreme Council of Antiquities, 2007.

Stadelmann, Rainer. "The Copper Statues of Pepy I in the Egyptian Museum." *Bulletin of the Egyptian Museum* 2 (2005a): 125–142.

Stadelmann, Rainer. "A New Look at the Tombs of the First and Second Dynasties at Abydos and Sakkara and the Evolution of the Pyramid Complex." In *Studies in Honor of Ali Radwan*, edited by Khaled Daoud, Shafia Bedier, and Sawsan Abd el-Fatah, 361–376. Cairo: Supreme Council of Antiquities, 2005b.

Stadelmann, Rainer. "Userkaf in Saqqara und Abusir. Untersuchungen zur Thronfolge in der 4. und frühen 5. Dynastie." In *Abusir and Saqqara in the Year 2000*, edited by Miroslav Bárta and Jaromír Krejčí, 529–542. Prague: Academy of Sciences of the Czech Republic, Oriental Institute, 2000.

Stadelmann, Rainer. "Représentations de la famille royale dans l'Ancient Empire." In *L'art de l'Ancient Empire égyptien: Actes du colloque organisé au museé du Louvre par le Service culturelles*, edited by Christiane Ziegler and Nadine Palayret, 169–192. Paris: La documentation Française, 1999.

Stadelmann, Rainer. "The Development of the Pyramid Temple in the Fourth Dynasty." In *The Temple in Ancient Egypt: New Discoveries and Recent Research*, edited by Stephen Quirke, 1–16. London: British Museum Press, 1997.

Stadelmann, Rainer. "König Teti und der Beginn der 6. Dynastie." In *Hommages à Jean Leclant*, vol. 1, 327–336. Cairo: Institut Français d'Archéologie Orientale, 1994.

Stadelmann, Rainer. "Beiträge zur Geschichte des Alten Reiches: Die Lange der Regierung des Snofru." *Mittleilungen des Deutschen Archäologischen Instituts Abteilung Kairo* 43 (1987a): 229–240.

Stadelmann, Rainer. "Königinnengrab und Pyramidenbezirk im Alten Reich." *Annales du Service des Antiquités de L'Égypte*, 71 (1987b): 251–260.

Stadelmann, Rainer. *Die Agyptischen Pyramiden: Vom Ziegelbau zum Weltwunder*. Mainz am Rhein: Philipp von Zabern, 1985.

Stadelmann, Rainer. "Khaefkhufu = Chephren: Beiträge zur Geschichte der

4. Dynastie." *Studien zur Altägyptischen Kultur* 11 (1984): 165–172.

Stadelmann, Rainer. "Das vermeintliche Sonnenheiligtum im Norden des Djoserbezirkes." *Annales du Service des Antiquités de L'Égypte* 69 (1983): 373–378.

Stadelmann, Rainer, and Nicole Alexanian. "Die Friedhöfe des Alten und Mittleren Reiches in Dahschur." *Mitteilungen des Deutschen Archäologischen Instituts Abteilungen Kairo* 54 (1998): 293–318.

Stasser, Thiery. *La mére royal Seshseshet et les débuts de la Vie dynastie*. Brussels: Édition Safran, 2013.

Strong, Anise. "Incest Laws and Absent Taboos in Roman Egypt." *Ancient History Bulletin* 19 2005): 31–41.

Strudwick, Nigel. *Texts from the Pyramid Age*. Atlanta: Society of Biblical Literature, 2005.

Strudwick, Nigel. *The Administration of Egypt in the Old Kingdom*. London: KPI, 1985.

Sweeney, Deborah. "The Vizier Amenemhat at Wadi Hammamat – a Macbeth Moment?" Göttinger Miszellen 238 (2013): 107–124.

Tallat, Pierre. "Ayn Sukhna and Wadi el-Jarf: Two Newly Discovered Pharaonic Harbours on the Suez Gulf." *British Museum Studies in Ancient Egypt and Sudan* 18 (2012): 147–168.

Tallet, Pierre, and Gregory Marouard. "The Harbor of Khufu on the Red Sea Coast at Wadi al-Jarf, Egypt." *Near Eastern Archaeology* 17 (2014): 4–14.

Tassie, Geoffery. "The Ancient Egyptian Hairdresser in the Old Kingdom." *Mitteilungen des Deutschen Archäologischen Instituts Abteilungen Kairo* 17 (2017): 255–275.

Tidyman, Richard. "Further Evidence of a Coup d'État at the End of Dynasty?" *The Bulletin of the Australian Centre for Egyptology* 6 (1995): 103–110.

Tietze, Christian, and Mohammed Abd el Maksoud. *Tell Basta: Ein Führer über das Grabungsgelände*. Potsdam: Universitätsverlag, 2004.

Traunecker, Claude. "Kamutef." In *The Oxford Encyclopedia of Ancient Egypt*, edited by Donald Redford, 221–222. Oxford: Oxford University Press, 2001.

Trigger, Bruce. "Monumental Architecture: A Thermodynamic Explanation of Symbolic Behavior." *World Archaeology* 22 (1990): 119–132.

Tristant, Yann, and Béatrix Midant-Reynes. "The Predynastic Vultures of the Nile Delta." In *Before the Pyramids: The Origins of Egyptian Civilization*, edited by Emily Teeter, 45–54. Chicago: University of Chicago Press, 2011.

Troy, Lana. "Religion and Cult in the Time of Thutmose III." In *Thutmose III: A New Biography*, edited by Eric Cline and David O'Connor, 123–182. Ann Arbor: University of Michigan Press, 2006.

Troy, Lana. *Patterns of Queenship in Ancient Egyptian Myth and History*. Uppsala: Acta Universitatis Upsaliensis, 1986.

Ullmann, Martina. "Thebes: Origins of a Ritual Landscape." In *Sacred Space and Sacred Function in Ancient Thebes*, edited by Peter Dorman and Betsy Bryan, 3–26. Chicago: The Oriental Institute of the University of Chicago, 2007.

Uphill, Eric. "The Royal Ka Houses of Egypt: A Survey." *Journal of the Ancient Chronology Forum* 5 (1992): 77–88.

Valbelle, Dominique. "Pharaonic Regality: The Nature of Power." In *The Pharaohs*, edited by Christiane Ziegler, 97–111. London: Thames and Hudson, 2002.

Valloggia, Michel. *Abou Rawash I*. Cairo: Institut Français d'Archéologie Orientale, 2011, 2 vols.

Valloggia, Michel. "The 'Unfinished' Pyramids of the Fourth Dynasty." In *The Treasures of the Pyramids*, edited by

Zahi Hawass, 224–235. Vercelli: White Star, 2003.

Van Dijk, Jacobus. "Retainer Sacrifice in Egypt and in Nubia." In *The Strange World of Human Sacrifice*, edited by Jan Bremmer, 135–156. Leuven: Peeters, 2007.

Van den Boorn, Guido. *The Duties of the Vizier: Civil Administration in the Early New Kingdom* (Studies in Egyptology). London and New York: Kegan Paul International, 1988.

Van Neer, Wim, Mircea Udrescu, Veerle Linseele, Bea de Cupere, and Renée Friedman. "Traumatism in the Wild Animals Kept and Offered at Predynastic Hierakonpolis, Upper Egypt." *International Journal of Osteoarchaeology* 27, (2017): 86–105.

Van Wetering, Joris. "The Royal Cemetery of the Early Dynastic Period at Saqqara and the Second Dynasty Royal Tombs." In *Egypt at Its Origins: Studies in Memory of Barbara Adams*, edited by Stan Hendrickx, Renée Friedman, Krzysztof Cialowicz, and Marek Chlodnicki, 1055–1080. Leuven: Peeters, 2004

Vandenbeusch, Marie, Aude Semat, and Margaret Maitland. *Pharaoh, King of Ancient Egypt*. Cleveland: Cleveland Museum of Art, 2016.

Vandier, Jacques. *Mo'alla, La Tombe D'Ankhtifi et la Tombe de Sébekhotep*. Cairo: Institut Française d'Archéologie Orientale, 1950.

Vasiljević, Vera. "Der König im Privatgrab des Mittleren Riches." *Imago Aegypti*, 1 (2005): 132–143.

Verner, Miroslav. *Abusir: The Necropolis of the Sons of the Sun*. Cairo: American University in Cairo Press, 2017a.

Verner, Miroslav. *The Statues of Raneferef and the Royal Sculpture of the Fifth Dynasty*. Prague: Charles University, Faculty of Arts, 2017b.

Verner, Miroslav. "Pr-twt – The Cult place of Raneferef's Statues." In *Rich and Great. Studies in Honour of Anthony J. Spalinger on the Occasion of his 70th Feast of Thoth*, edited by Renata Landgráfová and Jana Mynárová, 325–330. Prague: Charles University Faculty of Arts, 2016.

Verner, Miroslav. "The Miraculous Rise of the Fifth Dynasty: The story of Papyrus Westcar and Historical Evidence." *Prague Egyptological Studies* 15 (2015a): 86–92.

Verner, Miroslav. "Sanctuary *Meret* and the Royal Cult." In *Royal versus Divine Authority, 7. Symposium zur ägyptischen Königsideologie*, edited by Filip Coppens, Jiří Janák, and Hana Vymazalová, 325–330. Wiesbaden: Harrassowitz, 2015b.

Verner, Miroslav. "Thoughts on the Fifth Dynasty Sun Temples." *Mitteilungen des Deutschen Archäologischen Instituts Abteilung Kairo* 70/71 (2014/2015): 457–462.

Verner, Miroslav. *Sons of the Sun: Rise and Decline of the Fifth Dynasty*. Prague: Charles University in Prague, 2014.

Verner, Miroslav. "Contemporaneous Evidence for the Relative Chronology of Dyns. 4 and 5." In *Ancient Egyptian Chronology*, edited by Erik Hornung, Rolf Krauss, and David Warburton, 124–143. Leiden: Brill, 2006.

Verner, Miroslav. "The Pyramids of the Fifth Dynasty." In *The Treasures of the Pyramids*, edited by Zahi Hawass, 236–259. Vercelli: White Star, 2003.

Verner, Miroslav. *Abusir: Realm of Osiris*. Cairo: American University in Cairo Press, 2002.

Verner, Miroslav. "Who was Shepseskara, and when did he reign?" In *Abusir and Saqqara in the Year 2000*, edited by Miroslav Bárta and Jaromír Krejčí, 581–597. Prague: Academy of Sciences of the Czech Republic, Oriental Institute, 2000.

Verner, Miroslav. *The Pyramids: The Mystery, Culture, and Science of Egypt's*

Great Monuments. New York: Grove Press, 1997.

Verner, Miroslav. *Abusir III: The Pyramid Complex of Khentkaues.* Prague: Universitas Carolina Pragensis Academia, 1995.

Verner, Miroslav, and Vladmír Bruna. "Why Was the Fifth Dynasty Cemetery Founded at Abusir?" In *Old Kingdom, New Perspectives: Egyptian Art and Archaeology 2750–2150 BC*, edited by Nigel Strudwick and Helen Strudwick, 286–294. Oxford: Oxbow Books, 2011.

Verner, Miroslav, and Vivienne Callender. *Abusir VI: Djedkare's Family Cemetery.* Prague: Czech Institute of Egyptology, Faculty of Arts, Charles University, 2002.

Vogel, Carola. "Fallen Heroes? Winlock's 'Slain Soldiers' Reconsidered." *Journal of Egyptian Archaeology* 89 (2003): 239–245.

Vörös, Gyózó, and Rezsó Pudleiner. "Preliminary Report of the Excavations at Thoth Hill, Thebes: The Temple of Montuhotep Sankhkara (Season 1995–1996)." *Mitteilungen des Deutschen Archäologischen Instituts Abteilung Kairo* 53 (1997): 283–287.

Voss, Susanne. "Untersuchungen zu den Sonnenheiligtümern der. 5. Dynastie." Ph.D. dissertation, University of Hamburg, 2004.

Vymazalová, Hana. "The Administration of the Royal Funerary Complexes." In *Ancient Egyptian Administration*, edited by Juan Carlos Moreno García, 177–196. Leiden and Boston: Brill, 2013.

Vymazalová, Hana. "The Economic Connection between the Royal Cult in the Pyramid Temples and the Sun Temples in Abusir." In *Old Kingdom, New Perspectives, Egyptian Art and Archaeology*, edited by Nigel Strudwick and Helen Strudwick, 295–303. Oxford: Oxbow Books, 2011.

Waddell, William. *Manetho.* Cambridge, MA: Harvard University Press, 1971.

Ward, William. *Essays on Feminine Titles of the Middle Kingdom and Related Subjects.* Beirut: American University of Beirut, 1986.

Ward, William. *Index of Egyptian Administrative and Religious Titles of the Middle Kingdom.* Beirut: American University of Beirut, 1982.

Warden, Leslie. "Centralized Taxation during the Old Kingdom." In *Towards a New History for the Egyptian Old Kingdom*, edited by Peter Der Manuelian and Thomas Schneider, 470–495. Leiden and Boston: Brill, 2015.

Way, Thomas von der. "Excavations at Tell el-Fara'in / Buto in 1987–1989." In *The Nile Delta in Transition: 4th – 3rd millennium BC: Proceedings of the seminar held in Cairo, 21–24 October 1990, at the Netherlands Institute of Archaeology and Arabic Studies*, edited by Edwin van den Brink, 1–10. Tel Aviv: Israel Exploration Society, 1992.

Wegner, Josef. "The Barque of Wenut-Shemau at the Sed-Festival: An Old Kingdom Temple Relief from Herakleopolis." *Journal of the American Research Center in Egypt* 53 (2017): 139–180.

Wegner, Josef. "A New Temple: The mahat of Nebhepetre at Abydos." *Egyptian Archaeology* 46 (2015): 3–7.

Weill, Raymond. "Monuments nouveaux des premieres dynastie. Un temple de Noutirkha à Héliopolis." *Sphinx* 15 (1911): 9–26.

Weinstein, James. "Foundation deposits in Ancient Egypt." Ph.D. dissertation, University of Pennsylvania, 1973.

Welc, Fabian, and Leszek Marks. "Climate Change at the End of the Old Kingdom in Egypt around 4200 BP: New Geoarchaeological Evidence." *Quaternary International* 324 (2014): 124–133.

Wendrich, Willemina, and René Cappers. "Egypt's Earliest Granaries: Evidence from the Fayum." *Egyptian Archaeology* 27 (2005): 12–15.

Wengrow, David. *The Archaeology of Early Egypt: Social Transformation in North-East Africa, 10,000 to 2650 BC.* Cambridge: Cambridge University Press, 2006.

Wenke, Robert. *The Ancient Egyptian State: The Origins of Egyptian Culture (c. 8000-2000BC).* New York: Cambridge University Press, 2009.

Werner, Edward. "The God Montu: From Earliest Attestations to the End of the New Kingdom." Ph.D. dissertation, Yale University, 1985.

Wildung, Dietrich. "Zur Deutung der Pyramide von Medum." *Revue D' Égyptologie,* 21 (1969a): 135–145.

Wildung, Dietrich. *Die Rolle ägyptischer Könige im Bewusstsein ihrer Nachwelt I.* Berlin: Bruno Hessling, 1969b.

Wilkinson, Alix. *The Garden in Ancient Egypt.* London: Rubicon Press, 1998.

Wilkinson, Alix. "Symbolism and Design in Ancient Egyptian Gardens." *Garden History* 22, (1994): 1–17.

Wilkinson, Toby. "Power and Authority in Early Dynastic Egypt." In *Another Mouthful of Dust: Egyptological Studies in Honour of Geoffrey Thorndike Martin,* edited by Jacobus Van Dijk, 543–557. Leuven: Peeters, 2016.

Wilkinson, Toby. "The Early Dynastic Period." In *A Companion to Ancient Egypt,* edited by Alan Lloyd, 48–62. Malden, MA: Wiley-Blackwell, 2014.

Wilkinson, Toby. *Lives of the Ancient Egyptians.* London: Thames and Hudson, 2007.

Wilkinson, Toby. "Before the Pyramids: Early Developments in Egyptian Royal Funerary Ideology." In *Egypt at Its Origins: Studies in Memory of Barbara Adams,* edited by Stan Hendrickx, Renée Friedman, Krzysztof Cialowicz,

and Marek Chlodnicki, 1129–1142. Leuven: Peeters, 2004.

Wilkinson, Toby. *Royal Annals of Ancient Egypt: The Palermo Stone and Its Associated Fragments.* London and New York: Kegan Paul International, 2000.

Wilkinson, Toby. *Early Dynastic Egypt.* London: Routledge, 1999.

Willems, Harco. "The First Intermediate Period and the Middle Kingdom." In *A Companion to Ancient Egypt,* edited by Alan Lloyd, 81–100. Chichester: Wiley-Blackwell, 2014.

Willems, Harco. "Nomarchs and Local Potentates: The Provincial Administration in the Middle Kingdom." In *Ancient Egyptian Administration,* edited by Juan Carlos Moreno García, 341–392. Leiden and Boston: Brill, 2013.

Willems, Harco. *Historical and Archaeological Aspects of Egyptian Funerary Culture: Religious Ideas and Ritual Practice in Middle Kingdom Elite Cemeteries.* Leiden and Boston: Brill, 2008.

Wilson, John. "Illuminating the Thrones at the Egyptian Jubilee." *Journal of the American Oriental Society* 56, (1936): 293–296.

Winlock, Herbert. *The Rise and Fall of the Middle Kingdom in Thebes.* New York: Macmillan Company, 1947.

Winlock, Herbert. *The Slain Soldiers of Neb-Hepet-Re Mentu-Hotpe.* New York: Metropolitan Museum of Art, 1945.

Winlock, Herbert. *Excavations at Deir el-Bahri, 1911–1931.* New York: Macmillan Company, 1942.

Winlock, Herbert. "Graffiti of the Eleventh Dynasty Temples at Thebes." *American Journal of Semitic Languages and Literatures* 58 (1941): 146–168.

Winlock, Herbert. "The Egyptian Expedition 1920–1921: III. Excavations at Thebes." *Metropolitan Museum of Art Bulletin* 16 (pt. 2) (1921): 29–53.

Wood, Wendy. "A Reconstruction of the Reliefs of Hesy-Re." *Journal of the*

American Research Center in Cairo 15 (1978): 9–24.

Wood, Wendy. "A Reconstruction of the Triads of King Mycerinus." *Journal of Egyptian Archaeology* 60 (1974): 82–93.

Woods, Alexandra. "*zšš w3d* scenes of the Old Kingdom revisited." In *Old Kingdom, New Perspectives: Egyptian Art and Archaeology, 2750–2150 BC*, edited by Nigel Strudwick and Helen Strudwick, 314–319. Oxford and Oakville: Oxbow Books, 2011.

Yoshimura, Sakuji, and Nozumo Kawai. "Finds of the Old and Middle Kingdoms at North Saqqara." *Egyptian Archaeology* 23 (2003): 38–40.

Yoshimura, Sakuji, Nozumo Kawai, and Hiroyuki Kashiwagi. "A Sacred Hillside at Northwest Saqqara: A Preliminary Report on the Excavations 2001–2003." *Mitteilungen des Deutschen Archäologischen Instituts, Abteilung Kairo* 61 (2005): 361–402.

Youssef, Mohammad. "New Scenes of Hunting a Hippopotamus from the Burial Chamber of Unas." In *Abusir and Saqqara in the Year 2010*, vol. 2, 820–822. Prague: Czech Institute of Egyptology, Faculty of Arts, Charles University, 2011.

Yoyotte, Marine. "The Harem in Ancient Egypt." In *Queens of Egypt: From Hetepheres to Cleopatra*, edited by Christiane Ziegler, 76–90. Monaco: Grimaldi Forum, 2008.

Ziegler, Christiane. "The Statues of King Khafre." In *Egyptian Art in the Age of the Pyramids*, edited by Dorothea Arnold, Christiane Ziegler, and James Allen, 252. New York: Metropolitan Museum of Art, 1999.

INDEX

Abu Gorab, 79
Abu Roasch, 58
Abydos
    Cemetery U, 12
    First Dynasty tombs, 13
Ain Sukhna, 136, 139
alignment between monuments, 79
alignments of Old Kingdom pyramids,
    77
Allen,
    James, 95
Amenemhat
    vizier, 137
Amenemhat I, 139
    pyramid complex, 207
Ankh Mesut, 147
Ankhenesmeryra, 106
Ankhenespepy I, 106
Ankhenespepy II
    marries Merenra, 114
    pyramid, 109

Bab el-Hosan., 127
Bab el-Tawfik
    Senusret I blocks, 160
Badarian, 8
Bapef
    priestess, 66
Bastet, 62, 83
    pottery statues, 54
    priest of, 44
Behenu, 114
Beit Khallaf tomb, 35
benben, 42, 80, 86
Bent Pyramid, 45
boat pits
    Khufu, 55
brother and sister marriage, 59, 66, 130,
    162
brother to brother succession, 67, 84
Bubastis
    ka-chapel, 100, 104
Building Inscription of Senusret I, 157
Buto, 9

cattle count
    Sneferu, 42
central administration, 163
climate change, 119
colossal statue
    first, 69
copper statues
    Hierakonpolis, 107
co-regency, 149
    Sixth Dynasty, 107
coregency
    early Twelfth Dynasty, 142
cult
    king's ka, 18, 133
cult of the sun god
    first, 20

daily rituals of the king, 91
decentralization, 119
decree, 100, 104, 109, 116, 117
Deir el-Bahari, 124
Dendera
    ka-chapel, 133
disappearance of sun temples, 89
divine filiation
    titles, 112
Djedkara Isesi, 93
Djoser
    later name of Netjerykhet, 31
domains, 48
    royal, 47, 118
Dry Moat, 33, 77, 189
Dynasty, 5, 12

eldest king's daughter, 45
eldest son, 60
    title of heir to throne, 45
Elephantine, 160
    small pyramid, 46
Ezbet Rushdi, 144

faience decoration, 84, 85
Fayum A, 6
Following of Horus, 25

203

foundations of divine kingship, 22
Friedman,
    Florence, 70–72
funerary forts, 89
    Early Dynastic, 14, 19
funerary temple
    Sahura, 82

Gabolde
    Luc, 130
Gebel Ahmar, 59
Gebelein
    Mentuhotep II, 134
Giza, 52
god Dua, 91
god Min at Coptos, 104
god's daughter, 41, 106
god's father, 130
Greatest of Seers, 39

harem, 101, 162, 163
Hathor, 51, 62
    Dendera, 134
    female counterpart of Ra, 21
    importance of, 161
    priestess of, 60, 66
Hathor and Neith, 63
Hathor cult at Thebes, 124
Hays
    Harold, 97
heb sed celebration, 86, 147
heb sed scenes, 53, 83, 86
heb sed temple, 48, 81
Heliopolis, 159
    sun god worship, 20, 38, 88, 96
Helwan, 19
henty-sha, 100
Henutsen, 58
Hesy-Ra, 39
Hetepheres I, 41
Hetepheres II, 56, 59, 65
Hetephernebty, 35
Hierakonpolis, 9–11, 80
    Tomb 100, 8
hieroglyphs
    oldest, 12
Horemakhet, 63
Horus, 22
Huni, 41, 46

I'h
    king's mother, 130
iconography of the queen, 58, 65
Ihy and Hetep
    Saqqara tombs, 140
Imhotep, 39
imiut-fetish
    Step Pyramid, 35, 36

Inenek, also called Inti, 111
Instructions of Amenemhat I, 142
Intef I, 121
Intkaues, 35
ipt nswt
    harem, 57
Iput
    mother of Teti, 94
Iput II, 116
iry-pat, 44
Itakayet.
    royal female, 147
Itja-tawy, 139, 160
ivory comb
    King Djet, 16, 20

Jánosi
    Peter, 143

ka-chapel
    Amenemhat I, 140
    mother of Pepy I, 104
Kai, 91
Kamutef
    Min, 127
Karnak
    Amen temple, 125
    Senusret I building, 154–157
Kawab, 56, 65
Khamaat
    marries official, 79
Khamerernebty I, 66
Khamerernebty II, 66
Khasekhem, 21
Khasekhemwy, 19
Khentetka, 59
Khentimentiu
    shrine Abydos, 105
Khentkaues II, 83, 85
Khentkaues titles, 74
Khentkaues's tomb, 73
Khuit II, 99
King Narmer, 10, 12
king's legitimacy, 149, 161
king's mother
    title of, 34
King's mother, Imi, 136
king's wife
    title of, 35
kingship
    source of, 11
kinship, 90
kinship terms, 64
Königsnovelle, 125

Landgráfová,
    Renata, 85
Lisht

reused blocks, 46, 54, 78
low Nile levels, 119
Loyalist Instructions, 158

Maadi
  culture, 8
Maat, 24, 41, 77, 82
Maghara, 116
Mahaa, 111
mahat
  Abydos, 135
Manetho, 5, 100, 118, 142
Master of Largess in the Mansion of Life, 52, 60
Menkauhor, 89, 93
Mentuhotep
  served Senusret I, 158
Mentuhotep II
  temple complex, 124–133
Mentuhotep III, 135
Mentuhotep IV, 136
Merenra., 107
Mereruka, 100
Meresankh III, 64
meret of Userkaf, 81
meret sanctuary
  Sneferu, 51
Meretites II
  also called Merut, 112
Meret-Nebty, 81
Meretneith, 16
Merimde, 7
Meritites I, 56
Merka, 26
Meydum, 42
Min
  cult of, with harem, 127
  Mentuhotep II as, 133
Montu-Ra, 130
Morales,
  Antonio, 97
mortuary temple
  Mentuhotep II, 132
Mother of two Kings of Upper and Lower Egypt, 84
myth of Osiris, 22

Nagada I, 8
Nagada II, 8
Nagada III, 9
neb hepet
  Sneferu epithet, 42
Nebemakhet, 65
Nebet
  non-royal woman, 112
Nebhepetra
  prenomen, 124
Nebuwenet, 111
Nedjeftet, 112
Neferhetepes, 60, 78

Nefermaat
  vizier, 43
Neferu (TT 319), 128
Neith
  goddess, 26
  marries brother, 115
  priestess of, 100
  royal female, 110, 116
Neithhotep
  First Dynasty, 14
Nekabu
  constructed ka-chapels, 104
Nekhbet, 83
Neolithic, 7
Nesu-Montu
  stela, 150
Netjeraperef, 52
Nitiqret or Nitocris, 98
nomes, 90
  beginning of, 27
North Saqqara
  First Dynasty tombs, 13, 18
Northern or Red Pyramid, 46, 47
Nymaathap, 34

obelisk
  of King Tet I, 16, 96, 100, 159
  Pepy I, 105
Omari, 7
One who is Over the Secrets, 90
Osiris, 127
  first evidence, 92
  grove of, 127
Osiris and Ra, 95
Otto
  Eberhard, 149
Overseer of all Royal Works, 43
Overseer of the harem
  title of Ihy, 140
Overseer of the priests
  given to nomarchs, 118
Overseer of Upper Egypt, 90
  given to nomarchs, 118

Papazian,
  Hratch, 106
Pepy I
  change of prenomen, 103
Pepy II
  length of reign, 117
per shena, 58
per weru, 82
Peribsen, 19
  political split, 22
  Seth name, 21
priestesses of Hathor
  chapels, 126
  sun and funerary temples, 88

INDEX

princesses marry officials, 90
propaganda, 162
Ptahshepses
    High priest of Ptah, 79
    vizier of Nyuserra, 89, 91
Punt, 79, 82
Pyramid Texts, 103
    Unas Pyramid, 94

queen
    main titles, 65
queen's titles
    of Neferu, 129
queenship as a duality
    Troy, 36

Ra
    in personal names, 39
Ra and Hathor
    parents of king, 80
Ra.
    creator god, 23
Ra's Delight
    Nyuserra, 85
Ra's Nekhen
    sun temple, 79
Raneb, 19, 20, 94, 184, 193
Raneferef, 84, 85
Rawer, 92
    vizier, Pepy I, 108
Reputnebu, 85
royal sibling marriage, 148

sacrificial burials
    human, 11, 13, 19
Sakhmet or Bastet, 50
Schatt er-Rigal, 129
Sebutet, 114
Sehetepibra
    reign of Senusret III, 159
Seila
    small pyramid, 46
Sekhemra
    last royal vizier, 68
Sekhet Iaru, 97
sema-tawy
    motif, 24, 83, 125, 134
    or Somtus, 134
sesh wadj
    ritual, 65, 110
Sesheshet, 98
setep-sa, 92
Setibhor
    queen, 93
Setka, 60
Shepseskaf, 68
Shepseskaf., 77
sibling royal marriage., 36

small pyramids, 46–47, 162
Smith
    Mark, 97
solar altar, 163
    Deir el-Bahari, 130
    Karnak, 130
Son of Hathor of Dendera, 134
son of Ra, 62
    title, 20, 56
Sphinx Temple
    Khafra, 63
Step Pyramid Complex, 32–34
suckling the king, 83
sun god worship, 34
sun temples
    precusor, 63

Tanis
    reused statue, 143
Tem
    tomb, 132
temple building, 162
Tetiankh-kem, 99
The One Who Sees Horus and Seth
    queen's title, 58
The Prophecy of Neferti, 138
The Story of Sinuhe, 142
Thoth
    priestess, 66
titulary
    royal, 23–24
Tjasepef
    priestess, 66
Tjetji,
    stela, 121
Tomb 507,
    Deir el-Bahari, 150
true pyramid, 42
twins, 82, 84
two bodies
    of the king, 24

unification, 5, 9
Userkara, 101

valley temple
    Khafra, 61
    Menkaura, 70
vizier, 26
    held by non-royal, 75
    in Eleventh Dynasty, 135
vulture headdress, 70, 74, 85, 116, 149

Wa'ankh Intef II, 121
Wadi al-Jarf, 52
Wadi el-Hudi, 136
Wadi Hammamat, 137
Watethathor, 100

Wedjebten, 117
Wehem Mesut, 139
Wemtetka, 45
Weni, 101, 115
Wepwawet, 54
weret hetes
   queen's title, 56, 102

Werkaura, 89
Westcar Papyrus, 76
wild animals
   sacrificed, 10

Zawyet al-Aryan, 61
Zawyet al-Meitin, 47